Clipper Programming

Brett Oliver
Jim Sheldon

Clipper Programming

Osborne **McGraw-Hill**

Berkeley New York St. Louis San Francisco
Auckland Bogotá Hamburg London Madrid
Mexico City Milan Montreal New Delhi Panama City
Paris São Paulo Singapore Sydney
Tokyo Toronto

Osborne **McGraw-Hill**
2600 Tenth Street
Berkeley, California 94710
U.S.A.

For information on translations or book distributors outside of the U.S.A., please
write to Osborne **McGraw-Hill** at the above address.

Clipper Programming

1234567890 DOC 998765432

ISBN 0-07-881758-7

To Elizabeth Oliver, my grandmother and inspiration.
Congratulations on your upcoming centennial birthday!

—Brett Oliver

To my mom and to the memory of my dad;

To my wife and best friend, Beth, who is a constant source of
love and support.

—Jim Sheldon

Publisher
Kenna S. Wood

Acquisitions Editor
Jeffrey M. Pepper

Associate Editor
Emily Rader

Technical Editors
Ira Emus
Hilde Oliver

Project Editor
Kathy Krause

Copy Editor
Dusty Bernard

Proofreading Coordinator
Nancy Pechonis

Proofreaders
Mick Arellano
Colleen Paretty

Indexer
Valerie Robbins

Quality Control Specialist
Bob Myren

Computer Designer
Stefany Otis

Cover Designer
Bay Graphics, Inc.

Contents at a Glance

Contents

Foreword

Brett and I have been good friends since the inception of Nantucket, back in 1984, and I am pleased to introduce his first book on one of our favorite subjects—Clipper.

In 1984, creating a compiler for dBASE was considered an all-but-impossible task, the result of which could at best have a small market of professional developers.

Since that time, several hundred thousand copies of Clipper have been sold worldwide. It is the number-one development tool for the dBASE community and has been used in critical situations such as Operation Desert Storm and various NASA projects. Its main duties, however, rest in the business community, where thousands of applications are in daily use.

Until this book, which makes Clipper accessible to beginners, Clipper programmers would normally spend time as dBASE programmers. Beginners would learn to program in dBASE, and only when they became frustrated with the lack of speed, as well as other limitations, did they look around for a better solution. Clipper runs faster, produces .EXE files, and introduces many programming language features to the dBASE community.

Brett Oliver and Jim Sheldon have brought the power of Clipper to the beginning programmer. Their gentle introduction to the concepts of programming and their use of a sample application as an orientation point help the reader understand real programs—not just snippets of code.

I hope you have as much fun learning Clipper as we at Nantucket did creating it.

Brian Russell
Vice President of Development
Nantucket Corporation

Acknowledgments

I would like to thank my wife Hilde for her significant contribution to this book. She checked the manuscript from cover to cover from the viewpoint of a novice. Comments like, "This is not clear," "You've lost me," and "You don't explain this anywhere" transformed the work from techno-babble into something someone could use! She held the fort, running our business and our family while I went gallivanting off to my favorite restaurant, notebook computer in hand!

I would also like to thank Hilde's mother, Agnes, for her immeasurable support. Vielen herzlichen Dank!

I thank my parents Edna and Ian, for encouraging my literary endeavors, and, through example, making me a compulsive reader.

I would like to thank my children, Scott, Jason, and Jonathan, for their patience as I disappeared inside the computer.

Of course I have to thank the wonderful people at Osborne/McGraw-Hill, including Jeff Pepper, my editor, who read my scratchings instead of watching the inflight movie. He corrected each of the first five chapters three times! He taught me how to "think" as a technical writer.

—Brett Oliver

Special thanks to Ryan and Daniel for all their love and patience and for understanding when I had to work instead of play.

Thanks to my brother, Tom, for his part in providing this opportunity and sharing his knowledge of the whole process.

Thanks to Jeff Pepper, Emily Rader, and Kathy Krause at Osborne/McGraw-Hill for their guidance and assistance.

Thanks to Merle Douglas for providing the flexibility and support to work on this book.

Thanks also to Jerry Cerny and Stu Tomlinson for their support and encouragement during my early years.

—Jim Sheldon

Introduction

Clipper is a software development system that provides all the facilities necessary to create complete application programs. Clipper was originally designed as a compiler for the popular language dBASE, but has since greatly expanded the basic dBASE command set and capabilities. Add-ons to the Clipper language that were developed by third-party vendors provide the programmer with the tools to perform a virtually unlimited number of tasks.

Many professional programmers have selected Clipper as their day-to-day language because of its ease of use, power, and flexibility. Clipper is also an excellent language for the beginning programmer. Each Clipper command performs considerable work, and even novice programmers can write very useful programs with only a limited knowledge of Clipper. Because beginning programmers can write applications quickly, they are encouraged to explore the language further and learn how to incorporate more difficult capabilities.

About This Book

Various exercises and examples are presented throughout the book. Sample sections of code are presented first and then dissected in the paragraphs that follow. Glance over the code, but do not get hung up on the meaning of a command or construct. Some code sections are presented to clarify a point, such as the example in Chapter 1 that demonstrates the difference between a compiler and an interpreter. The commands and constructs will be explained in more detail as the book progresses. The exact definition of each command is in the Clipper 5 reference guide.

How This Book Is Organized

Chapters 1, 2, and 3 focus on understanding general programming concepts and introducing you to the commands in the context of examples. When learning a language, such as English, the initial focus is on phrases, not words. Once you are comfortable with complete statements such as "Good day," you can focus on the variations of the word "good" and the word "day." In the same way, you should focus on grouping and general meaning first. If you don't feel that you fully understand all of the nuances of a command in the early chapters, don't worry. The commands are grouped and fully explained in Chapter 7, so if you feel that the dissection was not clear enough in earlier chapters, feel free to jump to Chapter 7 or refer to the Clipper 5 reference guide.

Chapters 4, 5, and 6 cover the basic skills required to develop a simple application. These chapters provide you with the skills necessary to create menus, data entry screens, reports, and system maintenance utilities.

Chapter 7 is a reference section of Clipper capabilities. The focus is on the differing importance of the various commands and functions and how they work together. You may use this chapter to gain an understanding of the various capabilities of Clipper and the various methods that may be used to achieve results.

Chapter 8 concentrates on fine-tuning an application. You accomplish this using memory management, data-driven techniques, compile and link options, and various programming techniques.

Chapter 9 covers the skills that go hand-in-hand with developing successful applications, such as professionalism and communication. Chapter 9 also discusses the problems and challenges associated with presenting the application to the user and the ongoing maintenance and development of the application. This includes techniques to avoid problems in the first place, as well as ways to handle problems and new developments if they arise.

Chapter 10 provides an overview of Clipper's advanced features, such as code blocks, user-defined commands, compiler macros, the ability to interface with C and with assembly language, and object-oriented programming.

The Goal of This Book

The goal of this book is to provide background information and initial assistance to allow the new Clipper programmer to become proficient in the use of Clipper. Use this book as a companion to the books you receive with Clipper 5. Switch on the computer and try the examples. This book will have served its purpose if you are comfortable programming in Clipper by the end of it.

Conventions Used in This Book

Text you should type from the keyboard is shown as **boldfaced** text.

Keyboard commands and function keys are printed in small capital letters, like this: ENTER, F2, and ESC.

When two or more keys should be pressed simultaneously, they are joined by a hyphen. For example, "Press CTRL-W" means to hold down the CTRL key and press W.

Clipper-defined functions and commands are in uppercase type.

User-defined functions and commands are in lowercase type.

Disk Offer

***I**n the development of applications, it makes sense to use software tools where appropriate. You may have seen advertising on screen, report, and application generators. What are they and how do they work for you?*

Application Generator Software: What is...

...an Application Generator?

An application generator is a software product that allows the user to easily design a complete business application. It creates a running application.

...a Screen Generator?

A screen generator is a subset of an application generator. It allows the user to design an entry screen. The program will create another program that presents that screen to the user. Some screen generators allow for the definition of the underlying database structures.

...a Report Generator?

A report generator is similar to a screen generator, except that the focus is on how the report will look in the printout. A report generator assumes that there is an existing database of data that will be manipulated by the report.

...a Menu Generator?

A menu generator allows the user to create menus and sub-menus that will then call the application's different screens and reports.

...a Data Dictionary?

A data dictionary is a database that holds information on the structures of all the other databases in the application. It can also hold information such as help messages, tests to be performed, actions to take, and so forth—for each item in the system, whether it is an entry point on a screen, a location under the report generator or even a key element invisible to the user. Its main purpose is to maintain system integrity by having *one* point of reference. New databases can be built referencing a data dictionary.

...Interactive?

Interaction refers to the user's operation of the software. With an interactive menu designer, the menu choices created by the user become *immediately* active and usable. Interaction is the fastest way to design a system.

...Data-driven?

Data-driven is the concept of depending on information in a database for the way a program behaves.

For example, suppose an entry point in a screen has a test "state must be CA, NE, OR." All input is screened, and only those entries that match the above condition are allowed. Data-driven means the test resides in a field in the data dictionary and is popped out and used at run time. The advantage of having it reside in the data dictionary rather than in the code itself is that the test can be changed to include more states without your having to recompile the program.

...an Object?

In software terms, an object is a combination of data and actions that are to be performed on that data.

Take, for example, a window. An object has a *method* for drawing the window, and it also has *data*, such as the coordinates of the corners and the color of the window. Usually an object can change itself depending on messages it receives.

...Context-sensitive Help?

Context-sensitive help is information that is available that pertains to the item under the cursor. A data dictionary makes this kind of help easily available.

...Data-driven Versus Code-driven?

A data-driven screen is a screen that a program creates by reading information in a database.

A code-driven screen is a screen that a program creates from sections of code.

Changes to a code-driven system must be re-compiled and re-linked (and possibly debugged) before the system can be used, since you're changing the system's code.

The data-driven screen and system are ready to go after the changes have been made, since only the data gets changed, not the code.

Is a Data-driven System Slow?

A data-driven system is slightly slower in operation than a code-driven system, but on today's faster computers this is irrelevant.

Why Would I Want To Use an Application Generator?

There are several reasons why you might find an application generator useful:

- ❏ You'll be able to develop applications quickly.
- ❏ You'll be able to make changes easily.
- ❏ You'll be able to avoid repetitive tasks, such as hard-coding screens.
- ❏ You can be assured of system integrity.
- ❏ You'll be able to participate in the design throughout the design process.
- ❏ You'll be able to prototype.

One of the authors of this book, Brett Oliver, has spent several years developing a Clipper-based application generator that has all of the features mentioned above.

In demonstrations, Brett has produced a fully operational entry screen, including support menus and the underlying data-structure, in five minutes!

His product, Schooner, comes complete with an operational Customer Tracking System to show how easy this product is to use.

It is not only a useful tool but it also allows you to explore the concepts of data-driven and code-driven systems. It defaults to data-driven operation, but the source code for a screen code generator and the source code for the run-time engine of the data-driven system are included.

Access to more than 10,000 lines of Clipper source code, along with a clearly-written 320-page manual, will allow you to fully understand this exciting subject.

To order Schooner, or to obtain further information, contact Quicktek:

Phone: 805-494-9129

Fax : 805-497-4282

Write : 224 Whiteside Place

Thousand Oaks, CA 91362

Schooner retails for $195.

CHAPTER

Clipper Essentials

Clipper is a programming language, an interpreter, a compiler, and a rich development tool from which to build effective applications. This chapter starts out by explaining what is meant by "language," "compiler," "interpreter," and a host of other terms and winds up with a quick database primer. In this book you will learn by doing. You will see a lot of code early on in this book. This code will be used to build a full-fledged database application.

Clipper as a Language

A *programming language* is a group of instructions or commands that work together in many ways similar to a language such as English. The computer must be able to interpret and act on each command. The language should include all the tools necessary to enable the programmer to communicate fully with the user.

What defines a language? In theory, you could say that DOS—the operating system and its instructions—is a language. You could say that the spreadsheet functions in Lotus 1-2-3 form a language. However, operating systems and integrated packages are seldom called languages. The line between a programming language and simply a group of commands can be fuzzy, but you can make the distinction by answering the following question: Will the "programming language" produce a product for others to use, or is it an environment modification tool?

An operating system such as DOS is geared to do specific tasks at a very low level. There is a program in DOS called COMMAND.COM that interprets your keystrokes and turns them into instructions the machine understands. This is the program you see in action first. It is the program that puts the C:> symbol on your computer screen when the computer starts up.

DOS also makes it possible to group the commands in what is called a batch file. A *batch file* is a text file with the .BAT extension. DOS runs the instructions in a batch file the same way it runs individual commands. DIR, CD, and CLS are examples of DOS commands. DOS does not constitute a programming language because it has a limited number of commands and insufficient capabilities.

Your computer understands many levels of languages. At a very low level there is a language called machine language. The *machine language* controls the screen, reads input from the keyboard, and handles traffic to and from the hard disk, floppy disk, and memory, as well as peripheral devices such as the printer.

Machine language is represented in the computer as a series of 0's and 1's. However, giving the computer instructions as a series of 0's and 1's, such as 0110111011110, is a very difficult way to program. To make things easier, you can use a higher level language called *assembly language*. An assembly language instruction, such as MOV AX,BX, is still cryptic but is more workable for programmers. A program called an *assembler* translates the command MOV AX,BX into 0's and 1's. There are two ways to perform this translation process: compiling and interpreting. When a program is *compiled*, every text-based instruction, such as MOV AX,BX, is converted into machine code and stored in one place, called an *executable file*. You can then *execute* (run) the program at any time by typing the name of the newly created file. When a program is *interpreted*, each instruction is translated and then immediately given to the computer to run. As you will see, Clipper combines aspects of both types of translation.

Clipper is considered a language because it has more than 350 commands and functions that are broad in their capabilities and are used to create products for others.

New Terms

As a word of caution, in computer languages the words "function," "procedure," "program," and "routine" all refer to a set of instructions implemented by the computer. The word *program* is a general term and can refer to one program or a group of programs that work together. A *routine* is a small program that usually performs one specific activity. A *function* is similar in scope to a routine and usually returns a single value. A *procedure* is considered a single program but is often larger than a function or a routine. However, you can have large functions and small procedures, thus clouding the definition. You don't need to worry about the different names used to represent a set of instructions.

Interpreter Versus Compiler

In order to fully understand Clipper and its strengths, a little under-standing of the benefits of interpreters and compilers is in order. From the programmer's point of view, the difference between an interpreter and compiler is speed. The translation process takes time. When instruc-tions in a program need to be repeated, as often occurs with programs, a group of instructions that are translated one time, as in a compile, will be faster than a group of instructions that are retranslated over and over again, as happens with an interpreter.

To clarify the distinction between a compiler and an interpreter, it is necessary to look at files. Typically, you store the information on your computer on a hard disk or a floppy disk. To make it easy to find things, everything is stored in files. There are two kinds of files: data files and executable files.

Data files hold information that is available to the user. A spreadsheet, a customer list, and *source code* (a program you have written) are all stored as data files. The other kind of file is an executable file. This is a file that only the computer understands, and the computer executes it. A *compiler*, such as Clipper, is an executable file. It takes a text or data file, such as a program you have written, and turns it into an executable file. An *interpreter*, which is also an executable file, takes your source code and runs it immediately. It does not turn it into an executable file. This means your program is not able to run on its own; it always requires the interpreter to run the program. A major disadvantage of this is that the interpreter, such as dBASE, must be purchased by the end-user, which increases the overall cost of their software package.

In summary, there are two major points that distinguish a compiler from an interpreter. First, the translation process is done once with a compiler as compared to multiple times with an interpreter. Second, a compiler produces an executable file that will run independently of the compiler.

Clipper and dBASE

Clipper started as a compiler for the popular database language dBASE. Clipper allowed the dBASE instructions to execute much more quickly since a compiler converts text-based instructions into instructions closer to the machine's language. In other words, Clipper was a tool dBASE programmers used to speed up dBASE programs.

Clipper has expanded upon the original dBASE instruction set to include many powerful commands that only the Clipper compiler recognizes. The relatively late acceptance of Clipper as a programming language was due in part to the late acceptance of dBASE as a programming language. When dBASE II (there was never a dBASE I) was introduced, it was perceived as a database manipulator as opposed to a real language, like those with more general capabilities, such as BASIC and Pascal. It was only because of the incredible popularity of dBASE II that dBASE was reluctantly accepted as a programming language.

dBASE and Clipper are easy to use and are extremely effective in getting the job done in a short period of time. They will beat other computer languages, such as COBOL or C, in developing any application involving databases and user interfaces. These tasks happen to be about 70 percent of the activities for which computers are used.

If you program in C or assembly language, which are considered languages closer to the built-in machine language, you probably have tried to create higher level commands such as those already available in dBASE and Clipper. However, some high-level languages, such as COBOL, are exceedingly verbose. A revolving loan application that requires 650,000 lines of COBOL code requires only 25,000 lines of Clipper code—and the Clipper version is more functional and much easier to use!

The Interpreter and Compiler Revisited

This section expands on the brief explanation of compiler and interpreter just given and shows you an example of Clipper code in action. Clipper was defined as a compiler, which is not quite correct. To understand why, you need to know a little more about interpreters and compilers.

An interpreter reads a line of text instructions and *parses* the line (isolates each word), looking for words it understands. It then matches those words to a table of programs that correspond to those words. The interpreter then runs the appropriate program. It is called an interpreter because it invokes commands one line at a time.

A compiler performs pretty much the same task as the interpreter except that instead of running the appropriate program, it writes the commands out to a file that will be run later. This breaks out the translation process as a separate action from the run process. Thus, compiled programs run more quickly than interpreted programs. This is especially true when you have a repetitious use of commands. The interpreter has to retranslate commands that it processed just moments before. The compilation process does not perform the translation process at *run time* (when you run the program) and thus, logically, takes less time to perform the same task.

Let's take a look at an example that illustrates this concept.

```
CLEAR
x := 1
DO WHILE x < 5
    ? "My first Clipper program says 'Hello world' five times"
    x := x+1
ENDDO
RETURN
```

This example clears the screen by using the Clipper CLEAR command and stores the number 1 to a variable; a *variable* is like a container for storing values. The := tells Clipper that you want to put the value 1 into the variable x. The Clipper statement DO WHILE evaluates the expression $x < 5$, which means, "Is the value inside x less than 5?" If the expression is TRUE (as it is in the first attempt since 1 is less than 5), it runs the instructions between the DO WHILE and ENDDO statements. There are two instructions in this example. The first uses the Clipper command ? to print on the screen the message that is between quotes and then move the cursor down one line. The second instruction, x := x+1, tells Clipper to increase the value of the variable *x* by one. The value inside *x* will increase until the statement x < 5 is no longer TRUE, at which point the program jumps to the command RETURN. This command tells Clipper you are finished with this particular program.

The output from the the program is shown here:

```
My first Clipper program says 'Hello World' five times
My first Clipper program says 'Hello World' five times
My first Clipper program says 'Hello World' five times
My first Clipper program says 'Hello World' five times
My first Clipper program says 'Hello World' five times
```

Parsing

As you can see from the preceding example, there can be intense repetition of commands. Every command line has to be parsed—that is, it has to be broken into its components, and the components have to be checked to see if they are acceptable and if they work together as a team.

Even a simple program like the preceding one involves a series of steps. If the translation is necessary every time the program loops back from the ENDDO to the DO WHILE, you will have a very slow program indeed.

Macros

Macros are one of the elements that give dBASE and Clipper programmers so much flexibility. A *macro* is a string variable (a series of characters enclosed in quotes) that is translated at run time instead of compile time (when the program is compiled). This means you can hide instructions inside a macro, and Clipper will not translate those instructions until it is actually running the application. The advantage of this method is flexibility. Clipper permits you to use macros in place of expressions or to perform text substitution within strings.

Allowing the use of macros was a major liability for the designers of Clipper. Not only did they have to produce a program that created an executable file that DOS would recognize as legitimate and run correctly, they also had to bury a small *macro compiler* inside every user's final executable file. The job of this macro compiler was to read the contents of macros and execute the functions and tests referred to inside the macros. This is an example of what a macro looks like:

```
var1 := "SECONDS() < 43200"
IF &var1
   ? "Good Morning"
ELSE
   ? "Good Afternoon"
ENDIF
```

The macro symbol & says, "Look inside the variable following the macro symbol and use what is evaluated as a programming instruction," and that is what this macro compiler does. It is acting as an interpreter since it evaluates program instructions at run time. It now looks as if Clipper is an interpreter since an interpreter, by definition, immediately runs what it finds. In the preceding example, the expression "SECONDS() < 43200" is stored inside the variable called *var1*. The Clipper SECONDS() function calculates the number of seconds that have occurred since midnight. 43200 is the number of seconds that have elapsed from midnight to noon. If the value returned from the SECONDS() function is less than 43200, then the time must be morning. The Clipper IF statement tests the contents of *var1* (using the macro symbol &), and if the result of that test is TRUE, the instructions between the IF and the ELSE are executed. If the result of the test is FALSE, the instructions between the ELSE and the ENDIF are executed.

Chapter 7 demonstrates how powerful this macro capability is; this example simply illustrates how blurred is the line between "compiled" and "interpreted."

Interpreting and Compiling Combined

What good, then, is a traditional interpreter, such as dBASE III or QuickBASIC? It is a nice way to test small programs. An interpreter makes it easy to *interactively* (one command at a time) query the contents of *databases* (text files that store data such as names and addresses). It is a good platform for learning the basic commands. Interpreters will be around for a long time in one form or other because it is necessary to allow flexibility in how code is produced.

Interpreters are often buried in programs such as Windows, which has a WIN.INI file that contains instructions on how Windows should behave. The WIN.INI file is read when Windows is first run. This file provides information such as which printer you have, where your fonts are located, and so forth.

This combination of compiled and interpreted code gives power without sacrificing flexibility. You can use macros in situations where the user must be able to change the way the program acts without having to actually modify the source code. As a good example of this, suppose the user has a report that prints names and addresses of customers. The user wants only certain records to print but wants to be able to specify the criteria by which customers are included in the report. For example, the user may want to print only customers who live in California. Before the report is run, the program prompts the user for the desired criterion (a state code, for example). The report criterion is then used to build a macro string to be used in the report.

Macros are frequently used in reports to allow the user to change the condition in which detail lines will print. The programmer does not want the user to type the actual string to be used as the macro since this could easily result in a run-time error. The program could be written to prompt the user with a series of questions and build the macro string based on the answers to the questions. In this way the report criteria are not *hard coded* (converted to machine-level instructions) but are built by the program at run time, stored in a macro string, and then evaluated as the report is running.

Clipper permits the compiled code and interpreted code to work together to get the job done. Some pieces of code *must* run quickly and other pieces *must* be flexible. In either case, your code is executed by routines contained in the Clipper library. The *Clipper library* is the group of programs provided in Clipper that executes your Clipper commands. The additional flexibility provided by macros is well worth the added overhead of the translation process.

What Makes Clipper Special

dBASE has always been a valuable language, and Clipper seems better yet. One reason for Clipper's success is the work done by Brian Russell and Rich McConnell, the creators of Clipper.

Brian used to spend a great deal of time on requests for new commands; if he had a request for a menu-type command, for example, he would work with it until it was perfected. In the beginning, he simply had to get any command to work in order to establish the mechanics of the compiler. Then he had to get commands working that duplicated the dBASE command set. That was a challenge in itself. Finally, for a short period, he had the luxury of making up commands. This is where his conservative approach paid off. Others might have added everything—including the SET KITCHEN SINK ON command—but Brian was very careful about which commands to include and how they would work. As the request for commands increased, he probably spent a lot of time saying no.

What makes Clipper special is the inclusion of powerful yet simple commands. Other manufacturers of compilers don't always have the overall picture. They might add commands, work around them, or say you can use a particular feature—but only under certain circumstances.

Clipper commands have few restrictions. Other languages have difficulty implementing certain commands and functions because of their internal structure. A language is always changing, and Clipper 5 allows you to add commands to the Clipper language. By designing each command as a separate entity and by having very precise and simple rules on how each command will work with the rest of the commands, you can build a robust and expandable language compiler.

An Object-oriented Language

Nantucket is marketing Clipper as a dBASE compiler, but in fact it is more of an object-oriented engine. *Object-oriented language* is a new approach to building software that offers powerful techniques for producing flexible and easy-to-maintain applications. Programs and data are combined to form an object, such as a window; you control objects by sending them messages to tell them how they should behave. Object-oriented languages allow new objects to be created at run time.

With the inclusion of many C-type features, Nantucket has attempted to "go for the gold." If you had to create the *perfect* computer language, it would be as friendly as dBASE, as flexible as C, and as innovative as object-oriented languages. You would then take the 200,000 users of the original Clipper with you by giving them backward compatibility with the original version. You wouldn't make it too different on the first pass so they could adjust to the changes at a comfortable pace. And you would keep the architecture open enough to allow for new developments, such as multimedia databases and SQL (Structured Query Language). Nantucket has succeeded in this strategy.

What Skills Are Needed to Master Clipper?

To master Clipper, you need to

❑ Be familiar with floppy disks, hard disks, the keyboard, and the screen

❑ Understand the terms "memory," "processor", and "program"

❑ Be able to use the following DOS commands: COPY, DEL, CD, MD, RD, and DIR

❑ Know how to run a program from the DOS prompt

❑ Be able to check available disk space

Chapter 2 discusses specific hardware and software requirements for Clipper.

You also need to be able to edit programs in a text file. Clipper provides a simple program editor called PE.EXE that you can use use to create and modify source code. At a minimum, you should know how to perform the following actions:

❑ Create a new file

❑ Load a file

❏   Save a file

❏   Insert and delete text

❏   Block copy, block move, and block delete

❏   Navigate the file by using cursor keys

It is also essential that you understand what you or others *do* in business. Because Clipper focuses on the creation of business software, it makes sense for you to know the basics of business and be able to apply common sense as you develop applications.

Aptitude and desire, rather than knowledge of DOS, are perhaps the most valuable prerequisites for learning Clipper programming. You will certainly be able to write simple programs by the end of this book. If you're persistent, you'll be able to write good programs and possibly even make money writing them.

Knowing the Business

As already mentioned, it's important for you to know how business works. Here is an example.

Joe runs a business. He sells shoes. A customer comes into his shop and buys a pair of shoes. In California, which is where Joe has his shoe shop, he has to charge the customer 8.25 percent sales tax, which he gives to the government. The government wants to know how much money he made so they will know how much sales tax and income tax to collect. Joe must record the transaction of selling the shoes somewhere so he can look at it later with his accountant. He also wants his customers to come back and buy another pair of shoes from him at a later date, so he keeps the name and address of each customer.

When it comes time to send out a flyer to his customers to tell them about a shoe sale he is having, he needs to print labels with the customers' addresses on them. If Joe buys a computer and puts in the names and addresses of the customers, and also notes in the computer every transaction (each time he sells shoes), including how much money he received, he will be able to print labels on a printer with the names and addresses of his customers. He will also be able to print out a report of how much money he made and how much sales tax he collected.

Database Primer

The computer keeps information like Joe's in a file called a database. A database is like a long list, usually of names and addresses, but sometimes of transactions, with dollar amounts.

Each customer might have one record in this database. A *record* is a section of a database. One record could be used to store the information of one customer. The information is further broken down into *fields*. A record is made up of many fields; one field might hold the last name of the customer, another the first name, another the city, and another the phone number. Each record has the same structure as the next. There may be many records in a database. A second database could contain the customer's transactions—one for every time he or she bought a pair of shoes. You would then have a *lead database* containing each customer's name and address and a *support database* containing customer transactions.

As records are sliced into different fields, you give each field a name. For example, you could have a First Name field and a Last Name field. The customer's address could be broken up into a Street field, a City field, a State field, and a Zip field for the ZIP code. This makes finding the information easier.

Each customer has one record in the lead database and potentially *many* records in the support database. Let's say you need to be able to find a customer's name and address *and* his or her transactions. You can store the customer's name in the support database as well as in the lead database—so you can find him or her in both databases—or you can give each customer a unique number, like 21, and then include the number 21 in every transaction record belonging to that customer.

To assign a number to each customer, you would add a Customer ID field in both the lead database and the support database. You could then look for the customer by name in the lead database, find the customer ID number there, and then switch to the support database and look for the customer's transactions by customer ID. This type of setup is sometimes referred to as a *relational database*. Both files are considered as one database. You can display all the information together on the screen, to be edited, printed out, and so on. Using a relational database is the most common way of keeping track of customers in a business.

This is probably as much as you need to know about running a business—you don't have to worry about the advertising, market share, or product support to use Clipper effectively!

Key Points

Defining a Language

A programming language can be identified by how it answers the question "Will the programming language produce a product for others to use or is it an environment modification tool?"

What is Clipper?

Clipper is a programming language, an interpreter, a compiler, and a rich development tool which allows users to build effective applications.

Origin and Design of Clipper

Clipper appeared on the scene to speed up the dBASE language, which ran too slowly in interpreted form. Clipper is a well designed program that should remain prevalent in the language field for some time to come.

continues . . .

The Difference Between an Interpreter and a Compiler

With a compiler, the translation process is done only once for each piece of code. An interpreter, on the other hand, must translate the code each time it runs a program. A compiler produces an executable file which will run independently of the compiler.

Macros

A macro is a string variable that is translated at run time (when you run the program) instead of at compile time. Clipper permits the compiled code and interpreted code to work together to provide great flexibility to the programmer.

Basic Skills Needed for This Book

You will need some basic DOS and text editor skills, along with a desire to learn, in order to get the most out of this book.

CHAPTER

Getting Started

You can develop software using Clipper on virtually any personal computer with a hard disk. However, attempting to compile and link on a machine with anything less than a 286 processor can be very frustrating. Setting up the appropriate hardware and software environment can greatly enhance your productivity. This chapter discusses hardware considerations, software utilities, text editors, Clipper environment setup, an overview of the Clipper development cycle, and Clipper development utilities.

Hardware Considerations

Hardware is the physical equipment that makes up a computer system. The right hardware combination can make a considerable difference in the time it takes to compile and link programs. You should be able to buy a 386 clone with a 40-megabyte (MB) hard disk, a 1.2MB floppy disk drive, and a monochrome monitor for around $1000. It may be worth an additional $200 to get a VGA color card and monitor.

Microprocessor

The *microprocessor* is the brain of the computer. It monitors and directs all the activity of the computer and is the single most important factor in determining the speed of a computer. There have been many different microprocessors developed and there are always "new and improved" ones due to be released. Following is a list of processors from least powerful to most powerful: 8086; 286; 386-SX; 386; 486.

Another important factor regarding microprocessors is the megahertz (MHz) rating. *Megahertz* is the unit of measurement associated with the speed at which instructions can be processed. The higher the MHz, the faster the processor. This measurement may be used to compare processing speeds of the same processor, but it should not be used to make speed comparisons between different processors. There are other factors that affect the speed in addition to the MHz rating. For example, a 486 processor running at 33MHz will outperform a 386 processor running at 33MHz. This is due to the advanced architecture of the 486 processor.

Memory

Computer *memory* is a temporary high-speed storage area where data and programs reside while they are being processed. When you run an executable file, that file is loaded into computer memory from the hard disk. The processor reads instructions in memory rather than on the much slower hard disk. Both the Clipper linker and programs compiled in Clipper take advantage of *extended memory,* which is memory above the standard 640K. More memory makes linking your programs faster, and DOS 5 and above, allows you to load some DOS files and other memory-resident programs into extended memory.

Hard Disk

A *hard disk* is the storage medium for programs and data. The basic minimum you will need is a 20MB hard disk. Clipper 5 takes 6MB of storage. You could cut Clipper down to some basic programs and libraries and it would then come out to less, but it's not worth the effort. Other applications, such as Windows, WordPerfect, and dBASE IV, use around 5MB of disk space. DOS uses about 1MB. You can see how quickly the disk space can get filled up. If you are using one or more of these applications with Clipper, a 40MB hard disk or more may be necessary.

Video Display

There are many video board and monitor types. In general, the two have to match, although you can purchase multifunction video boards that allow a wide variety of monitors to be used with a simple switch adjustment. Clipper will work under any video type, but VGA is the preferred choice. Clipper also has functions that allow your software to detect video types—monochrome, CGA, EGA, or VGA. VGA offers the best *resolution*, which is the degree of clarity or, more specifically, the number of pixels (dots) per square inch.

Software Essentials

DOS and Clipper 5 are the primary software requirements for anyone wanting to program in Clipper. Become acquainted with the various DOS commands; you will spend a great deal of time dealing with the DOS prompt. There are many other utilities and enhanced editors that can make the job of programming much easier. Most of these utilities are very flexible because they allow the passing of parameters.

Parameters are variables within a batch file or program that receive values passed from outside that batch file or program. An example of a parameter would be the filename passed to the DOS DIR command, such as TEST.PRG, which is a parameter used within the DIR program to display the appropriate file listing. If you type **dir test.prg**, a directory listing of those files matching the parameter will be displayed.

File masks are often passed as parameters. These are used to specify a pattern of files to be acted on by the program. The standard wildcard characters are ? and *, and you may use them in place of characters to create a search pattern. A common example would be to pass *.PRG when you want to perform an action on all files ending with a .PRG extension. You use the * character to specify one or more characters, and you use the ? character to specify a single character. Using the DIR example, if you typed **dir *.prg**, the *.PRG would be a file mask passed as a parameter to the DIR program.

DOS Utilities

There are many DOS utilities that provide different capabilities. Even though you can do without them, they are really valuable tools. These utilities are available as shareware on electronic bulletin boards or as part of a package such as Norton Utilities or PC Tools. Most are now included in DOS 5.

File Search Utility

You use the file search utility to find files residing on a hard disk. A file mask or a specific name of a file may be passed as a parameter, and the program will display any matches found. Some names of file search utilities are WHEREIS.COM, WHERE.COM, and FF.EXE.

Text Search Utility

Sometimes you may need to search for text within files. A text search utility accepts a file mask and a text string as parameters and looks in the matching files for any matches of the text string. The text search utilities usually display the matching text highlighted within its surrounding text. You might use this type of utility, for example, when you have modified a function and that function is called throughout all your programs. You can use the text search utility to get a listing of all the files that need to be modified because of the change in the function.

DOSEDIT.COM

There is a utility called DOSEDIT.COM that sets up a *buffer* (temporary storage area in memory) of DOS commands that you have typed at the keyboard. This allows you to recall previously executed commands by pressing the UP ARROW and DOWN ARROW keys instead of having to type the commands again. This utility also allows you to edit the command line—a great advantage over the normal destructive BACKSPACE key. For example, you might use the DOSEDIT.COM utility if you mistyped a command. You would simply press the UP ARROW key to recall the commands you just executed and use the LEFT ARROW or RIGHT ARROW key to move to and correct the error.

File Size Utility

Utilities are available that will total the number of bytes in a directory or a subset of the directory by passing a file mask as a parameter. Some names for this utility are SIZE.COM and DS.EXE. DOS 5 provides this utility as part of the DIR command.

File Sort Utility

There are utilities available that will sort your directories based on different attributes of the files, such as the filename, extension, date, and time. An example of the use of this utility would be to find out all the programs you had modified after a specified date. You could use the file sort utility to sort the directory by date and time and then perform the DIR command to see which files were updated last.

Text Editor

Clipper comes with a simple text editor called PE.EXE (for "program editor"). However, you may want to consider other alternatives since it has very limited features. There is a vast array of text editors to choose from, such as Norton Editor, Brief, Edix, and Kedit. Most programmers have a favorite editor and believe the one they use is the best—probably because they are comfortable with it rather than because it contains superior features.

Edix is a favorite text editor of some programmers and was used to create the first version of Clipper. Brief is the current favorite at Nantucket Development. You will want to find a text editor that has powerful features and is easy to use.

Remember that a text editor is not a word processor. Microsoft Word and WordPerfect are examples of word processors. Edix and Brief are examples of text editors. A *word processor* provides many features that you really don't need in a text editor, such as word wrap, multiple font styles, and centering. Word processors also embed control characters, margins, page length, and other information within documents. You don't want this kind of information in your programs, with the exception of carriage returns, line feeds, end-of-file markers, and possibly tabs. If you *must* use a word processor, remember to save your program as an ASCII text unformatted document or you will have big trouble compiling your programs.

There are some essential capabilities that a good text editor should have. You should be able to invoke the important commands with one or two keystrokes. Let's look at what kind of actions you are likely to do and then see what kind of editor will do the job.

All text editors should provide the ability to load and save files and to move about within the file with a minimum number of keystrokes. Following are some other features that are highly recommended. In addition, you should be able to run DOS commands from within the editor. Table 2-1 gives a sampling of the commands available in Edix and their functions.

TABLE 2-1

Some Edix Commands and Their Functions

Command	Function
F1	Jump to window 1
F2	Jump to/open window 2
F3	Jump to/open window 3
F4	Jump to/open window 4
ALT-O	Give the whole screen to window 1
ALT-B	Load buffer (prompts for buffer number) in current window
F5	Move cursor to beginning of line
F6	Move cursor to end of line
F7	Help
F8	Mark block beginning/mark block end/remove mark from block
F9	Delete line
F10	Search
ALT-F10	Search again
ALT-T	Search and replace
ALT-W	Write out the file to disk
ALT-X	Exit Edix

Search and Replace

The *search and replace feature* lets you scan a document for a particular character string. With a simple *search,* you type the character string, and the editor finds the next occurrence of the string in your document. You should not have to reenter the character string to continue the search. A *global search and replace* changes all occurrences of the character string with a replacement string you have entered. A *conditional search and replace* changes each occurrence of the character string with a replacement string only after you confirm each change. There may be times when you accidentally perform a global search and replace. Some editors provide an *undo feature* that allows you to restore your document to the way it was before the search and replace changes were made.

Block Editing

You need to be able to perform actions on a *block* of text. That is, the editor should allow you to mark a beginning point and an ending point in the document, with the text between those points considered a block. You should be able to move, delete, or copy the block. The search and replace capabilities should be able to operate either entirely within a block or entirely outside a block.

Multiple File Capability

You definitely require the ability to open more than one window and load programs in each of those windows. This is necessary if you are to copy code sections from one program to another—a regular occurrence in programming.

Keyboard Macros

Some editors allow the creation of *keyboard macros.* These macros are quite different from the macros used in Clipper. A keyboard macro is used to create a *hot key*—a single keystroke combination that replaces a long sequence of keystrokes. For example, you could set up a keyboard macro so that each time you pressed ALT-P, your editor would type the

Clipper command SET PRINT ON. Keyboard macros allow you to create a custom version of the text editor, with all the keys performing the actions previously assigned.

Setting Up the Clipper Environment

There are several things you must do before you begin to program in Clipper. You must have Clipper installed and the appropriate adjustments made to the DOS environment. You will also want to create batch files to assist you in performing repetitive tasks. The following section will show you how to set up your Clipper programming environment.

Installing Clipper

If you haven't already installed Clipper 5, make sure you have plenty of extra disk space. Even though Clipper will fit in about 6MB, additional space will be needed. Each executable file created by Clipper will take approximately 200 to 400K. Some large Clipper applications have executable files that require over a megabyte of disk space. Give yourself room to grow; you'll feel kind of silly if you have just enough room to install Clipper and no room to compile and link programs.

To actually install Clipper, insert DISK 1 and type **install**. The Clipper installation procedure is self prompting from that point on. It should create a subdirectory called CLIPPER5 and directories under CLIPPER5 called BIN, INCLUDE, LIB, PLL, SOURCE, and NG. Within the SOURCE subdirectory, there should be the following subdirectories: DBU, PE, RL, and SAMPLE.

Organizing Directories

It is a good idea to set up a subdirectory to hold utility files. If you do not already have one, change to the root directory by typing **cd ** and then type **md util**. You may optionally move the executable files located in the \CLIPPER5\BIN directory to this utility subdirectory. Put all your other utility programs (such as those discussed earlier in this chapter) into this same directory. You may also want to put your editor into this directory.

It is necessary to keep your files organized if you want to simplify the compile, edit, and link cycle. Often, you may work on more than one project at a time. It is important to keep the code for each project separate. This is done by making a directory for each project.

The DOS PATH Statement

You must be able to run the executable files that are in your utility directory and the Clipper executable files from any subdirectory. You achieve this by using the DOS PATH statement in your AUTOEXEC.BAT file. This is a batch file that automatically runs when your computer boots up. It runs DOS commands that you want performed each time you turn on your computer. This file is where you place the PATH statement, as shown here:

```
PATH=C:\UTIL;C:\DOS;C:\BATCH;C:\CLIPPER5\BIN;
```

When you type a command, DOS looks in the current directory first and attempts to run the executable file. If DOS cannot find the file in the current subdirectory, it looks in the subdirectories listed in the PATH statement. In this example, it would look in the C:\UTIL, C:\DOS, C:\BATCH, and C:\CLIPPER5\BIN directories in an attempt to find the executable file. You can update your PATH statement to include any sub-directories you wish.

A DOS environment variable is created when you execute the PATH statement. An *environment variable* is a variable that can be assigned and detected at the DOS level and that resides in memory at all times once it has been set.

The LIB Statement

You will also want to include or modify the LIB statement in your AUTOEXEC.BAT file. The LIB statement tells Clipper where to look for library files when linking your program. It is similar to the PATH statement, but Clipper uses LIB to search for libraries rather than executable files. Here is a sample of the LIB statement that the Clipper installation program sets up:

```
SET LIB=C:\CLIPPER5\LIB;
```

File Handles

In the beginning, you will be working on small programs that use only a few database files, but at some point you may be opening a lot of database files. DOS assigns a file handle to each file that you open. A *file handle* is a space in memory that stores the information DOS needs to know about a file. DOS allows you to have only a limited number of files open at one time, but you can increase the number of file handles by making some adjustments to two files.

The first file you need to adjust is called CONFIG.SYS. This file, if it exists, resides in the root directory of your boot disk. The *root directory* is the highest level directory available and the first one normally encountered when running DOS. Other directories, called *subdirectories,* are attached below the root directory.

Using your editor, load the CONFIG.SYS file by typing the following command:

E CONFIG.SYS

(This book assumes that your editor is called "E".)

If you have a CONFIG.SYS file, there should be at least two lines similar to the following:

```
files=10
buffers=8
```

Change these two statements as shown here, or add them if they do not already exist.

```
files=55
buffers=8
```

The second file you need to modify is the AUTOEXEC.BAT file. The AUTOEXEC.BAT file should be modified to include the following line:

```
SET CLIPPER=F55
```

Before exiting and saving the AUTOEXEC.BAT file, make sure the Clipper installation program created the following lines:

```
SET LIB=C:\CLIPPER5\LIB
SET INCLUDE=C:\CLIPPER5\INCLUDE
SET OBJ=C:\CLIPPER5\OBJ
SET PLL=C:\CLIPPER5\PLL
```

Once you have exited and saved the file, you should have plenty of file handles to support the "file open" requests of your programs.

 Note You need to reboot your computer before these changes can take effect.

Batch Files

There are many actions involved in programming that you must repeat again and again, such as editing the program, compiling it, linking it, and running it. When you start programming, you can type the commands for editing a file, compiling a file, and so on, each time you need them, or you can enter the commands once in a batch file. You can then simply run the batch file by typing its name followed by the name of the program you are compiling and linking. The batch file is the only program file that does not need to be translated into machine code in order to run. The batch file is interpreted and run, line by line, by COMMAND.COM.

Let's create a batch file to handle the repetitive parts of the edit, compile, and link cycle. First, create a file called GO.BAT in your text editor. It should contain the following lines:

```
e %1.prg
clipper %1 /B
IF errorlevel=1 GOTO end
rtlink file %1 lib clipper, extend, dbfntx, terminal
```

```
IF errorlevel=1 GOTO end
%1
:end
```

The first line calls up the editor and the name of the program you want to edit. The %1 is a variable. Wherever the variable is mentioned, it will be replaced by a filename that you pass as a parameter to the batch file. If you typed **go myprog** at the DOS prompt, you would be running the GO.BAT program and passing the word "myprog" into the %1 variable. The value represented by %1 is called a parameter since it was passed to the program from outside the program. In this case, you will be passing as a parameter the name of the program you want to edit, compile, and link. When you type **go myprog**, where "myprog" refers to your Clipper program MYPROG.PRG, DOS will substitute the word "myprog," like this:

```
e myprog.prg
clipper myprog
IF errorlevel=1 GOTO end
rtlink file myprog lib clipper, extend, dbfntx, terminal
IF errorlevel=1 GOTO end
myprog
:end
```

DOS will run each line of this program as if it had been typed directly. The first line runs the editor and tells the editor to load your file, MYPROG.PRG. (Clipper programs all have an extension of .PRG.) The second line runs Clipper and tells Clipper to compile MYPROG.

The third line checks the DOS environment variable *errorlevel*, using the DOS IF command to see if Clipper failed to compile the program for some reason and set *errorlevel* to 1. If the compile did fail, the DOS GOTO command jumps to the DOS label :end. If the compile is successful, a file called MYPROG.OBJ is created. Rtlink, the Clipper linker, is executed; this links MYPROG to the library files CLIPPER.LIB, EXTEND.LIB, DBFNTX.LIB, and TERMINAL.LIB. If the linking action failed, then Rtlink sets *errorlevel* to a value of 1, which causes the program to go to the :end label. If the compile and link are successful, MYPROG.EXE is created. You can run this executable file by typing the name of the program, **myprog**. This is done in the sixth line of the batch file.

This procedure may seem confusing at first, but it is really simple in practice. Eventually, you will be writing batch files to do more than edit, compile, link, and run your Clipper programs. Refer to your DOS documentation for exact definitions and uses of the DOS commands and the use of batch files.

The Edit, Compile, Link, and Debug Cycle

Editing is the process of entering and modifying programs. This is where most mistakes are made. If you could write perfect code in the first place, you wouldn't be bothering with the edit, compile, link, debug cycle. You can probably write 10 lines without making a mistake—but try writing 100 lines without a mistake. This requires a great effort on the programmer's part.

Compiling is the process of having CLIPPER.EXE evaluate each line of your program. The compiler checks to see if the commands and functions are entered in proper syntax and produces error messages if they are not. The screen in Figure 2-1 shows an error message encountered on line 3 of the program called TEST.PRG. You must fix error messages before you can move on to the linking process.

Warning messages are also produced by the compiler. They alert you to potential problems if you decide to continue with the link process. The screen in Figure 2-2 shows an example of a warning message. In this

FIGURE 2-1   Program generating a compiler error

```
C:\MYPROG>GO TEST

C:\MYPROG>clipper TEST
Clipper (R) Version 5.01
Copyright (c) Nantucket Corp 1985-1991.  All Rights Reserved.
Microsoft C Floating Point Support Routines
Copyright (c) Microsoft Corp 1984-1987.  All Rights Reserved.
179K available
Compiling TEST.PRG
TEST.PRG(3)    Error C2002  Incomplete statement or unbalanced delimiters
1 error

No code generated

C:\MYPROG>IF ERRORLEVEL=1 GOTO end

C:\MYPROG>

C:\MYPROG>
```

case, an ambiguous variable was found in line 5 of the program called
TEST.PRG. Clipper defaults ambiguous variables to PRIVATE type visibility. Any variables that are not specifically declared are considered
ambiguous by the Clipper compiler. A more detailed discussion on
declaring variables is provided in Chapter 4.

Linking is the process of connecting all the programs required to run
your program. When you write your program. you are, in fact, making a
shopping list of other programs that will need to be available for the
commands in your program to work. For example, the CLEAR command
doesn't actually do anything except tell Clipper what you would like to
happen. Clipper reads the word "CLEAR" and understands that you want
to use the _CLRSCREEN() function and mentions that to the linker. The
linker finds the _CLRSCREEN() function sitting in the CLIPPER.LIB
library and makes a copy of it. That copy is then pasted into your
program. This process occurs for each command or function in your
program. The linker then assembles the whole thing as an executable
file, which is then ready to run.

Link errors usually result from the inability of the linker to find the
command or function you entered in your program. This may occur
because the command or function was mistyped or because the LIB
statement was not set up correctly. The screen in Figure 2-3 shows the
linker error message resulting from misspelling the Clipper function
called SETCOLOR() as SETDOLOR().

Debugging is the process of finding errors in your programs. There are
many possible types of errors that may not be discovered until run time.

FIGURE 2-2　　Compiler warning message

```
C:\MYPROG>clipper test /w /n /m
Clipper (R) Version 5.01
Copyright (c) Nantucket Corp 1985-1991.  All Rights Reserved.
Microsoft C Floating Point Support Routines
Copyright (c) Microsoft Corp 1984-1987.  All Rights Reserved.
250K available
Compiling TEST.PRG
TEST.PRG(5)    Warning C1004  Ambiguous reference, assuming memvar: 'VAR1'
1 warning
Code size 68, Symbols 64, Constants 12

C:\MYPROG>
```

FIGURE
2-3   Linker error message

```
250K available
Compiling TEST.PRG
Code size 48, Symbols 48, Constants 0

C:\MYPROG>IF ERRORLEVEL=1 GOTO end

C:\MYPROG>rtlink file test lib clipper, extend, dbfntx, terminal
.RTLink for Clipper  Dynamic Overlay Linker / Pre-Linker  Version 3.13
(C) Copyright Pocket Soft Inc., 1988-1991.  All Rights Reserved.


UNDEFINED SYMBOL(S) AFTER LIBRARY SEARCH:
       SYMBOL                                     FIRST REFERENCE
       _____                                     _____

       'SETDOLOR'                                 TEST.OBJ

warning wrt0022: .EXE may not execute properly -- undefined symbols
112K
1 warning message(s)

C:\MYPROG>IF ERRORLEVEL=1 GOTO end

C:\MYPROG>

C:\MYPROG>
```

Some will be *run-time errors,* which are problems that cause Clipper to terminate the program prematurely. Clipper then presents you with useful information, such as the error code and a brief description of the error. In addition, the program name and line number in which the error occurred are displayed. You would generate a run-time error if, for example, you attempted to print the value of a variable that you had not yet created.

Other errors are *logic errors* in your program. Logic errors are not run-time errors, but they do result in the program not behaving as you want it to. A good example of a logic error would be if your program calculated the wrong percentage of the tax owed on a transaction. Logic errors can be much more difficult to discover since you may not even realize that a problem exists.

Program testing is a crucial aspect in program development and considerable time should be set aside for testing your programs. You want to make sure that all the errors are out of a program before it is put into actual use. There are many techniques available for debugging programs. Clipper provides an interactive debugger called CLD.EXE, which allows you to step through your programs one line at a time.

To run the debugger on your program, type **cld myprog** at the DOS prompt. You can run your program as usual when using the debugger, but the debugger is always available when you press the ALT-D key combination. In addition, you can mark lines so the program will stop and allow you to use the debugging menus. The menus let you look at the contents of the existing variables, the names of the database files that are currently open, and so forth. You can easily check for errors by stepping through the program one line at a time if necessary. A more detailed discussion of the Clipper debugger is provided in Chapter 8.

Overview of Clipper

This section provides an overview of the Clipper programs. Refer to the *Clipper 5.0 Programming and Utilities Guide* for more information on each subject.

CLIPPER.EXE   CLIPPER.EXE is the Clipper compiler. It is the program that translates programs and produces object files. If you write a program called TEST.PRG, typing **clipper test** produces an object file called TEST.OBJ.

RTLINK.EXE   RTLINK.EXE is the Clipper linker. A *linker* takes the object files created by the compiler and merges routines contained in the library files and builds them into an executable file. A linker acts in much the same way as someone assembling a car. When the pieces of the car come up to the assembly line, the assembly-line worker attempts to assemble all the pieces. The car cannot be shipped out the door unless all the pieces are present. The same is true of a linker. It will not produce an executable file if all the pieces are not present.

RTLINK.EXE is a *dynamic overlay linker.* At one time, linkers placed all the necessary code in a single executable file. DOS loaded the entire file into memory when the program was executed. This presented problems since the maximum memory available for DOS programs is 640K, which is further reduced by COMMAND.COM and other memory-resident programs. *Dynamic overlays* allow programs larger than available memory to run by swapping programs in and out of memory as needed. When a call to a function is made, the Clipper *overlay manager* checks to see if that function is already in memory. If it is not, then it loads it from disk and replaces code residing in memory that is not being used at that time.

DBU.EXE   DBU.EXE is a database utility that you can use for creating database files, browsing data, creating index files, and performing a variety of utility functions on Clipper database files.

CLD.EXE   CLD.EXE is the debugger used to watch your code as it runs. The debugger allows line-by-line control of your code and makes problems easier to find. You can locate faulty code by controlling the features available in the debugger.

RMAKE.EXE   RMAKE.EXE is a utility you use to manage the compile and link cycle of Clipper applications. Batch files work well for simple projects, but it can become very difficult to maintain larger projects. RMAKE.EXE allows you to define the rules and files that make up a Clipper application. RMAKE.EXE then uses the DOS date and time stamps to determine if anything needs to be compiled or linked.

Key Points

Selecting the Right Hardware

Hardware is the physical equipment which makes up a computer system. The right hardware combination can give you a considerable advantage in the time it takes to compile and link programs.

The *microprocessor* is the brain of the computer. It monitors and directs all the activity of the computer and is the most important factor in determining the speed of a computer.

Computer *memory* is a temporary high-speed storage area where data and programs reside while they are being processed. Anything residing in memory is lost whenever you turn the computer off.

continues . . .

Key Points
(continued)

A *hard disk* is the storage medium for programs and data. It is considered permanent storage since it is not affected even when the computer is turned off.

The *video display* is the visual element of a computer system. The key components to the video display are video boards and monitors. There are many types of each.

Parameters

Parameters are variables within a batch file or program that receive values passed from outside of that batch file or program.

File masks are often passed as parameters to utility programs and are used to specify a "pattern" of files to be acted on by the utility program. Wildcard characters may be used in place of regular characters when creating the pattern.

Using Batch Files

Batch files can make the edit, compile, and link cycle much easier. You can store and run repetitive DOS commands rather than typing them out each time.

Adjusting File Handles

The number of file handles may be increased by modifying two files called CONFIG.SYS and AUTOEXEC.BAT.

continues . . .

Development Cycle

There are four steps involved in developing a program: editing, compiling, linking, and debugging, as described here.

❏ *Editing* is the process of entering and modifying programs.

❏ *Compiling* is the process in which the Clipper compiler evaluates each line of your program and attempts to create an object file.

❏ *Linking* is the process in which the Clipper linker connects all the programs required to run a program.

❏ *Debugging* is an attempt by the programmer to find errors in programs. The Clipper debugger is provided to make the job easier.

CHAPTER

Thinking About Design

*I*n this chapter the focus is on how to gauge your customer's intentions and on the development of good programming techniques. There are many techniques that make the development and maintenance of code easier. You need to develop the ability to program in such a way that you will be able to maintain the code and develop consistency and modularity. In addition, you must view projects from the top down, impose naming conventions, and document the code for future reference. This chapter will help you to start thinking like a professional programmer. Keep in mind that the examples are used only to demonstrate various concepts; don't worry if you do not understand the examples at this point.

What Are You Really Trying to Do?

Your goal in writing a Clipper application is to make the user more productive. The computer should automate time-consuming tasks and provide capabilities that would not otherwise be available. You are not trying to make the most amusing program or look like the smartest programmer. You can fool people for a while with a slick-looking system. However, if it is not easy to use and/or does not do the job intended, it will not be used. There are many aspects to developing a useful and maintainable Clipper application.

You must do a thorough job of determining exactly what the completed application should be. This is a very difficult task since the person paying you and the eventual users of the system may not even know what they want. Many users are fearful that the automation effort will make their jobs obsolete; therefore, they may be unwilling to cooperate and may give you incorrect or incomplete information.

You determine the requirements for a project by talking with everyone involved and observing the existing method you are attempting to automate. Some projects may require you to become an expert on the subject matter. Suppose you are going to write a program to keep track of helicopter maintenance records. The purpose of the program is to tell mechanics when to service the parts on helicopters. In this situation, you could be responsible for a helicopter crash if you don't become an expert in how the whole process works. Ultimately, it is your responsibility to find out everything there is to know about the subject matter.

There have been many instances where the programmer made a deal with the boss to produce product A and then proceeded to work closely with the end-user in evolving the product into B. When the boss came back and saw that the programmer had produced product B, which did not do what product A was supposed to do, the whole project was scrapped and the programmer was fired. On the other hand, there have been situations where product A was specified by the boss and implemented *exactly* as requested but was useless to the end users.

You have to learn to say no to requests that are technically wrong. The customer may say, "I want it to search six ways and give me all data on the screen at once, and...." Your job is to explain that it will take x resources in time and code to achieve that mechanism and to suggest suitable alternatives. Usually the moderator is time and money. You can tell your customer, "Sure, you can have the six-way search, but it will take x amount of time and y amount of money, and it will take $2y$ to maintain the software in the future." The customer must then decide which direction to go in.

Remember who is paying the bill and who is using the product. Sometimes you have to hold your tongue when customers ask for some things or exclude others. Your part in this puzzle is to make sure the ship doesn't hit the rocks. Will the internal design hold up to long-term abuse? Can you or someone else maintain the program later? There have been many instances where programmers were so compliant to bosses and users' requests that a monster of such proportion was created that it collapsed under its own weight.

Once you have a complete understanding of what you perceive the finished product should be, produce a document that reflects this. This document should be reviewed by everyone involved and be revised as many times as necessary until a full agreement is reached. This process reduces the possibility of misunderstanding. Misunderstandings may result in a great deal of additional work for you that may not be reimbursed.

As the project progresses, keep everyone posted of any changes from the original agreement. If you communicate well with all the parties involved, there will be few upsets. Your only problem at that point may be time. The majority of systems will take longer than estimated. This happens no matter how smart the programmer or systems analyst. Only the pessimists have a chance of being right. Take your most sincere guess as to how long it will take and then double that number. If the person requesting the job hears a programmer's guess, he or she should double that. This avoids "sticker shock" and severe upset. This is not because programmers are incompetent. The nature of software is that a program will become exponentially harder to implement and maintain the larger it becomes.

What Does the Customer Really Want?

It is difficult to gauge what the customer wants since the "customer" may be many people. Management does not usually know what it feels like to enter data all day long. The data entry person may not know what the long-term intentions of management involve. Some other member of some other department may be expecting a special report from the proposed system that is not included in the original design specification. The customer wants the end system to satisfy the requests of everyone involved. It is up to you to anticipate all of these needs. Your job is to rummage around and find all the loose strings associated with the proposed system, connect them all, assign importance to them or get the boss to assign importance to them, and present a coherent design that includes the requirements of all the necessary parties.

In some instances you may be working on an existing system to make corrections, or you may be a small programming cog in a bigger effort. In other instances, politics dictate that you cannot talk to everyone involved. In each of these cases, your hands are tied by circumstances; simply do the best job you can based on the information you are allowed to accumulate.

Ingredients for Success

There are many methods that facilitate the development of software systems. Not only do they enable you to write programs quickly, but they aid in program maintenance. Software *maintenance* is the process of fine-tuning programs. It means going back to fix a program that didn't work right, making an adjustment to a program to make it run more smoothly, or providing functions that did not exist before.

Good techniques will provide the ability to fix problems and incorporate new suggestions quickly. The customer will greatly appreciate this. Subsequent programmers will also benefit from the ability to delve into the code and make modifications themselves with little or no assistance from the original programmer.

Program as if every other programmer were coming to inspect your code. After a while you will be proud of your code. It will become "clean," "robust," "maintainable," and "modular," and you will have the satisfaction of knowing you have done a good job for the customer. In the long run, your reputation will get you more work at higher rates of pay, enabling you to tackle ever more challenging projects.

Modular Programming

Modular programming is defined as the process of breaking code sections into small *modules.* Ideally, these modules should be independent of all other modules, with the only information passing between the modules done through parameters or returned as the value from a function. This is known as the *black box approach.* Theoretically, two programmers given the same specifications should be able to produce modules that perform in exactly the same way, even though the internal logic may be quite different. Once the module has been tested thoroughly, you can put it in a library and never have to be concerned about the internal logic. At this point, you are concerned only with which parameters to pass and what the module actually does. It may take a little extra work to turn a section of code into a stand-alone module, but it is worth it. Attempt to think ahead and make the module as generic as possible.

The rule concerning modularity is, "If you can use the function without tinkering with the insides and without requiring knowledge of its actual internal structure, then it is modular." Modularity cannot be taken lightly as either a task or a design issue. The benefits of a modular design are substantial, and as these building blocks are developed, new code becomes easier and easier to implement.

The point is that the function can be used over and over, sometimes by different programmers working different projects, without anyone having to change the internals of the function. If an unusual situation requires a different version of the function, there are a couple of approaches to take. The first approach is to copy the module, make the necessary modifications, and then give the new module a different name. A second approach is to add additional parameters that will add functionality to the module but not affect the way it works for the existing calls to the module.

Most applications require the user to respond to questions asked by the program. The creation of a module to ask questions can be invaluable to both you and the user. You can simply pass the appropriate parameters to the module and let it do all the work. In the following example, the programmer passes the question as a parameter, and the dialog() function does all the work and returns the answer that the user typed.

```
answer := dialog("What is your name? ")
```

In this case, a user-defined function called dialog() is written to take care of positioning itself on the screen, possibly drawing a box, asking the question that you passed to it, and placing the result in a variable called *answer.* You could add additional parameters, such as the screen location in which you wanted the box to appear or perhaps a routine to make sure a valid name was entered.

You can add any number of features to the dialog() function with very little effort. The user benefits when the program has a consistent look and feel. If all questions to the user are handled through the same dialog() function, the user will recognize that when the screen generated by the dialog() function appears, it is "question time." You can create additional modules for other purposes that result in a consistent user interface.

Even though the modular approach lends itself to a more consistent user interface, you should make an effort to be consistent in your approach across modules. For example, the ESC key is normally used as an escape mechanism. The F1 function key is normally used as a help key. Users will come to depend on the ESC and F1 keys to perform their associated functions no matter what the users are doing. Some software manufacturers do not like to use the same keystrokes as others because they fear it may infringe on copyrights or because they want their interface to be unique. This causes endless problems with end users. Which key is the help key? Which key is the recalculate key? The best you can do is create your own standards as to how you want the user interface to be.

An important benefit of the modular approach is that it assists in isolating and correcting bugs. You need to make the change in only a single program instead of searching and fixing all the programs where a similar process is performed using a nonmodular approach.

Top-down and Bottom-up Design

Top-down design is the process of starting with the big picture and going into more and more detail as the design develops. The top-down approach is a common method of development. Automobile manufacturers design a beautiful car body first and then decide on where the engine and running gear are to be positioned. Once the basic shell and mechanical components are in place, the seat positions in relationship to surface areas are resolved. Finally, the color and design of smaller pieces such as the speedometer are considered. You may say that some of these pieces are designed simultaneously, but even here there is a top-down approach—big picture first, details later. Of course, while developing the top level, you must know what you are capable of doing at the lower level.

You first want to identify the major functions to be accomplished. Once those have been identified, then each of the major functions is broken up into lesser functions. This may continue for many levels until the modules are at the actual level at which coding can be done.

A *bottom-up design* occurs when the lower level routines are designed first, with the higher level routines built last. The databases may be defined first and the data entry screens next, and eventually everything is tied together through a menu system. It is very difficult to start by designing a database structure at the beginning of a project since the overall mechanics have not even been defined at that point. It usually means you have to dance back and forth between creating a database, creating a screen to enter data, making changes to the database structure, and so on, until the design is right.

There are appropriate situations in which to use bottom-up design. An example of this is if you are aware of routines that have already been developed. The upper level may be designed to accommodate these lower-level routines. A good programmer may also anticipate the lower-level routines that will be needed and begin work on them while higher-level routines are still being defined.

The top-down approach mimics the way the programmer or user would first experience the system and allows you to clarify the interface from a functional point of view. The top-down approach also resolves large issues first, such as which reports the customer wants, before going into finer details.

Naming Conventions

It is important to be particular when assigning names to files, database fields, memory variables, and function and procedure names. Developing a good method will make your programs more readable and avoids potential problems.

Avoiding Clipper Function and Command Names

There are 350 names of functions and commands that Clipper uses to represent its functionality—avoid using those names. Here is an example of a conflict:

```
say := "hi there"
@ 10,10 say say
```

The first line stores a character string "hi there" into a variable called *say*. The second line uses the Clipper command @ 10,10 SAY to display the character string inside the variable *say* on the screen ten lines down and ten columns over, starting from the top-left corner.

In this case, the first "say" is a Clipper keyword and the second "say" is the name of a variable. This will work because the SAY command is expecting an element following the word "say." Clipper may not be so forgiving in other instances.

Using Upper- and Lowercase

Notice that "say" was not uppercase in the preceding example. It doesn't have to be since Clipper is not case sensitive. But if you always write Clipper commands and functions in uppercase and your own commands and functions in lowercase, you will find it is much easier to differentiate the functions and commands you created from Clipper's commands and functions. The line

```
@ 10,10 SAY say
```

is much more readable even though there is a naming conflict.

Creating Unique Field and Variable Names

It is a good idea to precede the names of your functions and procedures with a character string identifying the person who developed the routine. For example, all routines developed by a programmer named Jim might start with "j_" and any developed by Brett might start with "b_". This will ensure that Jim and Brett do not create routines that have the same name.

You can differentiate between field names and variables in much the same way to avoid conflicts. Conflicts would not be a problem if you could always manage to give unique names to all your field names and variables, but that is a very difficult task. Clipper will give preference to a field name over a variable if you give them the same name. For example, if there was a variable called *lastname* and a field called lastname and you told Clipper to print "lastname" on the screen, the contents of the *field* called lastname would appear. This can become a headache.

There are ways around this potential headache. Clipper allows the stating of variables in the format m->*lastname,* where the m-> tells Clipper that the word following is a variable. This would allow the coexistence of a field called lastname and a variable called *lastname.*

Another alternative is to come up with a naming convention. You might make the first character uppercase for file and field names, and you can precede variables with characters to identify their type, as shown here:

l_fname	A variable with LOCAL visibility
g_fname	A variable with PUBLIC (global) visibility
s_fname	A variable with STATIC visibility
p_fname	A variable with PRIVATE visibility
Fname	A field name

The visibility of a variable is discussed in greater detail in Chapter 4. The important thing to note here is that a different naming convention is used for each type of variable. Here is a sample program using the preceding naming convention:

```
LOCAL l_fname := SPACE(20)
@ 10,10 SAY "Enter first name " GET l_fname
READ
SEEK l_fname
IF FOUND()
   CLEAR
   DO WHILE .NOT. EOF() .AND. l_fname == Fname
      ? Fname,Lname,Phone
      SKIP
   ENDDO
ENDIF
```

This sample program prompts the user to enter a first name into a data entry field. The variable called *l_fname* is declared to be LOCAL in the first line of the program. Since the variable name starts out with an "*l_*" it is easy to tell throughout the program that it is a LOCAL variable. The field names Fname, Lname, and Phone are easily identified since the convention used is first-character uppercase for field names.

First-character uppercase naming conventions may also be used for filenames, as the following example demonstrates.

```
USE Customer
INDEX ON Lname+Fname to Customer
```

This opens a file called Customer and creates an associated index file, also called Customer. (Index files are discussed in Chapter 4.) The fields called Lname and Fname are used to create the index file. How do you know the difference between field names and filenames if they are both first-character uppercased? Context! You always USE a filename and

INDEX ON field names to a filename. Thus, you can see whether field names or filenames are being used by studying the surrounding Clipper commands.

Naming Conventions for Filenames

It is a good idea to come up with a naming convention for filenames in addition to first-character uppercase. You could use the first two characters of the filename to describe the general system the database belongs to and the remaining characters to describe the purpose of the file. For example, the first two characters of the filename called APVENDOR indicate that it is an Accounts Payable database. VENDOR tells you it is the database used to store vendors. This naming convention allows you to easily differentiate between different systems that you may be maintaining. Here are some more examples:

UFHELP	Utility File/HELP file
GLACCT	General Ledger/master ACCounT file
ARCUST	Accounts Receivable/CUSTomer file
TBCUST	Time and Billing/CUSTomer file
PREMPL	PayRoll/EMPLoyee file

Using Descriptive Names

In the same way, you should use descriptive names for field and variable names. This example shows a program using a good naming convention:

```
LOCAL l_fname := SPACE(20)
@ 10,10 SAY "Enter first name " get l_fname
SEEK l_fname
IF FOUND()
   CLEAR
   DO WHILE .NOT. EOF() .AND. l_fname == Fname
      ? Fname,Lname,Phone
      SKIP
   ENDDO
ENDIF
```

The same code loses much readability if descriptive names are not used. You may remember what all the variables are used for right after writing it, but later you will need to familiarize yourself with the code before attempting to work on it. It is an even worse problem with large programs. Here is the same program with nondescriptive variable and field names:

```
LOCAL a := SPACE(20)
@ 10,10 SAY "Enter first name " get a
SEEK a
IF FOUND()
   CLEAR
   DO WHILE .NOT. EOF() .AND. a == b
      ? b,c,d
      SKIP
   ENDDO
ENDIF
```

Indenting

Code is much easier to read when indenting is used to offset certain sections of code. You use indenting when defining control structures such as DO WHILE/ENDDO, IF/ENDIF, DO CASE/ENDCASE and FOR/NEXT. It is important to indent even though Clipper does not require it. Note the difference in the readability in the following examples:

```
DO WHILE .T.
   DO CASE
      CASE season == spring
         IF garden
            DO plant
         ENDIF
      CASE season == fall
         DO harvest
      OTHERWISE
         DO nothing
   ENDCASE
ENDDO
```

This program is easier to read than the one that follows.

```
DO WHILE .T.
DO CASE
CASE season == spring
IF garden
DO plant
ENDIF
CASE season == fall
DO harvest
OTHERWISE
DO nothing
ENDCASE
ENDDO
```

It is best to plunge right in and make up names for variables, functions, constants, fields, and files and see what develops. When the code starts to look awkward in places, go back and rename variables and functions until they align more accurately. You will not get a perfect naming convention on the first pass, so don't worry about it.

Documenting Code

There is usually very little time to document your code. By naming the variables and functions as accurately as possible, you have performed a major step in the documentation of your code. However, there are times when even the most descriptive names cannot explain everything you are attempting to do in a program. Use the * to precede a line of comments. The // and the && tell Clipper to ignore anything following it. The following program demonstrates the use of the comment characters to place comments in your programs:

```
DO WHILE .T.
   DO CASE
      CASE season == spring
         *  check if there is a garden
         IF garden
            DO plant  && plant the garden
         ENDIF
      CASE season == fall
         DO harvest  // harvest the garden
      OTHERWISE
```

```
            && don't do anything
            DO nothing
      ENDCASE
ENDDO
```

When the comment characters occur first in a line, then the entire line is considered a comment. The * character may only be used to start a line. The && and // may be placed after Clipper statements and anything following will be considered a comment. A compiler error will result if you attempt to place the * character after a Clipper statement.

Don't bother commenting if it is obvious what the section of code is doing, but keep in mind that you or someone else may need to figure out what the section of code is doing at a later date. Good comments tell *what* the program is doing and *why*. The logic of a code section may be obvious at the time it is written but become obscure over time.

Sometimes it is necessary to make changes to existing programs. If you have time, make a comment about what was changed and why, and note the date it was changed. This could save time in the long run. For example, suppose you fixed a problem in a program and one week later a client calls with the same problem. The comments in your program could quickly tell you that the problem has already been fixed. If you had already sent them an update, you could remind them to install it, or you might explain a way to get around the problem temporarily. This eliminates the possibility of tracking down the same problem more than once.

The following example includes references to user-defined functions. Until now most of the functions mentioned have been Clipper functions, such as the SPACE() function. Examine the following section of code. Can you read it? Even if you do not understand everything about it, can you get a feel for what is happening? Notice that the variable names and, more important, the function names represent their purpose. You can get a good idea of what the task of a function is by looking at its name. You can tell what is stored in a memory variable, since it is named appropriately.

```
drawmenu()
answer := getprompt()
IF answer == nogood
   comment("We're shutting down")
   shutdown()
```

```
ENDIF
drawscreen("Customer")
openfile("Customer")
DO WHILE .T.
   action := getchoice()
   IF action == "ESCAPE"
      shutdown()
   ENDIF
   m_name := getname()
   SEEK m_name
   IF FOUND()
      DO CASE
         CASE action == add_key
            makerecord()
            getfields()
         CASE action == edit_key
            sayfields()
            getfields()
         CASE action == del_key
            delrecord()
      ENDCASE
   ENDIF
ENDDO
```

Clipper provides the ability to declare constants. *Constants* are entities to which you can assign unchanging values such as key codes. While memory variables must reside in a table in memory, and considerable internal housekeeping is associated with them, this is not so with constants. You have the ability to use mnemonic names for values while minimizing the memory requirements at the same time. Your programs can become more readable by using constants, as the following example illustrates.

```
IF last_key == K_UP
   DO stuff
ENDIF
```

is more understandable than

```
IF last_key == 5
   DO stuff
ENDIF
```

Clipper assigns a numeric value of 5 to the UP ARROW key. When you want to check to see what key the user pressed, you could compare the keypress with the number 5 or the constant called K_UP. If you use constants such as K_UP, the program becomes more readable.

Clipper provides many standard constant definitions for values such as numeric values of keystrokes. These *header files* may be included in your programs and the constants may be used in your programs. An example of a Clipper header file is inkey.ch, which is located in the \CLIPPER5\INCLUDE subdirectory. Here are some examples of constants from that file:

```
#define K_UP          5 // Uparrow
#define K_DOWN       24 // Dnarrow
#define K_LEFT       19 // Leftarrow
#define K_RIGHT       4 // Rightarrow
```

It is easy to see how constants may be used to make your program more readable. It may not be necessary to insert your own comments since it is fairly obvious what the section of code is doing.

Key Points

Goal of Clipper Applications

Your goal in writing Clipper applications is to make the end users more productive. You accomplish this by automating time-consuming tasks and providing capabilities that would not otherwise be available.

Becoming an Expert

As the programmer, you must become an expert on the subject matter for which you will be creating the program. You accomplish this by talking to as many people as possible and observing the existing method of operation.

continues . . .

System Description Document

A document describing the proposed system will reduce misunderstandings. The programmer must anticipate the needs of everyone involved and communicate the proposed system to the customer. This can only be done when a thorough job of determining the requirements has been completed. This document should be reviewed by everyone involved and revised as many times as necessary until a full agreement is reached.

Modular Programming

Modular programming is the process of breaking large code sections into smaller sections which can be reused over and over. It lends itself to a consistent user interface, but programmers should attempt to be consistent in their approach across modules.

Design Techniques

Top-down design is the process of starting with the big picture and going into more and more detail as the design develops. Bottom-up design is the process of starting with the detail and working towards the big picture. It is common to anticipate lower-level routines and work on them while the top-level routines are still being defined.

continues . . .

Naming Conventions

You should use naming conventions of filenames, field names, and variables to increase the readability of programs. Avoid using Clipper command and function names as variable names. Clipper commands and functions should be in uppercase and your own commands and functions should be in lowercase. Fields, variables, and filenames should be given descriptive names to make the program more readable.

Indenting

Indenting is the process of setting off code contained between Clipper control structures. It improves the readability of programs.

Documentation

You should use good documenting practices to make code more understandable and to identify the logic you used when you created the code. Other users may not be able to figure out why you did what you did; you yourself may forget after a time.

CHAPTER

Your First Application

*T*he basic idea behind a *database management system* is the creation of an automation process that gathers and stores data and then outputs that information in a useful format. This chapter uses a simple database management system—a customer tracking system—to illustrate the fundamentals of Clipper. This is a warm-up chapter. It covers the basic elements of a customer tracking system and concentrates primarily on developing menus and gathering some basic data. You will learn how to create a basic desktop-type layout on the screen. It will consist of a top menu bar, a pulldown menu, and a data entry screen.

Basic Concepts

Before you start to develop applications, you should be familiar with some basic concepts. The following sections briefly describe those concepts. Refer to the Clipper 5 reference guide for a more complete description of Clipper commands and functions used in the examples.

Variables

Variables are temporary storage areas that hold data. There are four basic types of variables in Clipper: numeric, character, date, and logical. You can use variables to store information while the program is working. A variable is initialized when it is first assigned a value. The value assigned determines the variable's type—either numeric, character, date, or logical. The type of a variable may be changed by assigning a value of a different type. Variables are also used to perform calculations and manipulations of the data.

Numeric Variables

You use *numeric variables* to store numbers. These numbers frequently represent financial figures such as revenue or payment amounts. This is where you cannot afford to make mistakes. Businesses rely heavily on the financial fields in a database. Misspelling a name or possibly transposing a number in a street address is minor compared to performing incorrect calculations when dealing with financial figures. You would be in big trouble if your program caused your customer's company to produce a $1000 vendor check when it should have been for only $10.

You should use numeric variables for a piece of data if you expect to perform mathematical calculations on the data. The hourly rate of pay of an employee, the number of hours he or she worked, and the percentages of tax deductions are examples of information that could be stored in numeric variables in the following manner:

```
STORE 7.35 TO l_rate
STORE 40 TO l_hours
STORE 0.045 TO l_taxperc
```

You perform mathematical calculations by using the following basic set of mathematical calculators:

+	Addition
−	Subtraction
*	Multiplication
/	Division

You can perform mathematical calculations on numeric variables to arrive at new values. Such a calculation, to determine the net pay due an employee, is shown here:

```
l_pay = l_rate * l_hours
l_taxamt = l_pay * l_taxperc
l_net = l_pay - l_taxamt
```

The first line arrives at the gross pay by multiplying the rate of pay (stored in *l_rate*) by the number of hours (stored in *l_hours*). The second line calculates the tax amount by multiplying the percentage stored in *l_taxperc* by the result of the first operation that was stored in *l_pay*. The net pay is calculated by subtracting the value stored in *l_taxamt* from the gross pay stored in *l_pay*. The result is stored in the numeric variable called *l_net*.

Character Variables

You use *character variables* to store strings of characters, such as a person's name, street address, and city. Character variables can accommodate very large strings but can also hold a single character. Here are some examples of storing data to character variables:

```
l_name = "Mickey"
l_city = "Orlando"
l_state = "FL"
l_answer = "Y"
```

You might use character strings to display text on the screen or to allow data input from the user. In most cases, it is up to the user of the application to enter the correct data in character data entry fields, but you should attempt to verify the data if there is a known set of valid responses.

Date Variables

You use *date variables* to store dates such as a person's birthdate or a transaction date. A special Clipper function called CTOD() may be used to initialize date variables, as shown here:

```
l_birth = CTOD("11/27/58")
```

The CTOD() function must be used in this case in order for the *l_birth* variable to become a date type. If it had not been used, *l_birth* would have been initialized as a character type. Some Clipper functions return a date type as their value, such as the Clipper DATE() function, as shown here:

```
l_currdate = DATE()
```

The DATE() function obtains the current date from the system clock of your computer. Keep in mind that this date is only as accurate as the date on your system clock. If the battery goes out, the DATE() function will not return a correct value. Most programs should display the current system date returned from the DATE() function to allow the user to verify that it is correct and modify it if necessary.

Logical Variables

Logical variables may be either TRUE or FALSE. You can use logical variables to control the logic within a program. By manipulating the value of the logical variable, you can keep track of certain conditions within the program. Clipper uses .T. to denote TRUE and .F. to denote FALSE, as shown here:

```
l_continue = .T.
g_demo = .F.
```

The first statement initializes the variable *l_continue* to a TRUE (.T.) value. This variable could be used to control flow of a program. The value of *l_continue* may change throughout the program and would, in effect, send a *flag* to the rest of the program indicating that the user did not want to continue.

Recall from Chapter 3 that "g_" is used to denote a global, or public, variable. The *g_demo* logical variable initialized in the preceding example could be used as a flag to indicate whether the application should be run as a demo or as a full-fledged application. The program might prevent the user from entering certain parts of the program if the *g_demo* variable were TRUE and allowing full access if it were FALSE.

Arrays

There is another type of variable called an array. An *array* is actually a collection of variables with the same name. Here is an example of how to create an array:

```
DECLARE var[100]
```

The number in the brackets is the number of elements in the array. In this case, the programmer is defining a variable called *var* that provides 100 elements in which to store data. Each of the elements may be assigned a value of character, numeric, logical, or date type. You can assign data to individual elements of the array by placing the number of the element in brackets, as shown here:

```
var[1] = "Jack"
var[2] = "Jill"
var[3] = 234.56
```

Clipper also supports multidimensional arrays that have multiple rows and, in addition, multiple columns. Here is an example of how to create a multidimensional array:

```
DECLARE var[5][5]
```

The programmer is defining 5 rows *and* 5 columns to the *var* array. This in effect creates 25 slots to store data. The columns could be used to represent various human attributes and the rows used to represent the individuals, as shown in Figure 4-1. You can then assign data to the array elements by enclosing the element numbers of the row and column in brackets, as shown here:

```
var[1][1] := "Jack"
var[1][5] := "Mary"
var[5][5] :=  144
```

You rarely access array elements by placing an actual number inside the brackets. Instead, you use a numeric variable to access the various elements within the array, as shown here:

```
x = 1
y = 1
? var[x][y]
```

This statement would be similar to

```
? var[1][1]
```

but would be much more flexible since the values of *x* and *y* may be changed by the program. It is common to traverse the whole array by using numeric variables. In this way, it would be easy to total a single column such as the weight column to get the total weight of all the persons contained in the array.

FIGURE
4-1

Representation of a multidimensional array

var[1][1]

	(Name) 1	(Age) 2	(Sex) 3	(Height) 4	(Weight) 5
1	Jack	30	M	69	145
2	Jill	21	F	73	165
3	Bill	25	M	65	140
4	Ted	37	M	72	162
5	Mary	20	F	67	144

var[1][5]   var[5][5]

Variables and Visibility

You will want to develop modules in such a way that the contents of the modules are hidden as much as possible. A module should not be influenced by other programs and, at the same time, a module should not influence other programs indirectly. The effect a module has on another module should be precise and predictable, as in this example:

```
x := getname()
```

getname() affects the current module only by changing the value of the variable *x*. One of the ways that programs can influence other programs is through variables. Controlling the *visibility* of variables is one way to reduce the effect that a module has on other modules. A variable can have one of four types of visibility—public, private, local, or static:

❏ A *public variable* is visible to every program in the system. Public variables are sometimes referred to as *global variables.*

❏ A *local variable* can be seen only by the function or procedure where it has been declared. It loses its contents upon returning to the calling program.

❏ A *static variable* is a special kind of variable. It must be declared immediately following the FUNCTION or PROCEDURE statement, and the value assigned will be used to initialize the variable the *first* time it is encountered. A static variable is visible only to the procedure or function in which it is declared; however, it retains its contents so that the next time that function or procedure is run those contents are again available.

❏ A *private variable* is similar to a local variable, except that it is visible by all programs that are called by the function or procedure in which the variable was declared. If a variable is not specifically declared, it becomes a private variable.

Here are two programs that demonstrate the concept of visibility:

```
PRIVATE message := "hi there"
DO func1
RETURN
```

```
PROCEDURE func1
@ 10,10 SAY message
RETURN
```

The procedure called func1 will print "hi there" because the variable *message* is visible; *message* is declared as a private variable. If *message* had been declared as local, a run-time error would have resulted when func1 attempted to print *message* since *message* was not visible to func1. There is really not much harm done in this example since func1 did not attempt to change the value of *message,* but that may not always be the case. It is important to manage your variable's visibility; otherwise the "bleed-through" effect might cause aberrant behavior in your code. If you know that the variable you are using in one routine is not going to be needed in the programs it calls, declare it local.

The following program demonstrates what can happen when you do not control visibility of variables:

```
m_age := "20"
DO func1
? "Jack is " + m_age + " years old"

PROCEDURE func1
m_age := "30"
? "Jill is " + m_age + " years old"
RETURN
```

This program will display Jack's age incorrectly. The "m_" prefix indicates a memory variable. The value of *m_age* was inadvertently changed by func1 when printing Jill's age.

The solution is to modify func1 in such a way that it cannot affect any variables outside it. Here is a revision of func1 that isolates it from its calling program:

```
PROCEDURE func1
LOCAL m_age := "30"
? "Jill is " + m_age + " years old"
RETURN
```

Declaring the *m_age* variable as local solved the problem in this case. You will avoid conflicts like this by declaring variables and controlling their visibility.

Passing Information Between Modules

Information may be passed between modules in many ways. The previous section on visibility described how variables declared as private and public may be changed at will by any subsequent modules that are called. Local and static variables may be changed by called programs by passing them as parameters. Parameters allow a module to modify variables used by its calling program. You do this by including a list of variables in the statement that calls a procedure or function. A list of receiving variables is declared within the function or procedure. These receiving variables are matched up one by one with the parameters passed.

The receiving variables may be declared within the function or procedure in two different ways. First, local variables are created if variables are declared as part of FUNCTION or PROCEDURE statements, as follows.

```
FUNCTION test(parm1,parm2)
* code goes in here
RETURN <value>
```

or

```
PROCEDURE test(parm1,parm2)
* code goes in here
RETURN
```

Second, if the Clipper PARAMETERS statement is used, private variables are created to accept the parameters passed by the calling program, as shown here:

```
FUNCTION test
PARAMETERS parm1,parm2
* code goes in here
RETURN NIL
```

or

```
PROCEDURE test
PARAMETERS parm1,parm2
* code goes in here
RETURN
```

The test procedure or function could be called in this way:

```
test(var1,var2)
```

The *var1* variable matches up with the receiving variable *parm1*. *var2* matches up with *parm2* in the same way. The original values of *var1* and *var2* would not change in the calling program even if the test procedure modified the value of *parm1* or *parm2* since the parameters were *passed by value*. This means that a copy of the variable is made and acted upon by the test procedure. The original variables remain unaffected.

The parameters may also be *passed by reference*, which allows their value to actually be changed and passed back to the calling program. When variables are passed by reference, the memory address of the variable is passed. Use the pass-by-reference operator (@) to pass variables by reference, as shown here:

```
test(@var1,@var2)
```

A procedure or function may also be called in this way:

```
DO test WITH var1,var2
```

The parameters are automatically passed by reference using this format. The called program can then modify the values of *var1* and *var2*. Avoid passing variables by reference as much as possible in order to control the visibility of variables.

The way a variable is passed can be rather confusing. Keep in mind that when you pass a variable by value, a new copy of that variable is created and acted on by the calling program. When you pass a variable by reference, you are just passing the memory address of the original variable. Any time you modify the value of the variable, you are modifying the original variable and not a copy of the variable.

Procedures Versus Functions

You may define a block of code as either a procedure or a function. The difference between the two is that a function may return a value or NIL, whereas a procedure will always return NIL. NIL is a new data type in Clipper 5. NIL indicates an unassigned variable or a meaningless value returned from a function.

Functions are more flexible than procedures since functions may be included in Clipper statements such as the @ SAY command covered later in this chapter. You use the @ SAY command to display information on the screen. Attempting to use the @ SAY command with a procedure will result in "NIL" being displayed since the procedure returns a value of NIL.

You terminate procedures and functions by using the RETURN command, which returns control to the calling program. The calling program is the one that called the current function or procedure. A function must return a value as part of the RETURN statement. The value may be of any data type, including NIL.

When creating a new module, a good question to ask yourself is, "Is the module going to return one and only one value?" If it is, declare the module as a function. Otherwise, declare it as a procedure. If a module needs to return more than one value to the calling program, use a procedure and pass the parameters you want to change by reference. This allows the called program to modify their contents.

Syntax Selection

Each new major upgrade of Clipper has resulted in numerous additions to the language. This provides you with many options when deciding which functions and commands to use or which statement syntax to use. Many functions and commands remain for compatibility reasons. These functions and commands allow programs written under previous versions of Clipper to run under Clipper 5 with little or no modification. An attempt should be made to choose the method that provides the best features. Here are some examples of Clipper SET statements that can be replaced with Clipper functions:

SET Statements	Functions
SET COLOR TO "W/B"	SETCOLOR("W/B")
SET CURSOR OFF	SETCURSOR(0)
SET CURSOR ON	SETCURSOR(1)

The functions in these examples provide greater benefits. For example, the SET CURSOR command allows you to turn the cursor off and on. The SETCURSOR() function allows you to turn the cursor off and on but also allows you to set the cursor to a variety of shapes. In addition, the function returns the current shape of the cursor. The great thing about having access to the current value is that you can easily write modules so that they restore the settings to whatever they were when the modules were first entered—even if the module changes the settings. For example, you may set the color by using either the SET COLOR command or the

SETCOLOR() function. The following example demonstrates the use of the SETCOLOR() function to restore the original color once the program is completed:

```
LOCAL mholdcol
CLEAR
@ 11,10 SAY "original color"
mholdcol = SETCOLOR("W/B")
@ 12,10 SAY "white characters on blue background"
SETCOLOR(mholdcol)
@ 13,10 SAY "back to original color"
```

In this example, the first line creates a local variable called *mholdcol*. The screen is cleared and "original color" is displayed. In the fourth line, the current color is returned to the variable *mholdcol* by calling the SETCOLOR() function. The SETCOLOR() function accepts the desired color as a parameter and sets the current color to white on blue. Once the program is done, SETCOLOR() is called again to restore the screen to the original color.

It is important to recognize the different styles available and realize the advantages of each approach. You may be required to convert your Clipper application so that it will run under dBASE. If this is a possibility, you will want to avoid code that could cause conversion problems.

The first program in an application must be a procedure. You may use either functions or procedures after that point. Ultimately, it is up to you to choose the style of commands, functions, and statement syntax that will meet your needs best.

Some statements may be worded differently but yield the same results. The following statements all increment the variable *var* by 1:

```
var := var + 1
```

```
var++
```

```
var+=1
```

These are all correct ways in which to increment *var*, but if you will ever need to run the program under dBASE, you had better stick with the first statement.

Decision Making

An application would not be very useful if it simply executed all the statements in the programs from beginning to end. The programs need to accommodate a wide variety of conditions and perform various sections of code depending on how those conditions are evaluated. The conditions may include user input and input from external devices, or maybe just the time of day obtained from the system clock. The programs must be able to make decisions based on the conditions. This is accomplished through the use of Boolean logic. *Boolean logic* provides the means by which you can control the flow of an application.

Following is a list of the various *logical operators* that are used as part of statements to control the flow of statement execution:

Operator	Conditions That Evaluate to a TRUE Value
.AND.	Both expressions are true
.OR.	One or the other expression is TRUE
.NOT.	One or the other expression is FALSE
$	The first expression is contained within the second expression

You use Boolean logic to control branching in programs. *Branching* occurs when a program separates in different directions depending on the evaluation of a condition.

Simple Branching

You should use the IF/ENDIF control structure if you need a section of code to execute only if a certain condition is met. The IF statement evaluates a single condition and then performs a section of code if the condition evaluates to TRUE. Here is an example of the IF/ENDIF control structure using the .AND. operator:

```
IF leaf==green .AND. season==winter
   tree:=coniferous
ENDIF
```

In this example, Boolean logic is used to evaluate the condition following the IF statement. If the condition is evaluated to be TRUE, the statement(s) within the IF/THEN structure would be executed.

The ELSE statement may be used with the IF control structure to provide an alternate sequence of instructions to be executed if the expression evaluates to be FALSE, as in this example:

```
IF leaf==green .AND. season==winter
   tree:=coniferous
ELSE
   tree:=deciduous
ENDIF
```

In this case, there is a section of code to be processed no matter what the result of the condition is.

The following example demonstrates the .OR. logical operator. One expression or the other must be TRUE in order for the code between the IF and ELSE statements to be executed:

```
IF vehicle==fire_truck .OR. vehicle==ambulance
   * emergency code
ELSE
   * non emergency code
ENDIF
```

Clipper always evaluates two expressions at a time, even if there are more than two expressions in a single statement. For example, in a statement with three expressions, Clipper evaluates the first and second expression first and then evaluates that result with the third expression. You can use parentheses to control the order in which the expressions are evaluated. This can be very important, as shown here:

```
IF (vehicle==fire_truck .OR. vehicle==ambulance) .AND. lights_on
   * emergency code
ELSE
   * non emergency code
ENDIF
```

In this example, the entire expression will evaluate to TRUE if the vehicle is a fire truck and its lights are on. If it is a fire truck and its lights are off, the expression will evaluate to FALSE. The same statement would yield a different result without the parentheses. The expression would evaluate to TRUE if the vehicle is a fire truck and its lights are on, just as before, and the appropriate emergency code would be executed. However, if it were a fire truck and its lights were off, the expression would also evaluate to TRUE. The program would go ahead and perform the emergency code even though there was not an emergency. Clipper evaluated the statement in a different order:

```
IF vehicle==fire_truck .OR. (vehicle==ambulance .AND. lights_on)
```

In this case, the expression evaluates to TRUE since the vehicle is a fire truck. The right side of the equation does not even need to be considered since one of the conditions of the .OR. logical operator has already been met. The parentheses are required in order for the statement to evaluate correctly. Use parentheses to avoid any possible conflicts when there are more than two expressions to be evaluated.

Complex Branching

The CASE control structure is similar to the IF control structure, but CASE allows the evaluation of many different conditions. The program executes the code following the first CASE statement and continues until the next CASE, OTHERWISE, or ENDCASE statement. If none of the statements are TRUE, Clipper executes whatever follows the OTHER-WISE statement and continues until the ENDCASE statement. Here is an example of a case statement:

```
DO CASE
    CASE condition1
        DO stuff()
    CASE condition2
        DO stuff2()
    OTHERWISE
        DO default()
ENDCASE
```

If *condition1* is evaluated to be TRUE, stuff() will be executed. The program will then jump to the statement immediately following the ENDCASE statement. The CASE statement is useful when you need to evaluate many possible statements and branch control of your program to only one section of code depending on how the statements are evaluated.

It is always a good idea to provide default code that should be executed even if you think it will never be executed. You can simply display a message like this:

```
OTHERWISE
    ? "This should never execute!"
    INKEY(0)
ENDCASE
```

This code simply displays a message and pauses the program until a key is pressed. The message tells you that your program is not working like it is supposed to. These types of comments are especially helpful when you are testing an application; they may be removed once you are sure the program is working correctly.

Looping Structures

You use *looping structures* to repeatedly execute a series of instructions until a condition is met. Most programs will need to sequence a database one record at a time, from beginning to end. The DO/WHILE construct performs this task well, as shown here:

```
USE Testdb
DO WHILE .NOT. EOF()
   *   process the record
   SKIP
ENDDO
```

The first line of this example opens a database called Testdb and steps through it one record at a time. Clipper maintains a *record pointer* for each database you open. When a database is first opened, the record pointer is positioned at the first record. The Clipper function EOF() returns a logical variable indicating whether the record pointer is positioned beyond the last record. The statement DO WHILE *condition* will continue to process the statements between the DO WHILE and ENDDO statements as long as *condition* is evaluated to be TRUE. The Clipper SKIP statement causes the record pointer to move to the next record. In this case, .NOT. EOF() is the condition that is evaluated. The loop will continue to execute as long as the record pointer has *not* reached the end-of-file marker.

Here is another example of a DO WHILE/ENDDO loop:

```
LOCAL x := 0
DO WHILE x < 10
   * do something
   x++
ENDDO
```

The DO WHILE in this example continues as long as the condition $x < 10$ is evaluated to be TRUE. The first line initializes a local variable x to a value of zero. The variable x is incremented each time through the loop. At the point when the value of x is equal to 10, the DO WHILE/ENDDO loop is done and the program will execute the statement immediately following the ENDDO statement.

When you are writing looping structures, it is important to make sure the condition will cause an exit from the loop at some point. If you forget to put the SKIP statement inside a DO WHILE .NOT. EOF() loop, the loop will continue forever—or until you press ALT-C to terminate the Clipper program.

Creating Menus

The top-down approach to programming implies that you start with the user's view. Most applications present the user with a top-level menu of some kind. Some programs simply list the menu items with a number next to each menu item. The user then enters the number to make a choice. Clipper provides an easy way to create menus in which the user moves a highlight bar to make selections. These menus give a polished look to a finished application.

Organizing the Menu Items

Be sure you understand what the user is going to do with the system you are developing. Once the needs of the customer have been analyzed, you can come up with the main menu items for the application. The main menu categories needed for our customer tracking system are customer information, reports, and maintenance.

Here are some items that should appear on the CUSTOMERS menu:

CREATE
MODIFY
DELETE

Under REPORTING, you could have

CUSTOMER LIST
TRANSACTIONS by MONTH
TRANSACTIONS by CUSTOMER
OUTSTANDING ACCOUNTS
MAILING LABELS

Under MAINTENANCE, there could be

BACKUP DATA
RESTORE DATA
REINDEX FILES

It is also a good idea to create a menu system that visually assists in finding selections. The most frequently used items should be presented on the left, with the least used items to the right. By designing the menu choices in such a way as to present the big decisions early on (such as editing versus reporting) and then going into more and more detail with lower level menus, you emulate the way the user thinks. First you choose to buy shoes, then you find a shoe shop, then you find the men's or women's section, and then you find the jogging section. This zoom-in technique is how people deal with a lot of subjects; it's a good idea to stick with that analogy when designing systems.

Remember, if you run out of room for choices on a pulldown menu, you can also create submenus. The submenus will pop up to the left or right of the main menu, or perhaps below it. This design in the sample customer tracking system allows three choices across the top, with possibly ten choices per pulldown and ten choices per sub-pulldown. This works out to 300 menu choices, which should be sufficient for most applications.

Displaying the Menu Screen

The first task when displaying a menu is to clear the screen and display any appropriate headings. It is a good idea to get the mechanics of the menu down first and worry about the cosmetics later. Here are the first three lines of the menu program:

```
CLEAR
@ 0,65 SAY DATE()
@ 0,35 SAY "CUSTOMER TRACKING"
```

The first line simply clears the screen. It ensures that the screen is clear at the beginning of the program.

You use the @ SAY command to put strings of text on the screen, and you use it in conjunction with the @ GET command, which allows the input of data at a particular spot on the screen. (The @ in the @ SAY and @ GET commands should not be confused with the pass-by-reference operator, which is also @. Clipper looks at the context of the statement to resolve issues such as this.) Clipper calls the first line on the screen line 0 and the first column on the screen column 0. The screen is divided into 25 lines (0-24) and 80 columns (0-79).

The second line of the sample program displays the current date on the top line. This enables the user to visually check to make sure the system clock has the right time.

The third line of the program displays a heading indicating the purpose of the program. Once the program is complete, you can add additional @ SAY statements to add further help information to the menu.

Processing the Menu

The Clipper PROMPT command places strings on the screen in the same way as the SAY command. In addition, PROMPT works with the MENU TO command by allowing the user to move the cursor up and down (or right and left) through a group of PROMPT commands. The current item is switched to inverse video. *Inverse video* displays a bright background with dark characters, as opposed to the normal bright characters on a dark background.

Here is a sample program that uses the PROMPT and MENU TO commands to display a menu:

```
@ 1, 1 PROMPT "CUSTOMERS"
@ 1,30 PROMPT "REPORTING"
@ 1,61 PROMPT "MAINTENANCE"
MENU TO choice
```

When the user presses ENTER on a menu item, the number corresponding to the selected choice is stored to the *choice* variable. If the user presses ESC, a zero is stored to the *choice* variable.

Here is the combined menu program, which does nothing more than present the menu items and display the number of the choice selected, as shown here:

```
CLEAR
@ 0,65 SAY DATE()
@ 0,35 SAY "CUSTOMER TRACKING"
@ 1, 1 PROMPT "CUSTOMERS"
@ 1,30 PROMPT "REPORTING"
@ 1,61 PROMPT "MAINTENANCE"
MENU TO choice
@ 3,1 say choice
```

In this menu example, the user could move the highlight bar to one of the choices by using the LEFT ARROW or RIGHT ARROW key, and then select the choice by pressing ENTER.

Repeating the Menu

The problem with the preceding program is that it returns to DOS as soon as the user makes a selection. The menu should be repeated over and over until the user presses ESC, as shown here:

```
*   TEST.PRG
*
DO WHILE .T.
   CLEAR
   @ 0,65 SAY DATE()
   @ 0,35 SAY "CUSTOMER TRACKING"
   @ 1, 1 PROMPT "CUSTOMERS"
   @ 1,30 PROMPT "REPORTING"
   @ 1,61 PROMPT "MAINTENANCE"
   MENU TO choice
   IF choice = 0
      RETURN
   ENDIF
   @ 3,1 say choice
ENDDO
```

The DO WHILE statement causes the program to loop indefinitely. The "IF choice = 0" statement provides an escape route should the user press the ESC key. If the user presses ESC, the RETURN statement is executed; this returns control to the calling program (or DOS). If the user does not press the ESC key, the choice entered is displayed using the @ SAY command.

Initial Testing of the Menu

Since it is usually a good idea to test programs as you are developing them, this might be a good time to do it. By running the program, you can determine that the menu is looping correctly and is returning the correct value when the user makes a selection. You can make sure that the ESC key exits the menu.

If you want to try this program, go to the root directory and create a directory called CUST. Enter the preceding program using your text editor, and save the file as CUST.PRG. Use the GO.BAT batch file created in Chapter 2 to compile and link the program. At the DOS prompt, type this command:

go cust

Fix any compiler errors and recompile as many times as necessary until you are able to run the executable file called CUST.EXE. Adding features to your program one step at a time makes testing easier. When you add new code and it results in a bug, you can zero in on the problem by concentrating on the code that was just added.

Branching of the Menu

The next step is to place a CASE control structure to handle the user's selections and some *dummy procedures* that do nothing but say "You are here." The dummy procedures allow your program to compile and link without errors while at the same time giving you the ability to check if the menu program is actually calling and executing the procedures correctly.

Here is the main menu with calls to the dummy procedures:

```
DO WHILE .T.
   CLEAR
   @ 0,65 SAY DATE()
   @ 0,35 SAY "CUSTOMER TRACKING"
   @ 1, 1 PROMPT "CUSTOMERS"
   @ 1,30 PROMPT "REPORTING"
   @ 1,61 PROMPT "MAINTENANCE"
   MENU TO choice
   DO CASE
      CASE choice == 0
         RETURN
      CASE choice == 1
         entry()
      CASE choice == 2
         rpt()
      CASE choice == 3
         maint()
   ENDCASE
ENDDO
```

```
RETURN

PROCEDURE entry
@ 22,1 say "THIS IS PROCEDURE ENTRY"
INKEY(0)
RETURN

PROCEDURE rpt
@ 22,1 say "THIS IS PROCEDURE RPT"
INKEY(0)
RETURN

PROCEDURE maint
@ 22,1 say "THIS IS PROCEDURE MAINT"
INKEY(0)
RETURN
```

The CASE statement handles the user's selection and branches to the appropriate procedure unless the user presses the ESC key. Each procedure displays a message at row 22 and column 1 and uses the INKEY(0) function to pause until a key is pressed. Once a key is pressed, control is passed back to the main program, where the DO WHILE loop causes the menu to be displayed again. At this point, you know the main menu works and can concentrate on the lower level modules, one procedure at a time.

Adding Pulldown Menus

The same techniques used to develop the main menu can be used to develop the submenus. Allow the user to view the main menu while at the submenu if at all possible. This means setting the menu off to one side of the main menu.

Here is the basic format for a submenu:

```
PROCEDURE entry
LOCAL choice := 0
#DEFINE boxstring CHR(213)+CHR(205)+CHR(184)+CHR(179)+;
        CHR(190)+CHR(205)+CHR(212)+CHR(179)+CHR(32)
DO WHILE .T.
```

```
@ 2,0,6,10 BOX boxstring
@ 3, 1 PROMPT "CREATE"
@ 4, 1 PROMPT "MODIFY"
@ 5, 1 PROMPT "DELETE"
MENU TO choice
DO CASE
   CASE choice == 0
       RETURN
   CASE choice == 1
      makecust()
   CASE choice == 2
      editcust()
   CASE choice == 3
      delcust()
   ENDCASE
ENDDO
RETURN

PROCEDURE makecust
RETURN

PROCEDURE editcust
RETURN

PROCEDURE delcust
RETURN
```

The preceding section of code looks very similar to what was done with the main menu. Notice that the PROMPT coordinates are going down instead of across. The BOX command has been added, which will draw a box around the items in the menu. The numbers 2,0,6,10 refer to the top left (2,0) and bottom right (6,10) coordinates of the box.

Using Constants in the Menu

The constant *boxstring* is defined as a series of patterns. The statement is split into two lines using the semicolon, which indicates the statement continues on the next line. The #define statement is used to assign a value to a constant. (Remember that a constant is similar to a variable, except that it cannot change its value when the program is run.) Key codes are the most common use of constants. The key code 27, which represents the ESC key, can be assigned to a constant K_ESC, like this:

```
#define K_ESC 27
```

which then allows tests such as

```
IF key_hit == K_ESC
   RETURN   //  leave this screen
ENDIF
```

When the program is compiled, every occurrence of the symbol K_ESC is replaced with the constant value 27. A constant may look like a variable, but its value never changes. A constant does not need the internal programming overhead required for tracking variables; thus the program runs more quickly and takes up less internal memory space.

The CHR() function is used to represent the ASCII code as a symbol associated with the screen; for example, CHR(65) = "A", CHR(97) = "a", and CHR(32) = a blank space. The codes being assigned to the *boxstring* constant represent patterns that look like parts of a box, with CHR(213) representing the pattern for the top-left corner of a box. There are nine patterns used; top-left corner, top horizontal, top-right corner, right vertical, bottom-right corner, bottom horizontal, bottom-left corner, left vertical, and a character used to fill the contents of the box, in this case a blank, CHR(32). The BOX command requires this string of symbols in order to paint a box. As you become comfortable with this command you may refer to a file called BOX.CH, included with Clipper, that contains samples of other box patterns.

Controlling Visibility of the User's Choice

Looking again at the program, notice that *choice* has now been declared as local. The LOCAL statement indicates that this version of *choice* will be seen only by the current program, thus avoiding confusion with the *choice* variable in the preceding program. In this way, its visibility is controlled. You could use the *choice* variable in any other programs and not have to worry about the effect on the current module. The PROMPT command positions the cursor according to the contents of the *choice* variable. Visibility problems could result in the prompt's being positioned at the wrong main menu item when the user returns from a lower level menu.

Duplicating the Submenu

Don't attempt to rewrite your menu program each time you want a new menu. Simply copy the module and change the lines to accommodate your new submenu—for example, change the lines controlling the menu's placement on the screen, the menu items displayed using the PROMPT command, and the branching statements. In the customer tracking system example, the format used for the entry procedure could also be used for the rpt and maint procedures, as shown here:

```
PROCEDURE rpt
LOCAL choice := 0
DO WHILE .T.
   @ 2,30,8,59 BOX boxstring
   @ 3,31 PROMPT "   CUSTOMER LIST                "
   @ 4,31 PROMPT "   TRANSACTIONS by MONTH        "
   @ 5,31 PROMPT "   TRANSACTIONS by CUSTOMER     "
   @ 6,31 PROMPT "   OUTSTANDING ACCOUNTS         "
   @ 7,31 PROMPT "   MAILING LABELS               "
   MENU TO choice
   DO CASE
      CASE choice == 0
         RETURN
      CASE choice == 1
         comment("This is CUSTOMER LIST")
      CASE choice == 2
         comment("This is TRANSACTIONS BY MONTH")
      CASE choice == 3
         comment("This is TRANSACTIONS BY CUSTOMER")
      CASE choice == 4
         comment("This is OUTSTANDING ACCOUNTS")
      CASE choice == 5
         comment("This is MAILING LABELS")
   ENDCASE
ENDDO
RETURN
```

```
PROCEDURE maint
LOCAL choice := 0
DO WHILE .T.
   @ 2,61,6,79 BOX boxstring
   @ 3,62 PROMPT "  BACKUP DATA     "
   @ 4,62 PROMPT "  RESTORE DATA    "
   @ 5,62 PROMPT "  REINDEX FILES   "
   MENU TO choice
   DO CASE
      CASE choice == 0
         RETURN
      CASE choice == 1
         comment("This is BACKUP DATA")
      CASE choice == 2
         comment("This is RESTORE DATA")
      CASE choice == 3
         comment("This is REINDEX FILES")
   ENDCASE
ENDDO
RETURN
```

When you are ready to enter this code into a text editor, you may want to copy the code of the entry procedure to create the rpt and maint procedures. You will need to modify the @ BOX statement to draw the box at different coordinates. The PROMPT commands will need to be modified to handle the different location and menu options available under REPORTING and MAINTENANCE.

Database Maintenance

Database maintenance is one of the major tasks involved in creating an application. Good planning up front will reduce the changes you have to make to database structures in the future. Clipper comes with a utility called DBU.EXE that allows you to create database structures, copy files, browse data, and perform numerous other file maintenance tasks.

Analyzing Your Database Needs

After talking to your customer, you should have an idea of the fields you need for your system. Database field types are very similar to variable types, with the addition of one more, called a memo type. A *memo type* is actually just a very long string. Memo fields allow you to enter an extensive amount of text by pulling up a mini word processor. Clipper handles memo fields differently than other fields. Normally, all of the data is stored in a file with a .DBF (Data Base File) extension. When you add a memo field to a database, a separate file with a .DBT (Data Base Text) extension is created. Any time you edit a memo field, the data is stored in the .DBT file and a connection is established between the .DBT and .DBF files.

You must assign descriptive names to the fields in your database and also assign the type and length of each field. It is worthwhile to review the customer's existing customer records to get a good idea of the data you will need to store. In this way, you can also estimate how long the fields need to be. In time, experience will help you decide on field lengths and the fields you will need. It is always best to make the field lengths longer than you will need, since it is extra work to make them longer once the system is in place.

In a customer database, you want the customer's first and last names, complete address, and phone number. In addition, you want to have a unique ID for each customer. The Id field will be used to tie the customer record to records in the transaction file. You will need a field in the transaction file of the same type and length as the Id field in the customer database. You will also want a product name, description, quantity purchased, and the cost of each item in the transaction file.

Creating the Databases

You need to know how to create databases in order for your system to serve any useful purpose. To create a database, first change to your application directory and type **dbu** at the DOS prompt. You will be presented with an opening DBU screen. Press F3 and then select DATABASE by pressing ENTER. You are then prompted to enter the name of the field, the field type, and the field length, as well as the number of decimal positions (if the field is a numeric one). The screen in Figure 4-2 illustrates the fields used in the customer tracking system.

There is one additional field to add, called Phone. It is a character type field and has a length of 12. When using DBU, press the DOWN ARROW key when you are at the bottom of the field entry screen, and all the fields will scroll up. This allows you to enter as many fields as you need. Once you have entered all the database fields, press F4 to save the structure. "STRUCT" will be highlighted, and you should press ENTER to confirm. Type the name of your database (Customer in the example program) in the File box presented and press ENTER again. Press ENTER at the OK box to actually save the database to disk.

Create all the necessary databases for your application in the same way. In the customer tracking system, you would enter the Trans database fields shown in Figure 4-3 and follow the same steps as in the previous example.

FIGURE 4-2

Customer database structure

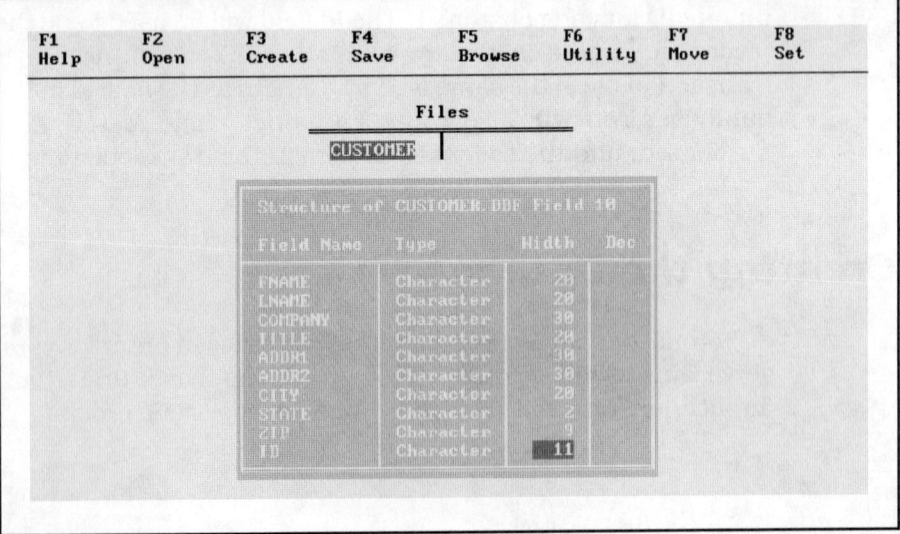

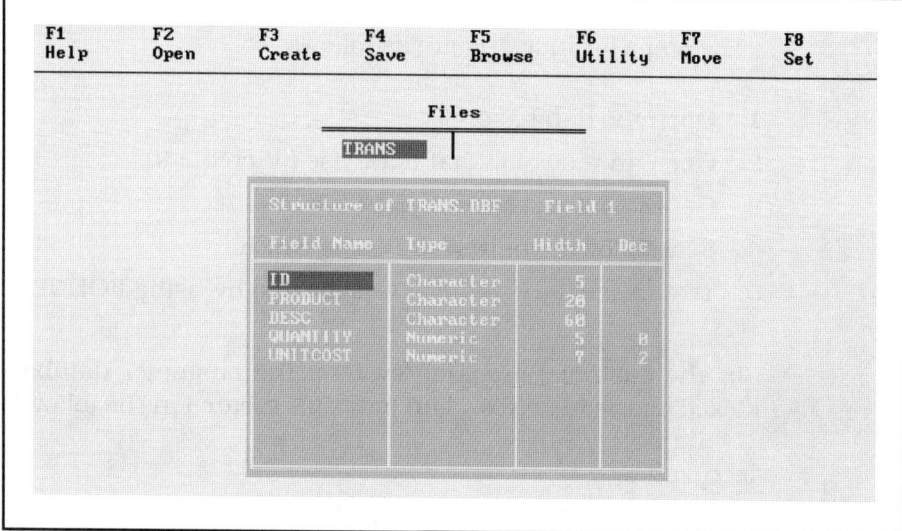

FIGURE 4-3 Transaction database structure

When you are entering the data types of fields, the character type is the default type. Pressing ENTER results in the field's being saved as character type. If you need to declare a field as a numeric, logic, date, or memo type, use the SPACEBAR to toggle through the various field types until the desired type is presented. In the customer tracking system, press the SPACEBAR when entering the Unitcost field until "Numeric" is displayed.

Numeric fields also require you to enter the number of decimal positions. Keep in mind that you have to add an extra character to the length of a numeric field to accommodate the decimal point.

Indexing

There are two ways to search for records in a database. The first is to do a sequential search starting at the top of the database and checking each record until you find a match. A better method is to *index* the file on certain key fields within the database. An index file provides you with the ability to look at your database in sorted order even though the database is not sorted in any particular order. An index file also allows you to perform quick searches by using the SEEK command.

The steps for indexing are as follows:

1. Open the database.
2. Open an index for that database (or create it).
3. Get the pattern to be sought.
4. Search for the pattern by using SEEK.
5. Test to see if the pattern was located by using FOUND().

In the customer tracking system, the customer database could be indexed on the Id field and an index file created in the following manner:

```
USE Customer
INDEX ON Id TO Customer
```

In the example, Id is the field to be indexed on. You can index on a single field or any combination of fields. An index file has an extension of .NTX. The example creates an index file called Customer that is sorted in ID order. This index could have been created by using DBU, but indexes are usually created within the application.

Creating an Index

To create the index file from within a program, you must first open the database. Indexing a file takes time and is normally done at the beginning of a program if the index does not already exist. If the index exists, you simply activate it by first opening the database and then switching on the index, like this:

```
USE Customer
SET INDEX TO Customer
```

This example opens the database called Customer and its associated index file called Customer. The database is then sorted by the index expression specified when the index was created.

Using an Index to Search

The SEEK command works with an indexed file to rapidly find a record where the key matches the pattern it is seeking. A *key* is an expression, usually a list of fields, that is used to build an index. In the following example, the key is the Id field. The index file will be built in alphabetical order using that field as its guide. An index could have just as easily have been built on the City field, the State field, or the Zip Code field. A single database may have many indexes associated with it. The following search() function demonstrates the use of an index file and the Clipper SEEK command:

```
FUNCTION search()
LOCAL l_id := SPACE(11)
@ 11,10 SAY "Enter Customer ID " GET l_id
READ
USE Customer
INDEX ON Id TO Customer
SEEK l_id
IF .NOT. FOUND()
   RETURN .F.
ENDIF
RETURN .T.
```

In this example, a local variable called *l_id* is created and initialized to 11 spaces. This variable prompts the user for input using the @ SAY/GET command combined with a READ statement. The database is opened with the USE command. The index file is created using the INDEX ON command. The SEEK command is then used to quickly locate any match for the key. The FOUND() function will return TRUE if there is a match found for the key entered by the user and FALSE if there is not a match found.

Multiple Indexes

Many times a database will have multiple indexes. The following command demonstrates how to open a database with multiple indexes:

```
USE Customer
SET INDEX TO Customer,Zip,Name
```

This example associates three indexes with the currently selected database and makes the Customer index active since it is the first index file listed. The order in which the indexes are listed determines the active index. The *active index* is the index that determines the order the database appears to be in, and it is also the index used by the SEEK command. The SET ORDER TO command could be used to change the currently active index. For example, SET ORDER TO 3 changes the active index to the customer name index in the preceding example.

Index Maintenance

Once you have created indexes for a database, Clipper will maintain them as long as you open them whenever you make changes to the database. One of the first things your program should do is to make sure all the appropriate indexes for your databases exist. The following code shows how to check to see if an index file exists and how to create it if necessary:

```
IF .NOT. FILE("Name.ntx")
    INDEX ON Lname+Fname TO Name
ELSE
    SET INDEX TO Name
ENDIF
```

The Clipper FILE statement returns a TRUE value if the filename passed as a parameter exists and FALSE if it does not exist. If the index file does not exist, then the program should create it using the INDEX ON command. The index file will be in effect after the INDEX ON command has completed. Otherwise, use the SET INDEX TO command to open the existing index file.

Whenever you open a database, it is extremely important to open all of the associated indexes. Problems could result if you add or modify records in a database without opening all of its index files. The index files would no longer correspond to the actual database. This is one of the ways in which an index file becomes *corrupt*. A corrupt index file can cause unpredictable results. For example, if you sequenced through your database from top to bottom, not all the records would be displayed. A corrupt index is easy to fix; you simply reindex the corrupt index file. However, it will not do any good unless you fix the source of the problem.

Data Entry

You enter data by using one or more @ SAY/GET commands followed by a READ statement. Nothing happens until the READ statement is activated. At that point, the user is given the ability to move freely between the pending GETs. The *pending GETs* are those @ GET commands encountered since the last READ command. Here is a simple program to demonstrate the data entry capabilities of Clipper:

```
LOCAL m_lname := SPACE(20)
LOCAL m_fname := SPACE(20)
@ 10,10 SAY "Enter first name " GET m_fname
@ 11,10 SAY "Enter last name  " GET m_lname
READ
```

The first two lines create local variables called *m_lname* and *m_fname* and initialize their values to 20 spaces. The next two lines add the two items to the pending GET list. The READ statement activates full-screen editing mode on the current pending GETs. If you leave off the READ statement, the user will never be prompted to enter the first and last names. The user can use the cursor keys to move back and forth between the two fields. Clipper provides several ways to save the current pending GETs. When you are on the last field, you can press ENTER, CTRL-W, or PGDN to save the values and exit the data entry screen.

Procedure to Add New Customers

As the next step in program development, you need to present a screen to users so they can add new records. Here is an expanded makecust procedure that performs this task:

```
PROCEDURE makecust
LOCAL m_holdscrn
SAVE SCREEN TO m_holdscrn
CLEAR
USE Customer
APPEND BLANK
@ 0,0,23,79 BOX boxstring
```

```
@ 0,20 SAY "CUSTOMER ENTRY SCREEN"
@ 1,2 SAY "Customer ID :" + Id
@ 2,2 SAY "First Name  :" GET Fname
@ 3,2 SAY "Last Name   :" GET Lname
@ 4,2 SAY "Company     :" GET Company
@ 5,2 SAY "Title       :" GET Title
@ 6,2 SAY REPLICATE("-",76)
@ 7,2 SAY "Address     :" GET Addr1
@ 8,2 SAY "            :" GET Addr2
@ 9,2 SAY "City        :" GET City
@ 10,2 SAY "State      :"
@ 20,20 SAY "Zip  :" GET Zip
@ 11,2 SAY "Phone       :" GET Phone
READ
RESTORE SCREEN FROM m_holdscrn
RETURN
```

This makecust procedure saves the current screen, clears the screen, opens a database called Customer with the USE command, and adds a new record to the database using the APPEND BLANK command. This procedure uses the @ SAY/GET command to paint a screen and initialize the fields to be entered. The READ command activates full-screen data entry. At that point the user may move the cursor freely among the various fields on the screen. Once the user is done, the original screen is restored. If the original screen is not restored then only a portion of the original pulldown window would display.

Revised Version of the Sample Database Program

When you write code, it is best to put certain types of code in specific places. The first lines of your program should be where you define your public variables, open general databases and indexes, and prepare the programming environment. Screen painting functions should be isolated from the actual entry section, and search routines are usually separated out as well. Following is a description of the various components of an application in the context of the customer tracking system. The complete listing is included at the end of the chapter.

Asking the User Questions

Your programs will frequently require the user of the application to respond with a yes or no. Here is a function that performs that task:

```
FUNCTION yesno(l_question)
LOCAL l_ans := .T.
@ 24,0
@ 24,0 SAY l_question GET l_ans PICTURE "Y"
READ
@ 24,0
RETURN l_ans
```

This function uses the last line on the screen to ask the user yes/no type questions. The @ 24,0 statement with no SAY or GET attached simply clears the whole line. It is used to remove any other data that may still be on that line. You should reserve line 24 to be used solely for asking questions and displaying comments, as discussed in the next section.

The PICTURE clause allows formatting of the characters presented using the SAY or GET command. In this example, the PICTURE clause turns .T. and .F. into "Y" and "N" and only allows "Y" or "N" to be input. Not only does it make more sense to the user to enter "Y" or a "N" than .T. or .F., but the user is also prevented from exiting the field until a valid answer is entered. The question that was passed as a parameter is presented on the screen and the answer is returned to the calling program using the RETURN statement.

Comments

You will frequently need to display messages to the user and wait for acknowledgment before continuing with your program. The last line of the screen may also be used for displaying comments. Here is an example of a program that displays comments to the user:

```
FUNCTION comment(l_comment)
@ 24,0
@ 24,0 SAY l_comment
INKEY(0)
```

```
@ 24,0
RETURN .T.
```

This is similar to the yesno() function, except that the data is presented and the program uses the INKEY() function to wait for the user to press any key on the keyboard. You can have the program wait for a specific period of time, as in INKEY(5) for a five-second wait, or forever, by using INKEY(0). INKEY() with no parameters passed to it returns immediately.

The Main Program

Recall that the main program of your application does not need to be declared as a function or a procedure. Its name is, in fact, the name of the DOS file itself, such as CUST.PRG in the following example. You can easily adapt the basic format of this program to any application you desire simply by modifying the PROMPT statements and the branching within the DO CASE/ENDCASE construct. The main idea is to present the user with the main menu over and over again until he or she presses ESC, at which time the program terminates. If the user presses ENTER while on a menu option, the program branches to the appropriate section of code.

```
* main program  - CUST.PRG

#DEFINE c_boxstrng CHR(213)+CHR(205)+CHR(184)+CHR(179)+;
        CHR(190)+CHR(205)+CHR(212)+CHR(179)+CHR(32)
LOCAL l_choice := 0
PRIVATE m_id
USE Customer NEW
IF .NOT. FILE("Customer.ntx")
   INDEX ON Id TO Customer
ELSE
   SET INDEX TO Customer
ENDIF
USE Trans NEW
IF .NOT. FILE("Transid.ntx")
   INDEX ON Id TO Transid
ELSE
   SET INDEX TO Transid
ENDIF
```

```
DO WHILE .T.
   CLEAR
   @ 0,65 SAY DATE()
   @ 0,35 SAY "CUSTOMER TRACKING"
   @ 1, 1 PROMPT "CUSTOMERS"
   @ 1,30 PROMPT "REPORTING"
   @ 1,61 PROMPT "MAINTENANCE"
   MENU TO l_choice
   DO CASE
      CASE l_choice == 0
         RETURN
      CASE l_choice == 1
         entry()
      CASE l_choice == 2
         rpt()
      CASE l_choice == 3
         maint()
   ENDCASE
ENDDO
RETURN
```

In this program, the DO WHILE loop causes the menu to be repeated over and over until the user presses ESC. The first line defines a constant called *c_boxstrng* that can be used by any procedure or function within the same file. The variable *l_choice* is defined as local so that there cannot be any conflict with other procedures or functions using the same variable name. A variable called *m_id* is declared as private, which makes it visible to any subsequent programs the preceding menu program calls. This action eliminates the need to pass the variable as a parameter to all the modules that need it.

The main program also opens the Customer and Trans databases and their corresponding indexes and also creates the indexes, if necessary. Note the word "NEW" at the end of the USE statements. Each database requires an area in which to operate. The word "NEW" indicates that this database is to be opened in a new work area. An alternative to using the NEW clause as part of the USE statement would be to use the statement SELECT 0. This statement sets the current work area to the next available area that docs not have a file opened. If neither NEW nor SELECT 0 was used, then Clipper would automatically close any database in the current work area and use that same work area to open the database.

The Clipper SELECT command allows you to specify a specific work area in which to open a database. Here is an example of how to use the SELECT statement to assign a work area before opening a file:

```
SELECT 1
USE Customer
```

The SELECT 1 command tells Clipper to select work area number 1. The Customer database is then opened in that work area by the USE command.

Note that the Trans database is also indexed by the Id field. This is because the Id field is used to connect the two databases. This will allow a connection to be made between the master customer record and all of its associated transaction records.

The Submenu

Submenus are very similar to the main menu except that the menu items are offset from the main menu items. It is good practice to allow users to see the main menu while they are currently in a submenu. In the following example, the submenu items are displayed vertically as opposed to horizontally. The submenu is presented to the user over and over until the user presses the ESC key. When that happens, control returns to the main menu. The name of the submenu function should correspond to the task to be performed. In this example, the function is named entry() since it is concerned with the entry of customer records. The submenu does very little of the actual work other than determining exactly what the user wants to do by calling various functions and asking a few questions. The main work is left up to the functions and procedures that the submenu calls.

```
FUNCTION entry()
#DEFINE c_escape 0
#DEFINE c_create 1
#DEFINE c_modify 2
#DEFINE c_delete 3
LOCAL l_holdscrn
LOCAL l_choice := 0
```

```
SET DELETED ON
SAVE SCREEN TO l_holdscrn
DO WHILE .T.
   RESTORE SCREEN FROM l_holdscrn
   @ 2,0,6,11 BOX c_boxstrng
   @ 3, 1 PROMPT "  CREATE  "
   @ 4, 1 PROMPT "  MODIFY  "
   @ 5, 1 PROMPT "  DELETE  "
   MENU TO l_choice
   IF l_choice == c_escape
      RETURN .T.
   ENDIF
   IF search()
      DO CASE
         CASE l_choice == c_create
            IF yesno(m_id + " already exists - edit Y/N ? ")
               modifycust()
            ENDIF
         CASE l_choice == c_modify
            modifycust()
         CASE l_choice == c_delete
            deletecust()
      ENDCASE
   ELSE     // customer does not exist
      DO CASE
         CASE l_choice == c_create
            createcust()
         CASE l_choice == c_modify
            IF yesno(m_id + " does not exist - add Y/N ? ")
               createcust()
            ENDIF
         CASE l_choice == c_delete
            comment(m_id + " does not exist!")
      ENDCASE
   ENDIF
ENDDO
RETURN .T.
```

Two variables called *l_holdscrn* and *l_choice* are declared as local. The variable *l_choice* stores the user's menu selection. The variable *l_holdscrn* is used in the statement SAVE SCREEN TO l_holdscrn to save the screen.

Each time the DO WHILE loop is executed, the program needs to restore the original menu screen, which it does by using the RESTORE SCREEN FROM command. Otherwise, it would display over the top of whatever was left on the screen.

When you delete a record by using the DELETE command, the record is not actually removed from the database. It is just *marked* as deleted. SET DELETED ON makes your program act as if the records that are marked as deleted do not exist to most Clipper commands and functions. In effect, the deleted records become invisible to your program. There is a Clipper command called PACK that will physically remove the records that are marked for deletion.

The command #DEFINE establishes the constants *c_create*, *c_delete*, *c_escape*, *c_modify*, and *c_boxstrng*. These constants can be used in tests and, in the case of *c_boxstrng*, in the BOX command.

Once the user has selected an action, the search() function developed earlier in the chapter asks the user to input a number. That pattern is then sought in the database using the SEEK command. The result of the search is passed back in the form of a logical value. The IF/ELSE/ENDIF statement branches to the appropriate DO CASE structure, depending on the result of the search() function.

In the first CASE statement, if *l_choice* == *c_create*, then the program is being asked to create a customer that already exists. The user is told this and asked if he or she wants to edit the record using the yesno() function. If the user responds with a "Y" for yes, the modifycust() function is run. If *l_choice* == *c_modify*, the modifycust() function is run. If *l_choice* == *c_delete*, the deletecust() function is run.

If the search() function fails to find a match of the ID number entered, the ELSE section of the IF/ELSE/ENDIF statement is executed. In this case, if *l_choice* == *c_create*, the entry() function will call createcust() since the program is creating a new customer record. If *l_choice* == *c_modify* and there are not any matches, the yesno() function is used to ask the user if a new record should be created. If the user answers "Y," createcust() is run. If *l_choice* == *d_delete*, the user is simply informed by the comment() function that there were not any matches to delete.

Searching for the Desired Record

Searching for records within a database is something all applications will need to do. The user is prompted for all or part of the key field in a database, which is usually an ID number or a name. The program then searches to find a match. Your program must then take the appropriate actions to process the selection. The following function demonstrates the entry of a customer's ID in order to find the record:

```
FUNCTION search()
LOCAL l_scrn1 := savescreen(10,10,12,50)
m_id := SPACE(11)
@ 10,10,12,50 BOX c_boxstrng
@ 11,11 SAY "Customer Id " GET m_id
READ
restscreen(10,10,12,50,l_scrn1)
SELECT Customer
SEEK m_id
RETURN FOUND()
```

This function prompts the user for a customer ID and then uses the SEEK command in an attempt to find any matches. The FOUND() function returns TRUE or FALSE depending on whether there was a match found. This function also uses the savescreen() and restscreen() functions to restore the original screen.

Creating a New Record

Creating a new record relies mainly on calls to other functions that perform the actual work of adding the record, displaying the data entry screen, and getting the data from the user. The following example demonstrates the many calls to other functions that perform the majority of work. All that is left is to store key record information, such as the customer ID number in this case.

```
FUNCTION createcust()
appendrec()
REPLACE Id WITH m_id
custscrn()
saycust()
getcust()
RETURN .T.
```

The first line of the createcust() function calls the appendrec() function, which adds a new record or makes an empty one available. The key field is filled in with data. The program then makes function calls to other modules to perform the remaining work.

There may be many times when you want to create your own unique ID. One way to do this is to use the record number in the master database as the master record's ID. The record number must be converted to a string value, as shown here:

```
m_id = LTRIM(STR(RECNO()+10000))
```

This would create a unique ID that is 11 characters long. The Clipper RECNO() function returns the current value of the record pointer. The STR() function converts a numeric value to a character string. The Clipper LTRIM() function removes leading spaces from the string returned from the STR() function. If a record is, for example, 23, the numeric image looks like this:

00000023

which STR() converts into

"   23"

and LTRIM() converts into "23". The number 10000 is added to the record number because you want the length of the image to be consistent as it helps during searching. The customer's ID number is actually derived from its record number. Keep in mind that using the record number to create an ID could result in problems if you ever physically delete records. You could end up with the same ID numbers assigned to different master records.

Modifying an Existing Record

To enable an existing record to be modified, you will want to display the data entry screen and field values and then prompt the user for the data. The following example demonstrates the use of function calls to perform all of those tasks. Because the work is split up into various modules, the functions may be used for multiple purposes, such as adding a new record or deleting a record, in addition to modifying an existing record.

```
FUNCTION modifycust()
custscrn()
saycust()
getcust()
RETURN .T.
```

The three function calls in the modifycust() function could easily have been added to the menu that called it. However, it is a good idea to separate it from the menu program so that the menu program does not get cluttered. In addition, you may want to expand on this function in some way, such as adding additional data entry screens.

Deleting a Record

When deleting a record, you want to make that record available for future use if possible. You do this by clearing out all the field contents and marking the record as deleted:

```
FUNCTION deletecust()
REPLACE Fname WITH "", Lname WITH "", Company WITH "",;
        Title WITH "", Addr1 WITH "", Addr2 WITH "",;
        City  WITH "", State WITH "", Zip WITH "",;
        Id WITH "",Phone WITH ""
DELETE
RETURN .T.
```

All of the fields are cleared and the Clipper DELETE command is used to mark the record for deletion. This makes the record invisible to the program. Also notice that this function uses one REPLACE command for all the fields in the database. This will run more quickly than if a REPLACE command were performed for each field.

Obtaining a Record

If possible, you should attempt to reclaim records that have been marked as deleted. If there are not any deleted records present in the database, you will need to actually add a new physical record to the database. Here is a function that demonstrates this process:

```
FUNCTION appendrec()
SET DELETED OFF
GO TOP
IF .NOT. EMPTY(Id) .or. EOF()
   APPEND BLANK
ELSE
   RECALL
ENDIF
SET DELETED ON
RETURN .T.
```

This function switches off the SET DELETED ON command set earlier and then goes to the first record in index order. This will probably *not* be the first physical record. Blank fields come before fields with data, so if there are any blank records, they will be at the top of an indexed file. The field is tested to see if it is blank using the EMPTY() function. If it is not empty or if there aren't any records in the database, a new record is added to the database. Otherwise, the deleted record, which can now be seen because of the SET DELETED OFF command, is "undeleted" by using the RECALL command. Finally, the SET DELETED ON command is issued to hide other blank records that are not needed at this time.

Data Entry Screen Cosmetics

Prior to allowing users to enter data, you will need to display some help information. This information tells users what they should be entering for each field. You may optionally draw lines and boxes to make the screen more appealing to users. Initially, you may just want to get the data entry screen working. You can expand on the cosmetics later.

Here is the function that displays field help information on the screen:

```
FUNCTION custscrn()
@ 0,0,23,79 BOX c_boxstrng
@ 0,20 SAY "CUSTOMER ENTRY SCREEN"
@ 1,2 SAY "Customer ID :"
@ 2,2 SAY "First Name  :"
@ 3,2 SAY "Last Name   :"
@ 4,2 SAY "Company     :"
@ 5,2 SAY "Title       :"
@ 6,2 SAY REPLICATE("-",76)
@ 7,2 SAY "Address     :"
@ 8,2 SAY "            :"
@ 9,2 SAY "City        :"
@ 10,2 SAY "State   :             Zip  :"
RETURN .T.
```

This function simply displays titles for each of the fields to be entered by the user. The @ SAY command is used to place the test on the screen. The REPLICATE() function repeats the symbol "-" 76 times across the screen in order to draw a line.

Displaying the Field Information

There will be times when you want to display only the actual field data, such as when the user is attempting to delete a record. This allows the user to visually inspect the data before performing the delete. The following saycust() function displays a record of customer data:

```
FUNCTION saycust()
@ 2,15 SAY Id
@ 2,15 SAY Fname
@ 3,15 SAY Lname
@ 4,15 SAY Company
@ 5,15 SAY Title
@ 7,15 SAY Addr1
@ 8,15 SAY Addr2
@ 9,15 SAY City
@ 10,15 SAY State
@ 10,31 SAY Zip
RETURN .T.
```

This function uses the @ SAY command to display the field values. There is not a problem here since all the fields are character type. If any of the fields were numeric, the PICTURE clause of the @ SAY command could be used to format the field.

Obtaining the Data from the User

The @ GET command is used to get field information from the user. There are a couple of options here. With the following getcust() function, the user makes changes directly to the field. As an alternative, you could store all the fields to memory variables and allow the user to make changes to the memory variables. In this way, you can verify at the end to make sure the user really wanted to make the changes before changing the actual field values. The user has the ability to act directly on the fields or store all the fields to memory variables.

```
FUNCTION getcust()
@ 2,15 GET Fname
@ 3,15 GET Lname
@ 4,15 GET Company
@ 5,15 GET Title
@ 7,15 GET Addr1
@ 8,15 GET Addr2
@ 9,15 GET City
@ 10,15 GET State
@ 10,31 GET Zip
READ
RETURN .T.
```

The function getcust() allows entry of data directly into the record. Note that the screen presentation and edit functions are split up so that if there is a need later on to add SCROLL as an option alongside CREATE/ EDIT/DELETE, the screen format would be painted only once, using custscrn(), and the contents of each record would be presented quickly using saycust() as the user scrolls by using the UP ARROW and DOWN ARROW keys. The user could then use getcust() to get the record by pressing ENTER.

Introduction to the Debugger

Clipper comes with a debugger called CLD.EXE. This is a program that basically allows you to view the inner workings of the program while it is running. Use the debugger to solve difficult program problems or just to thoroughly test your program. Type the following command at the DOS prompt to run the Clipper debugger:

cld cust

For the debugger to be run on a program, it needs to be compiled using the /B option, as shown here:

clipper cust /B

The /B parameter is included as part of the GO.BAT batch file used for compiling and linking your sample programs. Once you have entered the debugger, a menu of options is first presented. You can examine the various menu items or you can run the program by pressing F5. You may pull down the debugger menu by pressing ALT-D at any time while the program is running. The menu includes options for inspecting the names and structures of currently open databases and the keys of the open indexes. It can be set up to watch the contents of particular variables and let you step through your code line by line. Most programmers use debuggers because their code sometimes gets too complex to figure out in their heads; they have to get in there and watch the problem sections operate. So do not think of the debugger as esoteric; just use it as you would any of the other tools supplied.

Customer Tracking System

Here is a complete listing of the sample database application, incorporating what was covered in this chapter:

```
* main program  - CUST.PRG

#DEFINE c_boxstrng CHR(213)+CHR(205)+CHR(184)+CHR(179)+;
        CHR(190)+CHR(205)+CHR(212)+CHR(179)+CHR(32)
LOCAL l_choice := 0
PUBLIC m_id
USE Customer NEW
IF .NOT. FILE("Customer.ntx")
   INDEX ON Id TO Customer
ELSE
   SET INDEX TO Customer
ENDIF
USE Trans NEW
IF .NOT. FILE("Transid.ntx")
   INDEX ON Id TO Transid
ELSE
   SET INDEX TO Transid
ENDIF
DO WHILE .T.
   CLEAR
   @ 0,65 SAY DATE()
   @ 0,35 SAY "CUSTOMER TRACKING"
   @ 1, 1 PROMPT "CUSTOMERS"
   @ 1,30 PROMPT "REPORTING"
   @ 1,61 PROMPT "MAINTENANCE"
   MENU TO l_choice
   DO CASE
      CASE l_choice == 0
         RETURN
      CASE l_choice == 1
         entry()
      CASE l_choice == 2
         rpt()
      CASE l_choice == 3
         maint()
   ENDCASE
```

```
ENDDO
RETURN


FUNCTION entry()
#DEFINE c_escape 0
#DEFINE c_create 1
#DEFINE c_modify 2
#DEFINE c_delete 3
LOCAL l_holdscrn
LOCAL l_choice := 0
SET DELETED ON
SAVE SCREEN TO l_holdscrn
DO WHILE .T.
   RESTORE SCREEN FROM l_holdscrn
   @ 2,0,6,11 BOX c_boxstrng
   @ 3, 1 PROMPT "  CREATE  "
   @ 4, 1 PROMPT "  MODIFY  "
   @ 5, 1 PROMPT "  DELETE  "
   MENU TO l_choice
   IF l_choice == c_escape
     RETURN .T.
   ENDIF
   IF search()
     DO CASE
        CASE l_choice == c_create
           IF yesno(m_id + " already exists - edit Y/N ? ")
              modifycust()
           ENDIF
        CASE l_choice == c_modify
           modifycust()
        CASE l_choice == c_delete
           deletecust()
     ENDCASE
   ELSE     // customer does not exist
     DO CASE
        CASE l_choice == c_create
           createcust()
        CASE l_choice == c_modify
           IF yesno(m_id + " does not exist - add Y/N ? ")
              createcust()
           ENDIF
```

```
            CASE l_choice == c_delete
                comment(m_id + " does not exist!")
        ENDCASE
    ENDIF
ENDDO
RETURN .T.


FUNCTION search()
LOCAL l_scrn1 := savescreen(10,10,12,50)
m_id := SPACE(11)
@ 10,10,12,50 BOX c_boxstrng
@ 11,11 SAY "Customer ID " GET m_id
READ
restscreen(10,10,12,50,l_scrn1)
SELECT Customer
SEEK m_id
RETURN FOUND()


FUNCTION createcust()
appendrec()
REPLACE Id WITH m_id
custscrn()
saycust()
getcust()
RETURN .T.


FUNCTION modifycust()
custscrn()
saycust()
getcust()
RETURN .T.


FUNCTION deletecust()
REPLACE Fname WITH "", Lname WITH "", Company WITH "", ;
        Title WITH "", Addr1 WITH "", Addr2 WITH "",;
        City  WITH "", State WITH "", Zip WITH "",;
        Id WITH "",Phone WITH ""
DELETE
```

```
RETURN .T.


FUNCTION appendrec()
SET DELETED OFF
GO TOP
IF .NOT. EMPTY(Id) .or. EOF()
   APPEND BLANK
ELSE
   RECALL
ENDIF
SET DELETED ON
RETURN .T.


FUNCTION yesno(l_question)
LOCAL l_ans := .T.
@ 24,0
@ 24,0 SAY l_question GET l_ans PICTURE "Y"
READ
@ 24,0
RETURN l_ans


FUNCTION comment(l_comment)
@ 24,0
@ 24,0 SAY l_comment
INKEY(0)
@ 24,0
RETURN .T.


FUNCTION custscrn()
@ 0,0,23,79 BOX c_boxstrng
@ 0,20 SAY "CUSTOMER ENTRY SCREEN"
@ 1,2 SAY "Customer ID :"
@ 2,2 SAY "First Name  :"
@ 3,2 SAY "Last Name   :"
@ 4,2 SAY "Company     :"
@ 5,2 SAY "Title       :"
@ 6,2 SAY REPLICATE("-",76)
@ 7,2 SAY "Address       :"
```

```
@ 8,2 SAY "              :"
@ 9,2 SAY "City          :"
@ 10,2 SAY "State        :            Zip  :"
RETURN .T.


FUNCTION saycust()
@ 2,15 SAY Id
@ 2,15 SAY Fname
@ 3,15 SAY Lname
@ 4,15 SAY Company
@ 5,15 SAY Title
@ 7,15 SAY Addr1
@ 8,15 SAY Addr2
@ 9,15 SAY City
@ 10,15 SAY State
@ 10,31 SAY Zip
RETURN .T.


FUNCTION getcust()
@ 2,15 GET Fname
@ 3,15 GET Lname
@ 4,15 GET Company
@ 5,15 GET Title
@ 7,15 GET Addr1
@ 8,15 GET Addr2
@ 9,15 GET City
@ 10,15 GET State
@ 10,31 GET Zip
READ
RETURN .T.


PROCEDURE rpt
LOCAL choice := 0
DO WHILE .T.
    @ 2,30,8,59 BOX c_boxstrng
    @ 3,31 PROMPT "  CUSTOMER LIST            "
    @ 4,31 PROMPT "  TRANSACTIONS by MONTH    "
    @ 5,31 PROMPT "  TRANSACTIONS by CUSTOMER "
    @ 6,31 PROMPT "  OUTSTANDING ACCOUNTS     "
```

```
      @ 7,31 PROMPT "  MAILING LABELS            "
      MENU TO choice
      DO CASE
         CASE choice == 0
            RETURN
         CASE choice == 1
            comment("This is CUSTOMER LIST")
         CASE choice == 2
            comment("This is TRANSACTIONS BY MONTH")
         CASE choice == 3
            comment("This is TRANSACTIONS BY CUSTOMER")
         CASE choice == 4
            comment("This is OUTSTANDING ACCOUNTS")
         CASE choice == 5
            comment("This is MAILING LABELS")
      ENDCASE
   ENDDO
RETURN


PROCEDURE maint
LOCAL choice := 0
DO WHILE .T.
   @ 2,61,6,79 BOX c_boxstrng
   @ 3,62 PROMPT "  BACKUP DATA     "
   @ 4,62 PROMPT "  RESTORE DATA    "
   @ 5,62 PROMPT "  REINDEX FILES   "
   MENU TO choice
   DO CASE
      CASE choice == 0
         RETURN
      CASE choice == 1
         comment("This is BACKUP DATA")
      CASE choice == 2
         comment("This is RESTORE DATA")
      CASE choice == 3
         comment("This is REINDEX FILES")
   ENDCASE
ENDDO
RETURN
```

Key Points

Information is the Goal

Gathering information and outputting that information in some useful format is the real goal of the automation process.

Memory Variables

There are four basic types of variables in Clipper: numeric, character, data, and logical. You may use memory variables to store information while the program is working. Variables are also used to perform calculations and manipulations of the data.

Numeric data types are used to store numbers.

Character variables are used to store strings of characters, such as a person's name, address, and city. Character variables can accommodate very large strings or can hold a single character.

Date variables are used to store dates, such as a person's birthdate or a transaction date.

Logical variables may be either true or false and are used by a programmer to control the logic within a program.

Arrays of Variables

An array is a collection of variables with the same name and may be either one-dimensional or multidimensional.

continues . . .

Flexibility of Arrays

It is easy to traverse entire arrays by using numeric variables to access the various elements.

Controlling Visibility

A module should not be influenced by other programs and, at the same time, a module should not influence other programs indirectly. The effect a module has on another module should be precise and predictable. You accomplish this by controlling a variable's visibility.

A public variable is visible to every program in the system. Public variables are sometimes referred to as global variables.

A local variable can only be seen by the function or procedure where it has been declared. It loses its contents upon returning to the calling program.

A static variable is a special kind of variable that is initialized with a value the first time it is encountered and retains its contents so that the next time that function or procedure is run, those contents are again available.

A private variable is similar to a local variable, except that a private variable is visible to all programs that are called by the function or procedure in which the variable was declared. If a variable is not specifically declared, it becomes private.

continues . . .

Passing Parameters

Passing a parameter by value means that a copy of the variable is made and acted upon by the called procedure. When variables are passed by reference, the memory address of the variable is passed. A copy of the original variable is not made and the original value may be altered by the called program.

Naming a Block of Code

You may define a block of code as either a procedure or a function. The difference between the two is that a function may return a value or NIL whereas a procedure will always return NIL.

Clipper Evolution

Each new major upgrade of Clipper has resulted in numerous additions to the language. Many functions and commands remain for compatibility reasons. These functions and commands allow programs written under previous versions of Clipper to run under Clipper 5 with little or no modification.

Boolean Logic

Boolean logic provides the means by which you can control the flow of an application.

continues . . .

Order of Evaluation

Clipper always evaluates two expressions at a time even if there are more than two expressions in a single statement.

Performing Simple Branching

The IF/ENDIF control structure should be used if you need a section of code to execute only if a certain condition is met. The ELSE statement may be used with the IF control structure to provide an alternate sequence of instructions to be executed if the expression evaluates to be FALSE.

Performing Complex Branching

The CASE control structure is similar to the IF control structure, but it allows the evaluation of many different conditions.

Looping Structures

Looping structures are used to repeatedly execute a series of instructions until a condition is met.

continues . . .

Displaying Menus

The top-down approach implies that you start with the user's view. Most applications present the user with a top-level menu of some kind.

Adding Features

Adding features to your program one step at a time helps make testing easier.

Database Maintenance

Database maintenance is one of the major tasks involved in creating an application.

Indexing

Indexing provides the ability to easily tie multiple databases together and provides a very quick way to search for data.

Corrupt Index Files

It is important to open all the associated indexes of a database file. Corrupt index files could result when records are added or modified without opening all of the index files.

continues . . .

Performing Data Entry

You enter data by using one or more @ SAY/GET statements followed by a READ statement.

The pending GETs are those @ GET commands encountered since the last READ command. The user may move freely between the fields in the pending GET list.

The USE Statement

The USE statement opens a Clipper database file in the current work area. Providing the NEW clause will open the database in the first work area that is not used by any other database.

Deleted Records

The Clipper DELETE command marks records as deleted. The record is not physically removed from a database until the PACK command is issued. The SET DELETED ON makes your program act as if the records that are marked as deleted do not exist to most Clipper commands and functions. In effect, the deleted records become invisible to your program.

CHAPTER

Improving Your First Application

This chapter covers some of the more advanced components of an application. The key components as far as the customer is concerned are the entry of data and the extraction of that data in the form of reports. The system should allow data to be entered as quickly and as free of errors as possible. Usually the data encompasses more than one database. You must provide the connections between all the databases, both in the entry of the data and in reports.

Chapter 4 introduced a database application that included a top menu bar, several pulldown menus, one data entry screen, an action menu used to update client information, and a database to receive the data. This chapter presents a discussion of speed issues and the use of secondary databases.

Speed Issues

When discussing speed issues, it is best to look at how long the user waits for each action to occur. There are times when the keyboard limits entry speed or the printer limits output speed. From a coding point of view, this is considered "breathing space." You don't have to be a very clever programmer to write reports that execute more quickly than the printer can print the results. It is sometimes better to sacrifice a little bit of speed in order to write readable and maintainable code.

Data Entry Optimization

There are many issues to deal with regarding data entry. The data entry person does not want to be slowed down when entering a stack of forms. Users may become annoyed if they are slowed down by the program's performing validation checks. An alternative is to perform the validation after each record or perhaps after many records have been entered. In some applications, the validation is done while the user is at lunch or after he or she goes home for the evening. The errors can then be fixed when the user returns.

Users are accustomed to certain activities that consume time. They expect that the program itself may take time to load into memory. They expect that reports will take time to print. The key is to reduce the amount of time users have to wait. The users want to be able to get something started and then let the computer do its thing while they go to work on something else. Reports should query users with any pertinent questions prior to running. You do not want the report to stop printing before it is completed while additional information necessary to run the report is obtained.

If certain parts of the program take a long time and there is no way to get around it, then display information about the progress of the program, such as the percentage completed or the current customer being processed. Studies have shown that perceived time is less when some kind of progress information is displayed continually.

Code Optimization

In its simplest form, code optimization means merely reducing the size of the code or, more specifically, reducing the number of instructions required to achieve a particular result. There are times when this is not always clear. Occasionally, there are trade-offs involved with optimizing code. Elaborate schemes used to increase speed may be the most difficult to maintain.

You should use constants whenever possible. Variable names take up system memory since variables must reside in a symbol table. The *symbol table* is a list in memory of all the variable names and function names. In a small program it is irrelevant, but in a very large application the difference in memory usage may be critical.

Another rule for optimizing code is to use Clipper functions rather than your own code whenever possible. Clipper functions are written in the C language and have already been optimized. As an example, do not attempt to rewrite the Clipper PADC() function, which centers text on a given length. Your program would run much more slowly and would take up additional code space as well.

Chapter 4 discussed the difference between passing variables by reference and passing variables by value. Passing by reference is another way to increase speed since only the memory address is passed to the function or procedure. New copies of variables are created when you pass variables by value, and this takes extra time.

Database Considerations

How much you know about the basic way databases are structured and the way certain commands work can greatly affect the performance of an application. You must keep in mind that the sample databases used for testing an application are rarely as large as what will eventually be used by the customer. You should attempt to simulate the actual conditions an application will be run under.

Opening and Closing Databases

Opening and closing databases takes time. Try to open all the databases used for a particular section of code right at the beginning. Not only does this save the time of continually opening and closing databases, but it simplifies coding as well.

Commands to Avoid

There are commands in Clipper that should be avoided if at all possible. The SORT command physically sorts the data on the disk, and this task takes considerable time and disk space. The PACK command makes a new copy of the database that contains all the records except those marked for deletion. Your applications should reuse the records marked for deletion whenever possible, as described in Chapter 4. There are appropriate times to use the SORT and PACK commands. Monthly and year-end programs often use the commands to clean up the databases in an application.

The SET FILTER TO statement is a great Clipper feature when used correctly. However, you must keep in mind that it processes and evaluates each record in the database. The LOCATE FOR command also processes the database sequentially until the first match is found. This is a disaster if the record you are attempting to locate is the last record in a 1-million-record database. Use the SEEK command whenever possible to quickly locate records that match a search criterion. You may even want to create additional index files to take advantage of the SEEK command.

Knowing the Language

Another more subtle form of coding inefficiency is a lack of knowledge of the capabilities of the language. You must continually review the available Clipper and third-party functions and procedures available to you. In this way, you will be able to select the best possible approach to a problem, which will, in many cases, affect the speed of processing.

Where to Optimize

A slow computer can be made to look relatively fast and a fast computer can be made to look relatively slow, depending on how the program is written. When you test your program before giving it to the user, watch out for places where *you* get frustrated waiting. Those are the areas requiring further work. Keep in mind that your databases are probably only a fraction of the size of your customer's. Your test database with 5000 records and five index files may run fine. There may be a significant slowdown when the customer uses the application on a 150,000-record database with the same five indexes. When you add a record, the program must update the five indexes. The index structure is built like the roots of a tree; it branches into smaller and smaller sections. The bigger the database gets, the deeper the search must be to find where the new record fits into the root structure. This search takes time. Do this five times for each of the five indexes, and the user will be staring at the screen, waiting. This problem is amplified when the application is run on a network.

Don't worry about solving all the speed issues up front; it is not always possible. The user will present the real speed issues once the application is put into use. Concentrate on becoming a good problem solver and handle the problems as they arise.

Data Entry Validation

Data that has been entered incorrectly may cause strange behavior in programs. You do not want to write all kinds of special code to handle invalid data, but at the same time you do not want your programs to continue if invalid data is going to affect the logic. The easiest way to validate data is to provide control of the data as it is being entered. Fortunately, Clipper provides many ways to validate data.

PICTURE Functions

The most basic level of validation is to use the PICTURE clause of the @ GET statement to limit the keys a user may enter or to convert a lowercase entry to uppercase. Suppose you want the user to answer a question with a "Y" or an "N." You do not want the program to continue executing if the response is a "Z"; the logic within your programs would not work correctly. PICTURE functions provide a way to format data as it is entered. Table 5-1 shows some of the more commonly used PICTURE functions.

As an example, you could include the following PICTURE function to ensure that the user enters only alphabetic characters:

```
@ 12,10 GET Fname PICTURE "@A"
```

Recall that the GET statement places a variable or field into the pending GET list. The row and column (in this case 12,10) are included in the statement to indicate its placement on the screen. You will frequently want to provide a default answer to a data entry field. If you use the @K PICTURE function, the user could edit the default answer by pressing the cursor keys or save the default answer by pressing the ENTER key. Any other keystroke will immediately clear the suggested input value. Here is an example of the @K PICTURE function:

```
m_city = "Chicago            "
@ 12,10 get m_city PICTURE "@K"
```

In the preceding example, pressing the ENTER key would cause the original string ("Chicago   ") to be saved in the m_city variable. The user could use the RIGHT ARROW key to modify the name slightly if desired. Any other keystroke would wipe out "Chicago" and replace the first character in the input field with the keystroke entered. Note that the original value of m_city was padded with spaces. This is done to provide additional space in case the city takes more spaces than the default value.

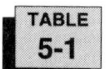

TABLE
5-1

Picture Function Symbols

Function	Variable Type	Action
A	Character	Allows only alphabetic characters
K	All types	Clears default value if first key is not a cursor key
!	Character	Converts all characters to uppercase

The following example uses the @! PICTURE function to convert all user input to uppercase:

```
m_state = "IL"
@ 12,10 GET l_state PICTURE "@!"
```

There are many instances where you will want an entire string to be entered in uppercase. The PICTURE function provides a good solution.

PICTURE Templates

The preceding example could also have been done by using a PICTURE template, as shown here:

```
@ 12,10 GET l_state PICTURE "!!"
```

When using a PICTURE template, you define the format of each character rather than the entire data entry field. Table 5-2 shows some of the more commonly used PICTURE templates.

It would be easy to force all numerics into a character data entry field by using the following PICTURE template:

```
m_zip = "          "
@ 12,10 get m_zip PICTURE "999999999"
```

This example would prevent the user from entering anything other than numbers.

TABLE
5-2

Picture Template Symbols

Template	Action
A	Allows only alphabetic characters
N	Allows only alphabetic and numeric characters
9	Allows only numeric characters
Y	Allows only "Y" or "N"
!	Converts lowercase characters to uppercase

The nice thing about PICTURE templates is that they may be mixed with characters, as in this example:

```
m_phone = "              "
@ 12,10 GET m_phone PICTURE "999-999-9999"
```

In this example, the user does not have to enter the dash in the phone number since it is provided by the PICTURE template. As the user types the numbers, the cursor skips over the dashes.

Sometimes you may want to force only the first character to be uppercase. You could do this by mixing PICTURE template characters, as shown here:

```
m_lname = "           "
@ 12,10 GET m_lname PICTURE "!AAAAAAAAA"
```

This PICTURE template will convert only the first character to uppercase and allow any alphabetic characters in the rest of the field.

If you needed to force the user to enter a "Y" or an "N," as would be required when asking a question, you could use the following PICTURE template:

```
l_answer = "Y"
@ 12,10 GET l_answer PICTURE "Y"
```

Although the preceding example is a "quick and dirty" way to force entry of a "Y" or "N" response, there is no way to notify users if they have made a mistake. Users may not realize that they're supposed to enter a "Y" or an "N." The cursor simply stays at the data entry field until a correct response is made.

Validation Using DO WHILE Loops

One way to force the user to enter an appropriate response is to use a DO WHILE/ENDDO loop and continue the loop until the user enters valid data. The following example asks a question until the user answers correctly:

```
LOCAL l_answer := "N"
DO WHILE .T.
   @ 17,28 GET l_answer PICTURE "!"
  READ
   IF l_answer $ "YN"
      EXIT
   ENDIF
   comment("invalid entry")
ENDDO
```

In this case, the code will continue to loop as long as the user's entry is not contained in the string "YN". Recall that the $ symbol is a logical operator that returns a true value if the expression on the left of the operator is contained within the second expression on the right. A message should be displayed notifying users that they made a mistake. The preceding example uses the comment() function developed in Chapter 4 to display the error message. The PICTURE template ! forces the contents of the variable to be entered as uppercase.

The problem with this kind of check is that it does not allow full-screen data entry. The user cannot move around freely among the various fields since only one field may be pending at a time.

The VALID Clause

A better way to handle the situation just described is with the VALID clause. The VALID clause enables you to provide a condition that must be met before the user may exit a field.

Here is a different version of the Yes/No field validation:

```
LOCAL l_answer := "N"
@ 17,28 GET l_answer PICTURE "!" VALID(l_answer $ "YN")
READ
```

This takes less code but does not tell the user what is wrong if an incorrect key is pressed. The VALID clause accepts a condition as its parameter and returns a logical value. The logical value determines if the user will remain on that field or proceed to the next one. Any expression may be inserted into the VALID clause, and the answer will determine the ability of the user to move on to the next field.

The VALID Clause and Generic User-defined Functions

VALID clauses will accept functions as well as expressions as parameters. This allows you a great deal of flexibility when designing data entry screens. Functions may be passed to the VALID clause rather than to an expression to not only validate the entry but to provide some feedback on errors. A user-defined function could be written to accept the condition and an error message as parameters. If the condition is not met, the function can display the message, as shown here:

```
FUNCTION error_chk(condition,message)
IF .NOT. condition
    comment(message)
    RETURN .F.
ENDIF
RETURN .T.
```

The preceding error_chk() function would be called like this:

```
l_answer := "N"
@ 17,28 GET l_answer PICTURE "!" ;
    VALID error_chk(l_answer $ "YN","Must enter Y or N")
READ
```

The condition parameter (l_answer $ "YN") is passed to the error_chk() function and evaluated. Recall from Chapter 4 that the semicolon indicates that the statement continues on the next line, as is done with the @ GET statement. If the statement evaluates to FALSE, the message parameter ("Must enter Y or N") is displayed using the comment() function. The error_chk() function then returns FALSE to the calling program, which in turn keeps the user on the same data entry field. This process continues until the user enters a correct value. When the user enters a correct value, the condition is evaluated to TRUE and the function returns TRUE.

The VALID Clause and Specific
User-defined Functions

It may be useful to write user-defined functions specifically for validating special data entry field types such as Yes/No types. A logical type variable could be returned from the function even though the user enters a "Y" or an "N." The user-defined function could then be used as part of the VALID clause. Here is a function used for asking Yes/No questions that returns a logical variable:

```
FUNCTION yesno(l_question)
LOCAL l_ans := "Y"
@ 24,0
@ 24,0 SAY l_question GET l_ans picture "!";
       VALID(error_chk(l_ans $ "YN","Answer must be a Y or N"))
READ
@ 24,0
if l_ans = "Y"
  RETURN .T.
endif
RETURN .F.
```

This function creates a local variable called *l_ans* of character type that is used to get the "Y" or "N" response from the user. The error_chk() function checks for a valid response and calls the comment() function to display an error message if necessary. The function then returns the appropriate logical variable, depending on the answer to the question. The yesno() function could easily be incorporated into branching statements such as IF/ENDIF, as shown here:

```
IF yesno("Are you ready to print ?")
  * print
ENDIF
```

This example passes the question to the yesno() function as a parameter. The yesno() function displays the question and forces the user to answer the question with a "Y" or an "N." A logical value is returned as part of the IF statement.

The Relational Database

A complete application usually incorporates a wide variety of interconnected databases. The databases used in Clipper are termed relational, which means that data is stored in simple tables with the relationships between different data items tied together by values in other tables.

An application usually has a *primary database*, such as a patient database, and numerous *secondary databases*, such as treatment, insurance, and billing databases. The field in the primary database used to connect the primary database with other databases is referred to as the *primary key*. Usually the primary key is in the form of a social security number, a part number, or some other unique identifying element. The primary key must be unique since there would be no way to make the correct connections if it were not. To illustrate this point, suppose there were two records in the primary database with the same ID number (primary key) and a record in the secondary database with that ID number. It would be a toss-up to determine which primary record the secondary record should be connected to.

If there is not a unique key available, one should be assigned. Using the last and first names as a primary key is not appropriate since there may be more than one person with the same name. In the United States, the government and banks use the social security number as the primary key. Americans can change their names, change their addresses, or change their relationships, but pandemonium would result if they were able to change their social security numbers. The social security number is the unique element that ties everything together.

The same principle applies in the computer world: Give them a number and you've got them. The program does not care if there are three Bill Smiths since each has been uniquely identified with a customer number.

Incorporating the Relational Database

Secondary databases present many problems. There could be many records with identical information or very similar information. Your main role is to provide an easy way to access the secondary records. In order to process the secondary database, the user selects a record in the primary database (such as a customer), and the program should then present a list of the associated secondary records (such as transactions).

In the sample application, the customer database is tied to the transaction database through the use of the Id field. Each customer is assigned a unique ID number. That ID number is stored for each transaction record created for that customer.

Finding a Match in the Secondary Database

The secondary database should have an index on the field that connects it with the primary database. Recall that an index file provides the ability to look at your database in sorted order even though the database is not physically sorted in any particular order. An index also allows you to perform quick searches by using the SEEK command. If an index were not used, each record in the secondary database would need to be processed in order to find all the matches. That would be very slow.

In the sample application, an index on the field called Id is created. The resulting index file called Transid is created and is used to find matching transaction records for a customer. This allows very quick access to an individual's transactions through the use of the SEEK statement, as shown here:

```
USE Customer NEW
USE Trans NEW
SET INDEX TO Transid
SEEK Customer->Id
IF FOUND()
   * process transactions
ELSE
   * there are no transactions to process
ENDIF
```

In this example, the Id field from the first customer record is used to search for matches within the Trans database. The SEEK statement will take only a split second to find a match, no matter how big the secondary database is. The Clipper FOUND() function is used after a SEEK to determine if any matches were found. The IF/ELSE/ENDIF construct is used to provide branching. The program branches one way if there were matches found and another way if there were no transactions.

Sequencing Through Secondary Records

Since there can be multiple matching secondary database records for a single record in the primary database, there has to be a way to traverse the secondary database and access those records. In the sample application, the database is sorted by ID number, and those ID numbers will be sequential. The idea is to find the first match and continue skipping records until the end-of-file marker is reached or the key value (ID number) changes, as shown here:

```
USE Customer NEW
USE Trans NEW
SET INDEX TO Transid
SEEK Customer->Id
IF FOUND()
```

```
    DO WHILE .NOT. EOF() .and. Trans->Id == Customer->Id
      * process transaction record
      SKIP
    ENDDO
ELSE
    * there are not any transactions
ENDIF
```

The preceding code section sequences through the records in the secondary database that are related to the current record in the primary database. The first part of the DO WHILE statement checks for the end-of-file marker. If EOF() returns .T., there are no more records in the database and you know you are done. If there are remaining records, the second part of the DO WHILE statement checks to make sure that the key relating the two databases has not changed. A change in the key field will cause the DO WHILE loop to terminate.

Selecting a Secondary Record

The preceding program demonstrated how to find the secondary records that match a primary record. Normally, you will want the user to be able to select from among the matches found or to add new secondary records. The user should be presented with a box and a scrolling bar in which to make the selection. These selection boxes are sometimes referred to as *pick lists*.

Providing a Path to Secondary Records

You first have to lead the user to the point where a secondary record may be selected. In the sample application, the whole process of customer transactions can be reduced to a single function call. You could modify the procedure that obtains the primary customer information to allow transaction processing by adding the following lines:

```
IF yesno("Edit Transactions Y/N ?")
    tranlist()
ENDIF
```

Since the user may not always want to process secondary records, the first line of the program uses the yesno() function to ask the user if he or she wants to edit customer transactions. Recall that the yesno() function prompts the user for a "Y" or "N" response and returns a logical answer. If the user answers "Y," the tranlist() function is called. The tranlist() function is considered a "black box" at this point. The method in which the transactions are handled is entirely up to you.

The idea here is to let the user select the record from the primary database and optionally allow editing of the primary record data. Once that has been completed, the user may be asked if he or she wants to process secondary transactions. If the user does want to process secondary transactions, then make a call to a function to perform that process.

This is an example of using the top-down approach since you are not concerned with the details of the tranlist() function at this time. The function to process the secondary transactions could do any number of things in any number of ways. Since applications may involve many secondary databases, the program may prompt the user as to which secondary database to process. If there is only one secondary database, the program could begin processing secondary transactions immediately. This whole process will work well as long as you have made the connection between the primary and secondary databases through the use of a key value supplied to both.

Selecting a Secondary Record

Clipper provides many methods for presenting multiple secondary records to the user. One method would be to use the @ SAY command to display the record number and some information in the secondary record. The following example calls the function procsec(), which uses the @ SAY command method.

```
USE Customer NEW
USE Trans NEW
SET INDEX TO Transid
SEEK Customer->Id
IF FOUND()
   procsec()
ELSE
```

```
   * there are not any transactions
ENDIF
```

In this example, the function procsec() (PROCess SECondary) is called if there were any secondary records for the primary customer database. This function should display the matching records in some format and allow the user to select one or to add a new one if desired. You could do this by displaying the record number and some information from the secondary record, as shown here:

```
FUNCTION procsec()
LOCAL m_linecnt := 3    // line counter
   CLEAR
   @ 1,1 SAY ALLTRIM(Customer->Fname) + " " + ;
           ALLTRIM(Customer->Lname)
   DO WHILE .NOT. EOF() .AND. Trans->Id == Customer->Id
     m_linecnt++
     @ m_linecnt,5 SAY STR(RECNO(),6) + " " + ;
                       DTOC(Trandate) + " " + Desc
     SKIP
   ENDDO
   * get the choice from the user
   * process the choice
RETURN NIL
```

In this example, the screen is cleared and some information from the primary record is displayed. The Clipper ALLTRIM() function trims blank spaces at the front and back of the Fname and Lname fields. The fields are displayed using their file aliases. An *alias* is assigned to a database when it is opened. The alias is usually the same name as the database file. An alias allows you to access fields even when you are in other work areas by placing the alias and the -> symbol in front of the field name. The example displays the customer's name in order to keep the user informed as to which primary record has been currently selected.

A DO WHILE loop is processed until the database either reaches an end-of-file marker or the Id field used to connect the two databases is not the same. Note that the @ SAY command uses the *m_linecnt* variable in place of a number. Since this variable is incremented for each record, it will cause information for each new secondary record to be displayed on a new line. This example uses the Clipper STR() function to convert the numeric value returned from the RECNO() function into a string with a length of 6. The Clipper DTOC() function converts *Trandate* from a date type to a character type so that it may be displayed. The transaction description is also displayed.

This may appear to be a good approach, but it presents several problems. Once the user has entered a record number, the program must ensure that it is a valid record number and that it is actually one of the numbers in the list that was presented. That would involve additional error checking by your program. In addition, this approach is not very professional looking.

A better approach would be to use the PROMPT command that is also used for menus to present the secondary records. Here is a revision of the previous example using the PROMPT command:

```
FUNCTION procsec()
LOCAL l_recarr[15]
LOCAL l_arrcnt := 0
LOCAL m_linecnt := 3
    CLEAR
    @ 1,1 SAY ALLTRIM(Customer->Fname) + " " + ;
              ALLTRIM(Customer->Lname)
    DO WHILE .NOT. EOF() .AND. Trans->Id == Customer->Id
      m_linecnt++
      @ m_linecnt,5 PROMPT STR(RECNO(),6) + " " + ;
                      DTOC(Trandate) + " " + Desc
      l_arrcnt++
      l_recarr[l_arrcnt] = RECNO()
      SKIP
    ENDDO
    MENU TO l_choice
    * process choice
RETURN NIL
```

In this example, the SAY statement was changed to a PROMPT statement and the method used to make a selection has been changed to the MENU TO command. The MENU TO command will return the menu choice selected, which may not correspond to the actual record number in the secondary database. Suppose the first item in the menu was actually record 100 in the database. There must be a way to know the actual record number of the choice. You accomplish this by using an array (*l_recarr*) to store the record numbers of the secondary records as they are displayed, using the PROMPT command. Each time a PROMPT command is issued, the array counter *(l_arrcnt)* is incremented and the record number of the item is stored in that array element, as shown here:

```
l_arrcnt++
l_recarr[l_arrcnt] = RECNO()
```

Once the record numbers have been stored in the array, it is easy to get the record number of the selected item. The menu choice would be used as the element number in the array, as shown here:

```
l_record = l_recarr[l_choice]
```

This method provides many benefits. Once the user has made the selection, you have the record number. There is no need to perform error checking such as making sure that the user entered a valid record number or that it was one of the record numbers listed. This method is also more visually appealing than just listing the secondary records would be.

The secondary record can be processed just like any other record once it has been selected. A data entry screen should be displayed and the variables or fields loaded as pending GETs by using the @ SAY/GET statement and activated by using a READ statement.

Adding a New Secondary Record

The preceding discussion concentrated on how to select an existing secondary record. There are really two different conditions you must handle. First, you must allow the user to add a secondary record if there are not any to begin with. Second, you must provide a way to allow the user to add a record while in the secondary record selection screen.

The SEEK command will return a FALSE value if there are no matches found. If there are not any matches found, the user should be asked whether he or she wants to add one. If the user does, the program should process the addition of a new transaction record, as shown here:

```
USE Customer NEW
USE Trans NEW
```

```
SET INDEX TO Transid
SEEK Customer->Id
IF FOUND()
   procsec()
ELSE
   IF yesno("Add a new record? ")
      addsec()
   ENDIF
ENDIF
```

In this example, if there are not any matches found, the statements between the ELSE and ENDIF statements will be executed. In that case, the user should be asked if he or she wants to add a record. This example uses the yesno() function developed earlier in this chapter to perform that task. If the user does want to add a record, a new record should be appended to the secondary database, the key data replaced, and a data entry screen presented to the user.

It is a little more difficult to add a new record if there are existing transactions. You want to be able to set up a hot key for the user to press to add a new record while in the secondary record selection screen. The idea is to use the Clipper SET KEY command to set up a hot key, as follows.

```
#include "inkey.ch"
PUBLIC g_lastkey := 0
SET KEY K_INS TO hotkeys
```

The file containing key code constants, called INKEY.CH, is included in the program by using the #include statement. Recall that the constant definitions included in INKEY.CH are used in place of the actual number assigned to the key. This makes the code more readable. A variable called *g_lastkey* is defined as public, which makes it available anywhere in the entire application. The SET KEY command accepts the keystroke (K_INS) and an assigned function (hotkeys()) as parameters. Once the key has been assigned in this way, the program will immediately execute the hotkeys() function when the user presses the INS key. Here is the hotkeys() function:

```
FUNCTION hotkeys()
g_lastkey := LASTKEY()
```

```
KEYBOARD CHR(K_PGDN)
RETURN NIL
```

The keystroke that caused an immediate branch to the hotkeys()
function is stored in the global variable *g_lastkey* by using the Clipper
LASTKEY() function. LASTKEY() returns the numeric value of the last
keystroke pressed. The KEYBOARD statement *stuffs* the keyboard buffer
with the characters specified. In this example, it stuffs the PGDN key into
the keyboard buffer. This acts the same as if the user had pressed the
PGDN key while in the PROMPT menu. The result is that the PROMPT
menu terminates. You must then determine what caused the exit from
the PROMPT menu, as shown here:

```
g_lastkey := 0
SET KEY K_INS TO hotkeys
MENU TO l_menupos
IF l_menupos == 0
   RETURN .T.
ENDIF
IF g_lastkey == K_INS
   addsec()
ELSE
   * user selected a record to edit
ENDIF
```

The variable *l_menupos* would return a zero if the user escaped from
the PROMPT menu. If the user did not escape, the global variable
g_lastkey is checked to see if the INS key was pressed. If it was pressed,
then the user wanted to add a new record.

The same function could be used if the user answered yes to the
question "Add a new record?" or if the user pressed the INS key while in
the secondary record selection screen. Here is the function that adds a
secondary record (ADD SECondary):

```
FUNCTION addsec()
   appendrec()
   replace Id with Customer->Id
   *  present the user with data entry screen
RETURN

FUNCTION appendrec()
```

```
SET DELETED OFF
GO TOP
IF .NOT. EMPTY(Id) .or. EOF()
   APPEND BLANK
ELSE
   RECALL
ENDIF
SET DELETED ON
RETURN .T.
```

In this example, the addsec() function calls on the appendrec() function to perform the work of obtaining an empty record for use. Recall from Chapter 4 that the appendrec() function attempts to reuse records that have been deleted. Once the empty record has been retrieved, the field that connects the primary and secondary databases is filled in. Once that has been completed, the screen for editing the secondary record is presented to the user. You usually do this by calling the same function used to edit the secondary records.

Deleting a Secondary Record

The method for selecting a secondary record to delete is very similar to that for adding a new record while in the PROMPT menu. A hot key is set up for the DEL key as follows.

```
g_lastkey := 0
SET KEY K_DEL TO hotkeys
SET KEY K_INS TO hotkeys
MENU TO l_menupos
IF l_menupos == 0
   RETURN .T.
ENDIF
DO CASE
   CASE g_lastkey == K_INS
      addsec()
   CASE g_lastkey == K_DEL
      delrec()
   OTHERWISE
      * user selected a record to edit
ENDIF
```

You turn a DEL key into a hot key by using the same hotkeys() function that the INS key uses. If the user presses the INS key or DEL key, the corresponding numeric code for that key is returned in the variable *g_lastkey*. A DO CASE construct is used since there is a need to process multiple conditions. If the user pressed the INS key, the addsec() function is performed. If the user pressed the DEL key, the delrec() function is performed. Otherwise, the user selected a record to edit.

The process of deleting the record is to clear out all the data within the record and use the Clipper DELETE command to mark the record as deleted, as shown here:

```
FUNCTION delrec()
REPLACE Id WITH "", Product WITH "", Desc WITH "",;
        Quantity WITH 0, Unitcost WITH 0,;
        Trans_date WITH CTOD("  /  /  ")
DELETE
RETURN .T.
```

You could use this example in the sample application. You could also easily modify it to suit any application by simply changing the field names. Note the Clipper CTOD() function used to initialize the date field called Trans_date. This function converts the character string " / / " to a date that can then be stored in the date field. A run-time error would result if this were not done.

Adding a Secondary Database to the Customer Tracking System

All the ideas discussed in this chapter allow you to incorporate secondary record processing into a database application. Following is a continuation of the customer tracking system developed in Chapter 4, with changes made to reflect ideas presented in this chapter. If you have been entering the customer tracking system, merge these modules with the modules described in Chapter 4 since only the ones that have changed are presented here.

The Main Program

The main program is usually the place to initialize constants and variables that will be used throughout the entire program. In addition, the main program should set up the appropriate Clipper environment by using the Clipper SET statements. Here is a revised version of the main program of the customer tracking system:

```
#DEFINE c_boxstrng ( CHR(213)+CHR(205)+CHR(184)+CHR(179)+;
          CHR(190)+CHR(205)+CHR(212)+CHR(179)+CHR(32) )
LOCAL l_choice := 0
PRIVATE m_id
PUBLIC g_lastkey := 0
#include "inkey.ch"
#include "set.ch"
SET DELETED ON
SET WRAP ON
SET SCOREBOARD OFF
opendbfs()                    // call function to open databases
#DEFINE c_escape 0
#DEFINE c_create 1
#DEFINE c_modify 2
#DEFINE c_delete 3
DO WHILE .T.
   CLEAR
   @ 0,65 SAY DATE()                    // display help information
   @ 0,25 SAY "CUSTOMER TRACKING"
   @ 1, 1 PROMPT "CUSTOMERS"            // initialize menu prompts
   @ 1,30 PROMPT "REPORTING"
   @ 1,65 PROMPT "MAINTENANCE"
   MENU TO l_choice                     // execute menu
   DO CASE                              // DO CASE construct begins here
     CASE l_choice == c_escape
        RETURN
     CASE l_choice == 1
        entry()
     CASE l_choice == 2
        rpt()
     CASE l_choice == 3
        sys()
   ENDCASE
```

```
ENDDO
RETURN
```

New SET statements, a public variable called *g_lastkey,* and #include statements were added to the beginning of the main program. Public variables should all be initialized at one place to provide easy reference. The public variable called *g_lastkey* is used during transaction processing to indicate that a hot key (either the INS key or the DEL key) was pressed.

Painting the Primary Record Screen

Once the primary record has been selected, the data entry screen should be displayed along with the field values. These routines may be used for editing data and displaying it for verification when the user wants to delete a record:

```
FUNCTION custscrn()
@ 7,4,18,50 BOX c_boxstrng
@ 7,20 SAY "CUSTOMER ENTRY SCREEN"
@  8,5 say "Customer ID :"
@  9,5 SAY "First Name  :"
@ 10,5 SAY "Last Name   :"
@ 11,5 SAY "Company     :"
@ 12,5 SAY "Title       :"
@ 13,5 SAY "Address     :"
@ 14,5 SAY "            :"
@ 15,5 SAY "City        :"
@ 16,5 SAY "State       :          Zip  :"
@ 17,5 SAY "Phone       :"
RETURN .T.


FUNCTION saycust()
@  8,18 SAY Id
@  9,18 SAY Fname
@ 10,18 SAY Lname
@ 11,18 SAY Company
@ 12,18 SAY Title
@ 13,18 SAY Addr1
@ 14,18 SAY Addr2
```

```
@ 15,18 SAY City
@ 16,18 SAY State
@ 16,34 SAY Zip
@ 17,18 SAY Phone
RETURN .T.
```

The custscrn() function paints the screen with headings, a box, and
field help information. The saycust() function displays the field values. It
would be easy to combine the two functions, but the flexibility would be
reduced.

Obtaining the Primary Record Data

You can add the ability to access secondary records to the function
used to edit the primary record data. Here is the getcust() function, which
demonstrates this idea:

```
FUNCTION getcust()
LOCAL l_finished := .F.
DO WHILE .NOT. l_finished
    @  9,18 GET Fname
    @ 10,18 GET Lname
    @ 11,18 GET Company
    @ 12,18 GET Title
    @ 13,18 GET Addr1
    @ 14,18 GET Addr2
    @ 15,18 GET City
    @ 16,18 GET State PICTURE "!!"
    @ 16,34 GET Zip
    @ 17,18 GET Phone PICTURE "999-999-9999"
    READ
    IF yesno('Edit Transactions Y/N ?')
        tranlist()
        SELECT Customer
    ENDIF
    l_finished = yesno("Finished Y/N ?")
ENDDO
RETURN .T.
```

A local variable called *l_finished* has been added to the getcust()
function. This variable controls the looping of the DO WHILE construct.
The *l_finished* variable will cause the loop to continue as long as the user
responds "Y" to the "Finished Y/N ?" question that is presented by using
the yesno() function. If the user answers "Y" to the question, the tranlist()
function is called. If the user answers "N" to the question, the value placed
in the variable *l_finished* will be FALSE. A FALSE value will terminate
the DO WHILE loop.

The effect of the DO WHILE loop, the *l_finished* logical variable, and
the yesno() question is to allow the user to edit the primary record and
associated secondary records as many times as necessary until choosing
to exit. Figure 5-1 shows the primary record data entry screen in the
sample application. Note that you do not allow edit of the Id field. This is
because the Id field is used to tie the primary record with the secondary
records. In the sample application, you would lose the connection
between the customer and the transactions if you allowed the user to
change the Id field.

FIGURE
5-1

Primary record data entry screen

Presenting the Secondary Records

There are many conditions to account for when presenting secondary records. Although this code may look complicated, you could easily modify it to suit your own application. Concentrate on the main flow of the logic.

```
FUNCTION tranlist()
LOCAL l_recarr[15]
LOCAL l_arrcnt
LOCAL l_screen1,l_screen2,l_screen3,l_toppos,l_menupos
SELECT Trans
SEEK Customer->Id
IF .NOT. FOUND()
   IF .NOT. yesno("No transactions - add one Y/N ? ")
      RETURN .F.
   ENDIF
   appendrec()
   REPLACE Id WITH Customer->Id
   l_screen1 := SAVESCREEN(15,1,22,78)
   transcrn()
   gettran()
   RESTSCREEN(15,1,22,78,l_screen1)
   RETURN .T.
ENDIF

l_toppos := RECNO()
l_screen2 := SAVESCREEN(3,49,18,79)
DO WHILE .T.
   l_arrcnt := 0
   @ 3,49,18,79 BOX c_boxstrng
   @ 24,0 SAY "INS to add, DEL to delete, ENTER to change, " + ;
            "ESC to exit"
   GOTO l_toppos
   l_count := 0
   g_lastkey := 0
   SET KEY K_INS TO hotkeys
   SET KEY K_DEL TO hotkeys
   DO WHILE Id == Customer->Id .AND. .NOT. EOF() .AND. ;
                         l_count < 15
      l_arrcnt++
      l_recarr[l_arrcnt] = RECNO()
```

```
            @ 4+l_count,50 PROMPT DTOC(Trans_date)+" " + ;
                           SUBSTR(Product,1,20)
            SKIP
            l_count := l_count+1
        ENDDO
        MENU TO l_menupos
        SET KEY K_INS TO
        SET KEY K_DEL TO
        IF l_menupos == 0
            RESTSCREEN(3,49,18,79,l_screen2)
            RETURN .T.
        ENDIF
        GOTO l_recarr[l_menupos]
        l_screen3 := SAVESCREEN(15,1,22,78)
        transcrn()
        DO CASE
            CASE g_lastkey == K_INS
                appendrec()
                REPLACE Id WITH Customer->Id
                gettran()
            CASE g_lastkey == K_DEL
                saytran()
                IF yesno("Delete Y/N ? ")
                    deltran()
                ENDIF
            OTHERWISE
                gettran()
        ENDCASE
        RESTSCREEN(15,1,22,78,l_screen3)
    ENDDO
RETURN .T.
```

The first lines of this function initialize the local variables used, select the transaction database, and then attempt to find the customer's ID by using the SEEK command.

If there are not any transactions for the customer, this section of the code is executed.

```
IF .NOT. yesno("No transactions - add one Y/N ? ")
    RETURN .F.
ENDIF
appendrec()
```

```
REPLACE Id WITH Customer->Id
l_screen1 := SAVESCREEN(15,1,22,78)
transcrn()
gettran()
RESTSCREEN(15,1,22,78,l_screen1)
RETURN .T.
```

The yesno() function asks whether a new transaction needs to be added. The program returns to the calling program (the program that called the tranlist() function) if the user answers "N" to the question. If the user does want to add a new transaction, the appendrec() function is called to obtain a new record. The screen is saved prior to calling the transcrn() and gettran() functions. Then the screen is restored prior to exiting back to the calling program.

If matches are found, the first record number is stored to the variable *l_toppos* and the current screen is saved. A DO WHILE loop is set up to run until the user is done processing the transactions, as shown here:

```
l_toppos := RECNO()
l_screen2 := SAVESCREEN(3,49,18,79)
DO WHILE .T.
   l_arrcnt := 0
   @ 3,49,18,79 BOX c_boxstrng
   @ 24,0 SAY "INS to add, DEL to delete, ENTER to change, " + ;
             "ESC to exit"
   *
   * (code here to handle transaction selection)
   *
   IF l_menupos == 0
      RESTSCREEN(3,49,18,79,l_screen2)
      RETURN .T.
   ENDIF
   *
   * (code here to process keystrokes)
   *
ENDDO
```

The local variable *l_toppos* stores the first record number so that a SEEK does not have to be performed each time through the loop. The screen is saved prior to the execution of the DO WHILE loop. The DO WHILE loop continues until the user presses the ESC key, in which case *l_menupos* equals zero. At that point, the screen is restored and the RETURN .T. statement returns to the calling program. A box is drawn and help information is displayed each time through the DO WHILE loop.

Here is the section of code that handles the selection of a transaction:

```
GOTO l_toppos
l_count := 0
g_lastkey := 0
SET KEY K_INS TO hotkeys
SET KEY K_DEL TO hotkeys
DO WHILE Id == Customer->Id .AND. .NOT. EOF() .AND. ;
                        l_count
   l_arrcnt++
   l_recarr[l_arrcnt] = RECNO()
   @ 4+l_count,50 PROMPT DTOC(Trans_date)+" " + ;
                SUBSTR(Product,1,20)
   SKIP
   l_count := l_count+1
ENDDO
MENU TO l_menupos
SET KEY K_INS TO
SET KEY K_DEL TO
```

The database record pointer is repositioned at the first record in the database that matches the current customer by using the *l_toppos* variable. The variables *l_count* and *g_lastkey* are both initialized to zero. The INS and DEL keys are set up as hot keys by using the Clipper SET KEY command. The corresponding record number for each menu item is stored in the array called *l_recarr* for use when a selection is made. Once the list of transactions is presented to the user, pressing either of those keys will result in the hotkeys() function being executed. The DO WHILE loop sequences the database one record at a time until the end-of-file marker is reached, the customer ID changes, or there are more than 15 transactions. The variable *l_count* is incremented for each transaction that is found and a PROMPT statement is issued. The MENU TO l_menupos statement will provide the user with a pick list of the available transactions, as shown in Figure 5-2.

When the user presses any key that causes exit from the PROMPT menu, the following section of code is executed.

FIGURE 5-2

Secondary record selection screen

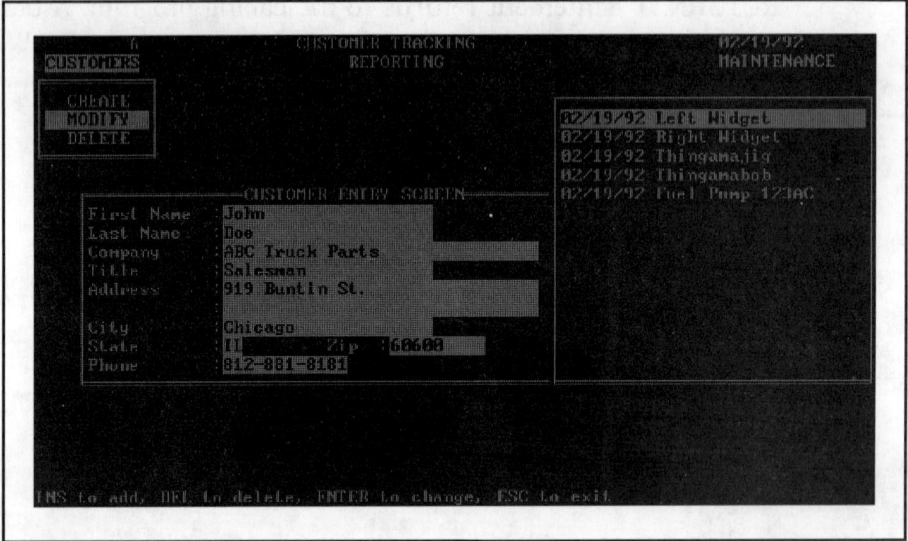

```
GOTO l_toppos
SKIP l_menupos - 1
l_screen3 := SAVESCREEN(15,1,22,78)
transcrn()
DO CASE
    CASE g_lastkey == K_INS
        appendrec()
        REPLACE Id WITH Customer->Id
        gettran()
    CASE g_lastkey == K_DEL
        saytran()
        IF yesno("Delete Y/N ? ")
            deltran()
        ENDIF
    OTHERWISE
        gettran()
ENDCASE
RESTSCREEN(15,1,22,78,l_screen3)
```

The first two lines of this code segment position the database record
pointer at the transaction record that was selected. The program then

saves the screen and presents the transaction entry screen. The CASE statement is executed and will perform the appropriate CASE statement, depending on which key terminated the MENU TO statement. If the user presses the ENTER key, the gettran() function will be called; this enables the user to edit the currently highlighted transaction.

If the user pressed the INS key, *g_lastkey* will be equal to the constant K_INS. The appendrec() function is called and the ID number is replaced with the current customer's ID number. The gettran() function is then called to enable the user to edit the transaction fields.

If the user pressed the DEL key, *g_lastkey* will be equal to the constant K_DEL. The current transaction field values are displayed and the user is prompted to make sure he or she really wanted to delete the transaction record. The record is deleted by using the deltran() function if the user answered "Y" to the delete question.

Note that this function uses the PROMPT/MENU TO combination to allow the user to select transactions. If there is a possibility of more than 15 transaction records, either the ACHOICE or TBROWSE scroller could be used. When you use ACHOICE, the items are loaded into an array and displayed by passing the array name and screen coordinates to the Clipper ACHOICE() function. TBROWSE is more complicated than either the PROMPT/MENU TO or the ACHOICE option.

Displaying the Secondary Record Screen

Secondary records may be handled in the same way as any other record once they have been selected. Here are the functions used to display the secondary record screen and data in the sample application:

```
FUNCTION transcrn()
@ 15,1,22,78 BOX c_boxstrng
@ 15,2 SAY "Transactions"
@ 16,2 SAY "Id           "
@ 17,2 SAY "Product      "
@ 18,2 SAY "Description  "
@ 19,2 SAY "Quantity     "
@ 20,2 SAY "Unitcost     "
@ 21,2 SAY "Total        "
RETURN .T.
```

```
FUNCTION saytran()
@ 16,15 SAY Id
@ 17,15 SAY Product
@ 18,15 SAY Desc
@ 19,15 SAY Quantity PICTURE "99999"
@ 20,15 SAY Unitcost PICTURE "9999.99"
@ 21,15 SAY Unitcost*Quantity PICTURE "9999.99"
RETURN .T.
```

These functions are split up so they may be used both for editing records and for displaying the information for the user to view if he or she wants to delete a record. Note that the saytran() function includes a calculated field (Total) that is calculated by multiplying the Unitcost field by the Quantity field.

The saytran() function demonstrates the use of the PICTURE clause to format data on the screen. An @ SAY PICTURE clause is very similar to an @ GET PICTURE clause except that it is used to display a numeric value on the screen or printer rather than to control the data being entered into a data entry field. The PICTURE template works in the same manner with the @ SAY command as with the @ GET command.

Obtaining the Transaction Data

When you are allowing the user to enter data, it is often a good idea to start a loop so that once the data has been entered, the loop will allow the user to modify the data again if necessary. That concept is illustrated here:

```
FUNCTION gettran()
LOCAL l_finished := .F.
DO WHILE .NOT. l_finished
   @ 16,15 SAY Id
   @ 17,15 GET Product
   @ 18,15 GET Desc
   @ 19,15 GET Quantity PICTURE "99999"
```

```
@ 20,15 GET Unitcost PICTURE "9999.99"
READ
@ 21,15 SAY Unitcost*Quantity PICTURE "9999.99"
l_finished = yesno("Finished with Transaction Y/N ? ")
ENDDO
REPLACE Trans_date WITH DATE()
RETURN .T.
```

The user is presented with the transaction data entry screen as long as he or she answers "Y" to the "Finished with Transaction Y/N ? " question. The total cost is calculated and displayed when the question is asked. The field called Trans_date in the transaction database is replaced with the current system date, using the Clipper DATE() function. The Clipper UPDATED() function could be used to change to Trans_date field only if any fields were changed. Figure 5-3 shows the transaction data entry screen.

Deleting Secondary Records

The deltran() function is called when the user presses the DEL key while in the PROMPT menu. The function is shown here:

```
FUNCTION deltran()
REPLACE Id WITH "", Product WITH "", Desc WITH "",;
        Quantity WITH 0, Unitcost WITH 0,;
        Trans_date WITH CTOD("  /  /  ")
DELETE
RETURN .T.
```

This function initializes all of the fields in the transaction record and marks the record as deleted. Any date field types must be initialized by using the CTOD(" / / ") syntax; otherwise, a run-time error will result. The record is marked for deletion by using the DELETE command. Recall that the DELETE command does not physically remove the record from the database. This allows the record to be reclaimed later when new secondary items are added.

FIGURE
5-3

Secondary record data entry screen

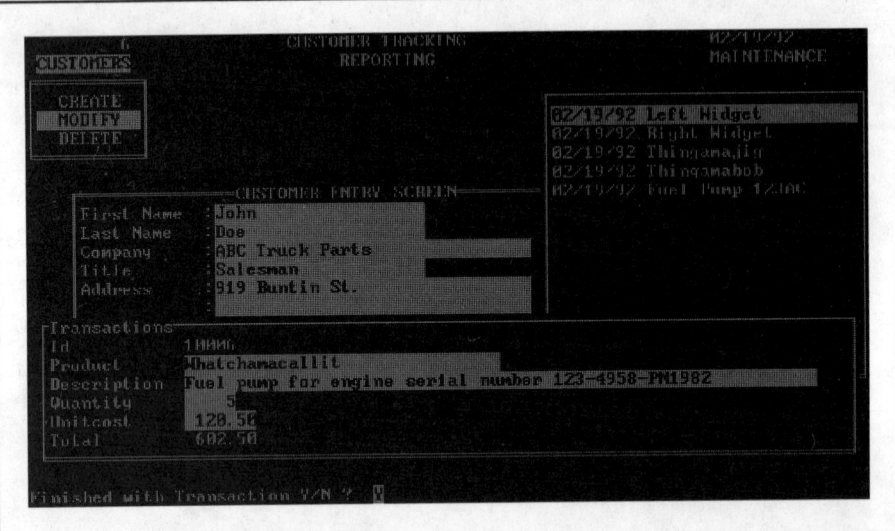

The Hotkeys() Function

You can set up keys to cause an immediate branch to a function. In the sample application, the INS and DEL keys were set up to branch to the hotkeys() function shown here:

```
FUNCTION hotkeys()
g_lastkey := LASTKEY()
KEYBOARD CHR(K_PGDN)
RETURN NIL
```

When the user presses the INS or DEL key, the program jumps from wherever it is to the hotkeys() function. The hotkeys() function places the key value in the global variable called *g_lastkey*. More important, the KEYBOARD command is used to force a PGDN keystroke into the keyboard buffer. The combined effect of this is to exit the MENU TO command with the appropriate key code stored in the *g_lastkey* variable.

The ability to set up keys in this manner is useful in many situations. For example, you could use it to pull up a pick list of states while entering the customer State field. You could also use it to provide utility programs such as calendars, calculators, and other pop-up type routines within your program. It is important to be very specific in the use of hot-key assignments. Common mistakes include forgetting to release the hot-key assignment or forgetting to reset the *g_lastkey* variable.

A Function to Open Databases

If your program opens many databases, it might be a good idea to pull out the code that opens databases and indexes into its own function, as shown here:

```
FUNCTION opendbfs()
USE Customer NEW
IF .NOT. FILE("Name.ntx")
   INDEX ON UPPER(Lname+Fname) TO Name
ELSE
   SET INDEX TO Name
ENDIF
USE Trans NEW
IF .NOT. FILE("Transid.ntx")
   INDEX ON Id TO Transid
ELSE
   SET INDEX TO Transid
ENDIF
SELECT Customer
RETURN .T.
```

This function opens the customer and transaction databases used in the sample application and creates index files if they do not exist.

Key Points

Sacrificing Speed

It is sometimes better to sacrifice a little bit of speed in order to write readable and maintainable code. Elaborate schemes used to achieve minimal speed increases may greatly increase the potential for future problems.

continues . . .

Slowing Down the Operator

Users may become frustrated if they are slowed down by the program's performing validation checks. An alternative is to perform the validation after each record or perhaps after many records have been entered. Ask all pertinent questions prior to running a report.

Perceived Time

Studies have shown that perceived time is less when some kind of progress information is displayed continually. This progress information could be in the form of a record number or a name, such as a customer name, that is currently being processed.

Code Optimization

In its simplest form, code optimization means merely reducing the size of the code or, more specifically, reducing the number of instructions required to achieve a particular result. This can be achieved by following these guidelines:

❑ Constants should be used whenever possible.

❑ Use Clipper functions rather than your own code whenever possible.

❑ Passing by reference is another way to increase speed since only the memory address is passed to the function or to the procedure.

continues . . .

Open Databases at the Beginning

Opening and closing databases takes time. Try to open all the databases used for a particular section of code right at the beginning.

Commands to Avoid

There are commands in Clipper that should be avoided if at all possible. The SORT command physically sorts the data on the disk, and this task takes considerable time and disk space. The PACK command makes a new copy of the database that contains all the records except those marked for deletion.

The SET FILTER TO statement is a great Clipper feature when used correctly. However, you must keep in mind that it processes and evaluates each record in the database. The LOCATE FOR command also processes the database sequentially until the first match is found.

The Real Speed Issues

The user will present the real speed issues once the application is put into use. Concentrate on becoming a good problem solver and handle the problems as they arise.

Data Validation

The easiest way to validate data is to provide control of the data as it is being entered. You can perform data validation by using PICTURE functions, PICTURE templates, and VALID clauses.

continues . . .

The VALID clause enables you to provide a condition that must be met before the user may exit a field.

Relational Databases

The databases used in Clipper are termed relational, which means that data is stored in simple tables, with the relationships between different data items tied together by values in other tables.

Primary Key

The field in the primary database used to connect the primary database with other databases is referred to as the primary key. Primary keys must be unique in order to work correctly.

Finding Secondary Records

A secondary record must be indexed on the field that is used to connect it to the primary database. You use the SEEK command to quickly locate matching secondary records.

Using Hot Keys

You can use the Clipper SET KEY command to set up hot keys such as the INS key (to allow addition of records) and the DEL key (to allow deletions).

CHAPTER

Reports and System Utilities

R eports are probably the most important element of an application since they present the user with information. Reports are sent to a printer or displayed on the screen in the form of lists and summaries presented in a specific order and matching some specified condition.

Chapter 4 introduced an example of a database application that included a top menu bar, several pulldown menus, one data entry screen, an action menu used to update client information, and a database to receive the data. Chapter 5 introduced secondary database processing to the application. This chapter covers the skills necessary to develop reports and system maintenance options.

The Basics of Writing Report Programs

As a programmer, you must be able to sort data, allow the user to select specific data, and make connections between various databases in the application. The output should be formatted in a way that is visually appealing to the user. Clipper provides the features necessary to process databases and produce reports and listings.

Output Method

There are two basic ways to output data either to the screen or to a printer. You can use the @ SAY command for specifying the location of the printed output by passing the row and column as part of the statement, as shown here:

```
@ 12,10 SAY "HI THERE"
```

This statement will print the text "HI THERE" on line 12, starting at column 10. Your program can jump around the screen freely to display text. For example, you could display text on line 20 and then display text on line 10 without any problem. However, this would be a problem when using a printer. Because the printer cannot move backward, it will eject a page in order to get to line 10.

You can also use the ? and ?? statements to display information on the screen or printer. These statements are followed by the expression to be printed, as shown here:

```
? "HI THERE"
```

The single question mark will perform a line feed prior to printing the expression. The double question mark will display the text at the current position.

With the @ SAY and ?/?? commands, you can combine expressions in the same statement by using the + operator, as shown here:

```
? "HI THERE" + " " + "JACK"
```

The + operator simply combines the various expressions. In this case, "HI THERE" is combined with a single space and "JACK".

Variables, Clipper functions, and user-defined functions can also be displayed as part of the @ SAY and ?/?? commands, as shown here:

```
? "TODAY'S DATE IS " + DTOC(DATE())
```

This example uses the Clipper DATE() function to display the current system date. Since the DATE() function returns a date type, it must be converted to a character type before it is displayed. You do this by using the Clipper DTOC() (date to character) function.

Using Clipper Functions to Format Data

There are many Clipper functions available to assist you in formatting data to display on the screen or output to the printer. The Clipper ALLTRIM(), RTRIM(), and LTRIM() functions are all used to trim spaces from a string. The LTRIM() function trims leading spaces. The RTRIM() function trims trailing spaces. The ALLTRIM() function trims leading and trailing spaces from the string. There will be many times when you do not want excessive space between pieces of data, such as between a first name and a last name, as shown in this example:

```
m_fname = "John           "
m_lname = "Doe            "
m_city  = "Chicago        "
? m_fname + " " + m_lname + " " + m_city
m_fname = "John           "
m_lname = "Andrews        "
m_city  = "New York       "
? m_fname + " " + m_lname + " " + m_city
```

The output from this would be

```
John            Doe             Chicago
John            Andrews         New York
```

The blank spaces between the first and last names should be removed. You can accomplish this with the ALLTRIM() function, as shown here:

```
m_fname = "John           "
m_lname = "Doe            "
m_city  = "Chicago        "
? ALLTRIM(m_fname) + " " + ALLTRIM(m_lname) + " " + m_city
m_fname = "John           "
m_lname = "Andrews        "
m_city  = "New York       "
? ALLTRIM(m_fname) + " " + ALLTRIM(m_lname) + " " + m_city
```

The output would look like this:

```
John Doe Chicago
John Andrews New York
```

This looks much better, but the city column no longer lines up. If your listing or report has columns, you will need to make adjustments since the columns will not line up after you use the TRIM statements. There are three Clipper commands that allow easy padding of spaces to a string so columns will line up correctly. The Clipper function PADC() accepts a string and the string length as parameters. The text is centered in the returned string. PADL() pads blank characters to the beginning of a string to make it the desired string length. PADR() pads blank characters to the end of a string to make it the desired string length, as shown here:

```
m_fname = "John              "
m_lname = "Doe               "
m_city  = "Chicago           "
? PADR(ALLTRIM(m_fname) + " " + ALLTRIM(m_lname),20) + ;
    " " + m_city
m_fname = "John              "
m_lname = "Andrews           "
m_city  = "New York          "
? PADR(ALLTRIM(m_fname) + " " + ALLTRIM(m_lname),20) + ;
    " " + m_city
```

This results in the following output:

```
John Doe            Chicago
John Andrews        New York
```

Note that the first parameter passed to the PADR() function is the trimmed value of the first and last names. The second parameter passed is 20, which results in a column 20 characters wide for the combined first and last names prior to printing the city.

You can use the SPACE() function to display blank spaces. This function eliminates the need to count the number of blank spaces within quotes. You simply pass the desired number of blank spaces as the parameter to the function, as shown here:

```
? "JOHN" + SPACE(10) + "DOE"
```

This results in the following output:

```
JOHN          DOE
```

You can use the STR() function to convert numeric data to string types. Here is an example of the STR() function:

```
var1 := 1234.56
var2 := STR(var1,7,2)
```

The first line of this example creates a variable called *var1*. That variable is then passed as the first parameter to the STR() function. The second parameter of the STR() function determines the desired string length. In this case, the length of the string returned would be seven characters. The third parameter indicates the desired number of decimal positions. When deciding on the string length, make sure you allow one place for the decimal point. If the length passed is longer than the number, the result will be padded on the left with spaces.

The TRANSFORM() function discussed in Chapter 7 can also be used to format data for reports. The TRANSFORM() function works in much the same way as the PICTURE clause in @ SAY and @ GET commands. TRANSFORM() functions or TRANSFORM() templates may be passed as parameters to format character, date, logical, or numeric values.

User-defined Functions in Reports

The data you want for your report may not be readily available. You can use user-defined functions to provide information to your report while eliminating the need for elaborate schemes to get the data. *User-defined functions* are functions that you write as opposed to those functions that are part of the Clipper language. As an example, you could use a user-defined function within the actual report to display the full spelling of the current month. Your report could include a CASE statement for each time it needed to print the month, or it could call on the following user-defined function:

```
FUNCTION strmonth(l_date)
LOCAL month := ""
LOCAL monthnum := substr(DTOC(l_date),1,2)
DO CASE
   CASE monthnum = "01"
     month = "January"
   CASE monthnum = "02"
     month = "February"
   CASE monthnum = "03"
     month = "March"
   CASE monthnum = "04"
     month = "April"
   CASE monthnum = "05"
     month = "May"
   CASE monthnum = "06"
     month = "June"
   CASE monthnum = "07"
```

```
       month = "July"
   CASE monthnum = "08"
      month = "August"
   CASE monthnum = "09"
      month = "September"
   CASE monthnum = "10"
      month = "October"
   CASE monthnum = "11"
      month = "November"
   CASE monthnum = "12"
      month = "December"
ENDCASE
RETURN month
```

This function accepts a date type as a parameter and gets the month number from the date. A CASE statement is used to return the month of the year spelled out rather than as a number. Making this a function allows the call to be included in a print statement, as follows.

```
? "The current month is " +  strmonth(DATE())
```

This would display the following output if the month were February:

```
The current month is February
```

It is common practice to use a one-character field to store coded data such as gender, payroll type, or payment type. To display a text value for the codes, you could use user-defined functions. The following example accepts the coded data as a parameter and returns the text value, which is then displayed in the report:

```
FUNCTION paytype(l_paycode)
DO CASE
   CASE l_paycode = "Q"
     RETURN("QUARTERLY")
   CASE l_paycode = "M"
     RETURN("MONTHLY")
   CASE l_paycode = "Y"
     RETURN("YEARLY")
ENDCASE
RETURN("UNKNOWN")
```

This example uses a CASE construct to return the appropriate text value for the code passed as a parameter. If the pay code is not found, the text value defaults to UNKNOWN. The user-defined function is easily incorporated into a print statement such as the following:

? "The payment method is " + paytype(*Fpaycode*)

where *Fpaycode* is a database field. The function converts the code to the appropriate text without the need to embed the CASE construct within the report itself.

In the preceding example, a CASE construct was used to convert the code into a text string. Many times the text string is stored in another database called a lookup table. A *lookup table* is a database used to store the description of a code. A database could be created to store the pay codes. Here is the structure of the lookup table:

Field Name	Field Type	Field Length
Fcode	C	1
Fdesc	C	30

The lookup table would have an index on the Fcode field. Here is a sample of a user-defined function that accesses a lookup table:

```
USE Paycode NEW
INDEX ON Fcode to Paycode
USE Employee NEW
DO WHILE .NOT. EOF()
   ? paytype(Fcode)
   SKIP
ENDDO


FUNCTION paytype(l_code)
LOCAL l_holdsel := SELECT()
LOCAL l_return := "UNKNOWN"
SEEK l_code
IF .NOT. EOF()
  l_return = Fdesc
ENDIF
SELECT (l_holdsel)
RETURN l_return
```

The main program opens the lookup table called Paycode and creates an index file (Paycode) on the field called Fcode. The Employee database is sequenced using a DO WHILE loop, and the descriptions of the pay codes in all the records are displayed using the ? command and the paytype() function.

The paytype() function preserves the current work area, using the Clipper SELECT() statement. The Employee database is the current database prior to entering the function, and the function should make that database the currently selected database upon completion. The SELECT() statement returns the current work area to a variable called *l_holdsel.*

The SEEK command is used to find the matching pay code to the pay code in the employee database. The value is returned from the function in a variable called *l_return.* Note that *l_return* is initializing a value of UNKNOWN in case a match for the code is not found.

The advantage of this approach over a CASE statement is that you can add and delete codes and change the descriptions simply by editing the record in the lookup table.

Sorting Data

Usually you will want your report to be sorted based on some criteria within the report, such as a customer's name or social security number. It is preferable to use an index already present if possible. In that case, it is easy to select the appropriate index file to run your report.

You can also create index files on the fly to be used during a report. Suppose you had a CUSTOMER file and you wanted to index on the customer's ZIP code. You would open the database and index on the ZIP code as follows.

```
USE Customer
INDEX ON Zip TO Zip
```

The data will be indexed on the ZIP code field. You then can sequence through the records by using a DO WHILE loop, as shown here:

```
DO WHILE .NOT. EOF()
  * process record
  SKIP
ENDDO
```

The INDEX ON command opens the index file and positions the record pointer at the first logical record. The DO WHILE loop will process all the records in the database.

Filters

A *filter* makes a database file appear as if it contains only the records that match a specified filter expression. You use the Clipper SET FILTER TO command to create filters on a database. You can prompt the user with questions and then set the database filter accordingly based on the user's answers. Suppose you want to allow the user to select only customers within a certain state to print on a report. Here is a sample of code to accomplish that task:

```
USE Customer
l_state := space(2)
CLEAR SCREEN
@ 12,10 SAY "Enter state code: " GET l_state
READ

SET FILTER TO Fstate = l_state
DO WHILE .NOT. EOF()
  * process record
  SKIP
ENDDO
SET FILTER TO
```

The user is prompted to enter a state code. The SET FILTER command filters out all records except those that match the state code entered by the user. The database may be processed as usual, using the DO WHILE loop. Only the records that match the filter condition will be processed within the DO WHILE loop. The last SET FILTER TO statement turns off the filter. Make sure you do this, or the rest of your application will be affected by the filter on the database.

Destination of Output

You use the SET CONSOLE command to toggle the display of text to the screen. The command SET CONSOLE OFF prevents any output from going to the screen. You should do this when a report is to be printed rather than displayed on a screen. Use the command SET CONSOLE ON to resume display to the screen.

Use the SET PRINT statement to direct output to a printer. The command SET PRINT ON echos to the printer any output normally directed to the console. The command SET PRINT OFF turns off the echo to the printer. Use this command when you want to direct output to the printer prior to the first print statement. It should be turned off right after the last print statement.

Displaying Progress Information

It is a good idea to display some kind of progress information while the report is being printed. You could slightly modify the comment() function developed in Chapter 4 to allow it to be used to display status information. The function must be modified so that comment messages do not get output to the report in addition to the regular printed output. The modified comment() function is shown here:

```
FUNCTION comment(l_comment,l_pause)

#include "set.ch"
LOCAL hold_print    := SET(_SET_PRINTER,.F.)
LOCAL hold_cons     := SET(_SET_CONSOLE,.T.)

IF l_pause = NIL
   l_pause = .T.
ENDIF
@ 24,0
@ 24,0 SAY l_comment
IF l_pause
   INKEY(0)
   @ 24,0
ENDIF
```

```
SET(_SET_PRINTER,hold_print)
SET(_SET_CONSOLE,hold_cons)
RETURN .T.
```

An additional parameter called *l_pause* has been added. If a TRUE value (.T.) is passed as a parameter, the function will work as before by displaying the message and waiting for a keystroke from the user prior to exiting the function. If the parameter is not passed, *l_pause* is initialized to TRUE by the following statements:

```
IF l_pause = NIL
   l_pause = .T.
ENDIF
```

If the parameter is not passed, Clipper assigns the local variable *l_pause* a value of NIL. If the value is NIL, the program defaults to TRUE. This eliminates the need to modify any existing calls to this function. The user will not be required to press a key if a FALSE is passed as the *l_pause* parameter. In addition, the line printed is not erased prior to exiting the function.

Since the comment() function will now be called from a report, you have to make additional modifications to ensure the message is displayed on the screen and not printed on the report. The following statements serve to modify the current Clipper settings while preserving the existing values in the local variables called *hold_print* and *hold_cons*:

```
#include "set.ch"
LOCAL hold_print   := SET(_SET_PRINTER,.F.)
LOCAL hold_cons    := SET(_SET_CONSOLE,.T.)
```

The #include statement causes Clipper to include the file called set.ch as part of the program. set.ch defines constants used for the various Clipper SET commands, such as SET PRINT and SET CONSOLE. By using the #include file, you can refer to the different settings by name (_SET_PRINTER or _SET_CONSOLE) instead of by number. The first parameter of the Clipper SET() function accepts the Clipper setting you want to access. The second parameter accepts the value you want to change it to. The function returns the current value of the setting. In the example, the SET PRINTER statement is changed to FALSE, which means it is turned off. The SET CONSOLE statement is changed to TRUE, which means it is turned on. The current values are stored in the variables *hold_print* and *hold_cons.* Prior to the function's being exited, the original settings are restored by using the following commands:

```
SET(_SET_PRINTER,hold_print)
SET(_SET_CONSOLE,hold_cons)
```

These are just a few of the settings that could be preserved, but they will suffice in most cases. As you saw, by preserving the current settings to variables, you are able to restore them later in the program.

Multiple Databases

When accessing multiple databases, you can use the database alias and the -> symbol to access field information from another work area. Here is an example of this principle:

```
USE Customer NEW
USE Trans NEW
? Customer->Fname
```

Even though the database in the current work area is Trans (the transaction database), you can easily access the field information from the Customer database by placing its alias (Customer) followed by the -> symbol.

Many reports use the secondary database as the primary source of data, with a line printed for each secondary record. The primary record must be matched up in order to access some of the primary information, such as name and address. The following example demonstrates this principle:

```
USE Customer NEW
INDEX ON Id TO Customer
USE Trans
DO WHILE .NOT. EOF()
   SELECT Customer
   SEEK Trans->Id
   SELECT Trans
   ?  ALLTRIM(Customer->Fname) + "   "
```

```
      ?? ALLTRIM(Customer->Lname) + "  "
      ?? Fdesc
      SKIP
   ENDDO
```

This example draws on the information from a secondary database (Trans) and a primary database (Customer). The SEEK command is used to make the connection between the databases. The alias of the primary database (Customer) followed by the -> symbol accesses field information from the primary database. The first print statement uses ? to start a new line. The next two print statements use ?? to display data on the same line.

Developing a Report

A report may draw information from a single database or may involve connections among many databases. The following example demonstrates a simple report that displays customer names and phone numbers on the screen:

```
USE Customer NEW
custlist()

PROCEDURE custlist()
DO WHILE .NOT. EOF()
   ? ALLTRIM(Fname) + " " + ALLTRIM(Lname) + "    " + Phone
   SKIP
ENDDO
RETURN
```

The main databases are usually opened at the start of a program. Function calls are made to the various submenus and reports. This example opens the Customer database and calls the report function called custlist(). Custlist() contains a DO WHILE loop that will continue as long as the end-of-file marker has not been reached. The Clipper ALLTRIM() function trims leading and trailing blank characters from the *Lname* and *Fname* variables.

When you are listing a report to the screen, it is always a good idea to pause after each screenful of data. A line counter can be initialized to perform that purpose, as shown here:

```
USE Customer NEW
custlist()

PROCEDURE custlist
LOCAL l_linecnt := 2
LOCAL l_max := 22
CLEAR SCREEN
? "Name                    Phone Number"
?
DO WHILE .NOT. EOF()
   l_linecnt++
   IF l_linecnt > l_max
      ?
      ? "Press any key to continue"
      INKEY(0)
      l_linecnt := 2
      CLEAR SCREEN
      ? "Name                    Phone Number"
      ?
   ENDIF
   ? ALLTRIM(Fname) + " " + ALLTRIM(Lname) + "   " + Phone
   SKIP
ENDDO
RETURN
```

The local variable *l_linecnt* is initialized to 2 to include the two lines used for the heading. Another local variable, called *l_max*, is initialized to 22, which is the maximum number of lines to display on a screen. The *l_linecnt* variable is incremented by 1 each time through the loop. If the line counter is greater than 22, a pause message is displayed and the INKEY() function is used to wait for a keystroke from the user. The line counter is reinitialized, the screen is cleared, and the heading is redisplayed.

You could modify this program slightly to accommodate a listing to either the screen or printer, as follows.

```
LOCAL l_destiny := "S"
USE Customer NEW
CLEAR SCREEN
@ 10,10 SAY "Destination S/P ? " GET l_destiny picture "!";
        VALID(error_chk(l_destiny $ "SP","Answer S or P"))
READ
custlist(l_destiny)

PROCEDURE custlist(l_destiny)
LOCAL l_linecnt := 2
LOCAL l_max := 22
SELECT Customer
GO TOP
IF l_destiny = "P"
  SET PRINT ON
  SET CONSOLE OFF
  l_max := 55
ENDIF

CLEAR SCREEN
? "Name                Phone Number"
?
DO WHILE .NOT. EOF()
    l_linecnt++
    IF l_linecnt > l_max
       IF l_destiny = "S"
          ?
          ? "Press any key to continue"
          INKEY(0)
       ENDIF
       l_linecnt := 2
       CLEAR SCREEN
       ? "Name                Phone Number"
       ?
    ENDIF
    ? ALLTRIM(Fname) + " " + ALLTRIM(Lname) + "   " + Phone
    SKIP
ENDDO
IF l_destiny = "P"
  SET PRINT OFF
  SET CONSOLE ON
```

```
ENDIF
RETURN


*
* (include error_chk and comment functions)
*
```

The program opens the Customer database and then prompts the user for the print destination. The answer stored in the variable *l_destiny* is passed as a parameter to the custlist() function. The number of lines per page is adjusted and the SET PRINTER ON statement is executed, which results in output getting sent to the printer. The SET CONSOLE OFF command suppresses the output to the screen. The pause message and INKEY(0) are performed only if the output is going to the screen. Once the report is completed, the SET PRINT OFF command terminates output to the printer. The SET CONSOLE ON command allows the display to be directed to the console again.

Incorporating Reports to the Customer Tracking System

All the ideas discussed in this chapter allow you to incorporate reports into a database application. Following is a continuation of the customer tracking system developed in Chapters 4 and 5. You can use these reports as a model for developing reports for your own applications.

The Report Menu

The report menu does little of the actual work besides determining which report the user wants to execute and making function calls. The main work is left up to the various report functions that the submenu calls.

```
FUNCTION rpt()
LOCAL l_choice,l_scr
SET MESSAGE TO 24 CENTER
```

```
SELECT Customer
SAVE SCREEN TO l_scr
DO WHILE .T.
   RESTORE SCREEN FROM l_scr
   @ 2,30,7,59 BOX c_boxstrng
   @ 3, 31 PROMPT "  CUSTOMER LIST              " ;
        MESSAGE "Print a list of customers"
   @ 4, 31 PROMPT "  MAILING LABELS             " ;
        MESSAGE "Print mailing labels"
   @ 5, 31 PROMPT "  TRANSACTIONS BY MONTH      " ;
        MESSAGE "Print monthly transaction totals"
   @ 6, 31 PROMPT "  TRANSACTION BY CUSTOMER    " ;
        MESSAGE "Print customers transactions"
   MENU TO l_choice
   DO CASE
      CASE l_choice == 0
         SELECT Customer
         RESTORE SCREEN FROM l_scr
         RETURN .T.
      CASE l_choice == 1
         r_cust()
      CASE l_choice == 2
         r_label()
      CASE l_choice == 3
         r_tranmnth()
      CASE l_choice == 4
         r_trancust()
   ENDCASE
ENDDO
RETURN .T.
```

The rpt() function uses the PROMPT command to display the report menu. A DO WHILE loop is performed repeatedly until the user presses the ESC key. The function returns to the calling program (the main menu) when the user presses the ESC key. The MESSAGE clause has been added to the PROMPT commands. The MESSAGE clause combined with the SET MESSAGE TO 24 CENTER statement results in the addition of help information for each menu item.

Customer Listing

The next example demonstrates the listing of field values in a single database from beginning to end. You could easily adapt this basic format to print listings in your own application.

```
FUNCTION r_cust()
*Print a list of customers
LOCAL l_page := 1
LOCAL l_line := 2
LOCAL l_reccount := 0
LOCAL l_lastrec := alltrim(str(RECCOUNT()))
SELECT Customer
GO TOP
CLEAR SCREEN
SET PRINT ON
SET CONSOLE OFF
? "Customer list                    Page "+LTRIM(STR(l_page))
?
DO WHILE .NOT. EOF()
   l_line++
   l_reccount++
   comment("Processing record " + alltrim(str(l_reccount)) + ;
          " of " + l_lastrec,.f.)
   IF l_line > 66
      l_line := 2
      l_page++
      EJECT
      ? "Customer list                 Page " + ;
        LTRIM(STR(l_page))
      ?
   ENDIF
   ? Lname,Fname,Company
   SKIP
ENDDO
SET PRINT OFF
SET CONSOLE ON
EJECT
RETURN .T.
```

This is the simplest of the reports mentioned here. The Customer database is selected and the record pointer moved to the top. Keep in mind that the customer database is indexed by *Lname+Fname*. The "top" refers to those customers whose last names start with "A."

The printer is activated with the SET PRINT ON command and switched off with SET PRINT OFF. What this means is that any output that would normally go to the screen will also go to the printer. The SET CONSOLE OFF command is issued to suppress output to the screen.

A DO WHILE loop is used to sequence through all the records in the database. The comment() function displays the status of the report. The function establishes variables to track the number of pages (*l_page*) and the number of lines (*l_line*) per page. Most printers allow about 66 lines per page. You should check your printer and assign the appropriate number for the counter limit. As each record is processed, the current line number is checked against the maximum count. If the statement

```
IF l_line > 66
```

is evaluated to be TRUE, the block of code is executed to process a new page. The page counter is incremented and the line number counter is reset to 2 to accommodate the two heading lines in the report. An EJECT statement is performed to eject the page in the printer. The heading is printed on the next page prior to the program's moving on with regular record processing.

Printing Labels

Most customer databases require the ability to print labels. Keep in mind that labels come in many sizes. You may need to adjust your label-printing program to print on a continuous-feed dot matrix printer or a single-sheet-feed laser printer. The following function demonstrates the basic flow of printing one-across labels:

```
FUNCTION r_label()
LOCAL l_filler := 0
LOCAL l_reccount := 0
LOCAL l_lastrec
SELECT Customer
```

```
GO TOP
l_lastrec := alltrim(str(RECCOUNT()))
SET PRINT ON
SET CONSOLE OFF
DO WHILE .NOT. EOF()
   l_reccount++
   comment("Processing record " + alltrim(str(l_reccount)) + ;
          " of " + l_lastrec,.f.)
   ? TRIM(Fname)+" "+Lname
   IF .NOT. EMPTY(Company)
      ? Company
   ELSE
      l_filler++
   ENDIF
   ? Addr1
   IF .NOT. EMPTY(Addr2)
      ? Addr2
   ELSE
      l_filler++
   ENDIF
   ? TRIM(City) + ", " + State + " " + Zip
   DO WHILE l_filler > 0
      ?
      l_filler--
   ENDDO
   ?
   SKIP
ENDDO
SET PRINT OFF
SET CONSOLE ON
EJECT
RETURN .T.
```

This function processes from the top of the database to the end, using a DO WHILE loop. Since the labels in this example require six lines to be printed, a variable called *l_filler* is used to determine the number of lines that are actually printed. The Clipper EMPTY() function determines if particular fields contain data. You do not want to print an address line if it does not contain data. Once the lines of data have been printed, additional blank lines are printed at the end to position the printhead at the top of the next label.

Printing multicolumn labels is more difficult since you cannot print the first label without knowing the data to print on the second or third column. Here is sample code to accomplish printing more than one column of labels:

```
LOCAL l_count : 0
DECLARE line[6]
DO WHILE .NOT. EOF()
   AFILL(line,"")
   count := 1
   DO WHILE .NOT. EOF() .AND. count < 4
      line[1] := line[1]+Lname+Fname+"     "
      line[2] := line[2]+Addr1+"              "
      l_count := 2
      IF .NOT. EMPTY(Addr2)
         l_count++
         line[l_count] := line[l_count]+Addr2+"           "
      ENDIF
      l_count++
      line[l_count] := line[l_count] + padr(ALLTRIM(City) + " ";
                     + State + " " + Zip,40)

      * fill remaining lines with spaces
      FOR i := l_count + 1 to 6
         line[l_count] := line[l_count] + SPACE(40)
      SKIP
      count++
   ENDDO
   ? line[1]
   ? line[2]
   ? line[3]
   ? line[4]
   ? line[5]
   ? line[6]
ENDDO
```

This example uses a one-dimensional array called *line* to store the values to be printed on a label until the data for three labels is gathered. The AFILL() function initializes the array to blanks. The AFILL() function accepts the name of an array and the desired value as parameters. It then inserts the value into each array element. Each element of the array corresponds to a line to be printed. A single element actually contains data for three different labels by the time the label is printed. At that time, the condition for the inner DO WHILE loop is evaluated to be TRUE and the lines are printed using the ? command. The program continues to load the data for three labels and print the labels until all the records in the database have been processed.

Note that a variable called *l_count* is kept in order to keep track of the line of the label that was just filled. This is done in the event that the Addr2 field does not have any data. (You would not want a blank line printed in the middle of the name and address.) The use of *l_count* allows the city, state, and ZIP to be inserted at the next available line. If you did not adjust for blank fields, the resultant label would look something like this:

John Doe
130 Hillcrest Drive

Glen Carbon, IL 62034

You do not want the extra blank space between the first street address and the city, state, and ZIP. You want the label to look like this instead:

John Doe
130 Hillcrest Drive
Glen Carbon, IL 62034

Printing Transaction Totals

The next sample report demonstrates the process of gathering data from a secondary database. The primary database is processed sequentially until the end-of-file marker is reached. The SEEK command locates any corresponding secondary records. Those are processed, using a DO WHILE loop, until either the end-of-file marker is reached or until the fields linking the primary and secondary records are no longer equal.

```
FUNCTION r_tranmnth()
*Print monthly transaction totals
LOCAL l_page  := 1
LOCAL l_line  := 999
LOCAL l_total := 0
```

```
LOCAL l_id,l_month,l_year
LOCAL l_reccount := 0
LOCAL l_lastrec
SELECT Trans
INDEX ON Id+DTOC(Tran_date) TO Temp
SELECT Customer
l_lastrec := alltrim(str(RECCOUNT()))
GO TOP
SET PRINT ON
SET CONSOLE OFF
? "Transaction totals by Customer        Page "+ ;
  LTRIM(STR(l_page))
?
DO WHILE .NOT. EOF()
   l_reccount++
   l_line++
   comment("Processing record " + alltrim(str(l_reccount)) + ;
          " of " + l_lastrec,.f.)
   IF l_line > 60
      l_line := 2
      l_page++
      EJECT
      ? "Transaction totals by Customer        Page "+ ;
         LTRIM(STR(l_page))
      ?
   ENDIF
   SELECT Trans
   SEEK Customer->Id
   IF FOUND()
      l_id    := Customer->Id
      l_month := MONTH(Tran_date)
      l_year  := YEAR(Tran_date)
      DO WHILE Customer->Id == l_id .AND. ;
             l_month == MONTH(Tran_date) .AND. ;
             l_year == YEAR(Tran_date) .AND. .NOT. EOF()
         l_total := Unitcost*Quantity
         l_line++
         SKIP
      ENDDO
      SELECT Customer
      ? Id,m_month+"/"+m_year,Company,Lname,Fname,tot_count
      l_total := 0
```

```
      SKIP
   ENDIF
ENDDO
SET PRINT OFF
SET CONSOLE ON
EJECT
SELECT Trans
SET INDEX TO Trans
RETURN .T.
```

This program sequences through the Customer database and then jumps to the Trans database to find all transactions that match the ID in the Customer record. It then skips through the Trans database, adding up the *Unitcost*Quantity* and storing the accumulating total in the *l_total* variable. Indexing Trans by date as well as by ID makes it possible to group the totals by month. The transaction file is processed one record at a time until the month changes. At that point, the program prints out the total accumulated for the month/year just processed.

Printing Each Customer's Transactions

The previous example simply totaled up data in the secondary records to print on the same line as the primary record. This sample report prints the primary record data and some data from each of the secondary matches:

```
FUNCTION r_trancust()
*Print customer's transactions
LOCAL l_page := 1
LOCAL l_line := 2
LOCAL l_id
SELECT Customer
GO TOP
SET PRINT ON
SET CONSOLE OFF
? "Print Customer's Transactions                    Page "+;
   LTRIM(STR(l_page))
?
DO WHILE .NOT. EOF()
   comment(padr("Processing customer " + alltrim(fname) + ;
```

```
                     " " + alltrim(lname),40),.f.)
        SELECT Trans
        SEEK Customer->Id
        IF FOUND()
           l_id := Customer->Id
           DO WHILE Customer->Id == l_id
              ?
              ? Lname,Fname,Company
              l_line+=2      // C Clipper increase by 2
              DO WHILE Customer->Id == l_id .AND. l_line < 60
                 ? Product,Desc,Tran_date
                 ? Unitcost,Quantity,Unitcost*Quantity
                 ?
                 l_line+=3   // increase by 3
                 SKIP
              ENDDO
              IF line_count >= 60
                 EJECT
                 ? "Print Customer's Transactions    Page "+ ;
                       LTRIM(STR(l_page))
                 ?
                 l_page++
                 l_line := 2
              ENDIF
           ENDDO
        ENDIF
        SELECT Customer
        SKIP
     ENDDO
     SET PRINT OFF
     SET CONSOLE ON
     EJECT
     RETURN .T.
```

This report prints a listing of transactions for each customer. The customer name is repeated if transactions for that customer continue onto a new page. This program also prints multiple lines of data representing each transaction. The interesting thing about this report is that after the first page header has been printed, all other headers are printed from the inner DO WHILE loop. This shows that there is no fixed way to do a report.

System Maintenance Utilities

You should attempt to provide everything necessary to keep the application going forever. You do not want the user to call you to fix problems for items that could easily be incorporated into the program. Index files occasionally get corrupted. This may happen because the user ran out of disk space, the power went off during a critical operation, or any number of other reasons. You can use a system maintenance menu to provide various system utility options, such as indexing files and backing up and restoring data. Other menu items might show the number of records and size of each database in the application or provide month-end or year-end options that clear out unused records.

Here is a sample System Maintenance menu. Simply expand on the various menu items to incorporate this into your own application.

```
FUNCTION sys()
LOCAL l_choice,l_scr
SET MESSAGE TO 24 CENTER
l_scr := SAVESCREEN(2,64,6,72)
DO WHILE .T.
   @ 2,64,6,72 BOX c_boxstrng
   @ 3,65 PROMPT "REINDEX" ;
        MESSAGE "Reindex databases"
   @ 4,65 PROMPT "BACKUP" ;
        MESSAGE "Save databases to floppy"
   @ 5,65 PROMPT "RESTORE" ;
        MESSAGE "Restore databases from floppy"
   MENU TO l_choice
   DO CASE
      CASE l_choice == c_escape
         RESTSCREEN(2,64,6,72,l_scr)
         RETURN .T.
      CASE l_choice == 1
         SELECT Trans
         REINDEX
         SELECT Customer
         REINDEX
      CASE l_choice == 2
         !backup c: a:
      CASE l_choice == 3
```

```
        !restore  a:  c:
    ENDCASE
ENDDO
RETURN .T.
```

The only new items in this function are REINDEX and the ! command. The REINDEX command reindexes any currently open indexes. Since all the necessary indexes are opened at the beginning of the program, this command should work correctly. The ! command is also called the RUN command. It is used to directly run commands as if it were at the DOS prompt. The DOS commands BACKUP and RESTORE are used in this example. If you choose to run programs other than DOS commands, be aware that you are in a Clipper program that is taking up system memory. Any programs you choose to run will have only the remaining system memory available to them. If you have 600K before running the Clipper program and the Clipper program takes up 300K, you will have only 300K left for any program you wish to run using the ! or RUN command.

Key Points

User-defined Functions in Reports

User-defined functions may be used to provide information to your report while eliminating the need for elaborate schemes to get the data. User-defined functions reduce the amount of code in the actual report while making the process readily available for new reports in the application.

Lookup Tables

A lookup table is a database used to store the description of a code. The advantage of using lookup tables is that you can add and delete code and easily change the descriptions by simply editing the record in the lookup table.

continues . . .

Sorting Data

Index files are used to sort data in a report. A file may be indexed on a single field or many fields. The Clipper SORT command may also be used but should be avoided since it performs a physical sort of the database—which takes a lot of time as opposed to an index.

Filters

The SET FILTER TO command allows the programmer to set a filter in a database. The programmer can prompt the user with questions and then set the database filter based on the user's answers. The filter makes a database file appear as if it contains only the records that match a specified filter expression.

Accessing Databases in Other Work Areas

When accessing multiple databases, the database alias and the -> symbol may be used to access field information from another work area. This eliminates the need to continually switch work areas while your report is running.

Displaying Progress Information

It is a good idea to keep the user notified of the progress of a report. This may be done by calling a function which displays the progress information (such as the record number currently being processed) and restores the Clipper environment when it is completed.

CHAPTER

A Look at the Tool Box

This reference chapter is designed to get you up and running in Clipper programming. The focus is on the importance of the various commands and functions and how they work together. Use the Clipper 5 reference guide to get a more detailed description of each command or function. Some commands and functions have been excluded because they duplicate newly introduced commands and functions.

Chapters 4, 5, and 6 introduced many Clipper commands and functions in the context of a sample database application. This chapter groups those commands by their use. Use this chapter to gain an understanding of the various capabilities of Clipper and the various methods you can use to achieve results.

Making Decisions

Chapter 4 discusses the use of the IF/ENDIF and CASE/ENDCASE control structures. In that chapter, these structures are used to evaluate conditions and branch programs to sections of code depending on the outcome of the evaluation of the conditions.

Use the IF/ENDIF control structure if you need a section of code to execute only if a certain condition is met or to execute an alternate section of code if the condition is not met. The IF statement evaluates a single condition and then performs a section of code if the condition evaluates to TRUE. The ELSE statement provides an alternate sequence of instructions to be executed if the expression evaluates to FALSE. The basic format for the IF/ENDIF construct looks like this:

```
IF condition
   * process if condition is true
ELSE
   * process if condition is false
ENDIF
```

The immediate IF() function is a variation of the IF/ENDIF construct that allows the entire construct to be placed in a single statement, as shown here:

```
result = IF(condition,result1,result2)
```

The IF() function evaluates the condition passed as the first parameter. If the condition is evaluated to be TRUE, the second parameter (*result1*) is returned as the value of the function. If the condition is evaluated to be FALSE, the third parameter (*result2*) is returned as the value of the function. The IF function is useful when you need to return one of two values depending on a certain condition.

The CASE control structure allows the evaluation of many different conditions. The CASE statement is useful when you need to evaluate many possible conditions and branch control of your program to only one section of code depending on how the conditions are evaluated. The basic format for the CASE statement looks like this:

```
DO CASE
    CASE condition1
        DO stuff()
    CASE condition2
        DO stuff2()
    OTHERWISE
        DO default()
ENDCASE
```

Looping Structures

You use looping structures to process certain code over and over until a certain condition is reached. The DO WHILE loop is used in menus, when sequencing through databases, and in any other situation where you want to repeat code over and over until a certain condition is met.

Many times the condition evaluated as part of the DO WHILE expression is always TRUE. When this occurs, there should always be an escape mechanism. The menu program introduced in Chapter 4 uses the DO WHILE loop to present the menu over and over until the user presses ESC, as shown here:

```
DO WHILE .T.
    CLEAR                           // clear the screen
    @ 0,65 SAY DATE()               // display the current date
    @ 0,35 SAY "CUSTOMER TRACKING"  // display heading
    @ 1, 1 PROMPT "CUSTOMERS"
```

```
@ 1,30 PROMPT "REPORTING"        // initialize menu items
@ 1,61 PROMPT "MAINTENANCE"
MENU TO choice                   // get the user's choice
DO CASE
   CASE choice == 0
      RETURN                     // ESCAPE key pressed
   CASE choice == 1
      entry()                    // process first menu choice
   CASE choice == 2
      rpt()                      // process second menu choice
   CASE choice == 3
      maint()                    // process third menu choice
   ENDCASE
ENDDO
RETURN
```

Recall that the menu items are initialized by using the PROMPT statements, and the MENU TO statement presents the user with a scrolling bar-type menu. The user's choice is returned in the variable called *choice* by the MENU TO statement. The DO CASE construct checks for the ESC key and executes the RETURN statement if ESC was pressed. The MENU TO statement returns a value of zero if the user has pressed ESC. Any other choices result in a call to the appropriate function. Once the function has been executed, the menu program picks up where it left off and presents the menu to the user again.

The DO WHILE loop is useful when you are processing records in a database. The program positions the record pointer to the desired record in a database and then processes until either the end-of-file marker is reached or some other condition is met. Sometimes you will want to process an entire database from the first record to the last. In that case, you would use a DO WHILE loop and check for the end of the file, as this example from Chapter 4 demonstrates.

```
USE Testdb
DO WHILE .NOT. EOF()
 *  process the record
  SKIP
ENDDO
```

The database is opened and a DO WHILE loop continues until the end-of-file marker is reached. The SKIP statement moves the record pointer through the records in the database. When the end-of-file marker is reached, the DO WHILE condition has been met and the loop terminates. Other conditions, in addition to checking for the end-of-file marker, can also be tacked onto the DO WHILE condition. When processing secondary records, the DO WHILE loop processes until either the end-of-file marker is reached or there are no more matches to the primary record, as shown in this example from Chapter 5:

```
USE Customer NEW
USE Trans NEW
SET INDEX TO Transid
SEEK Customer->Id
IF FOUND()
   DO WHILE .NOT. EOF() .and. Trans->Id == Customer->Id
     * process transaction record
     SKIP
   ENDDO
ELSE
   * there are not any transactions
ENDIF
```

The primary database and secondary database and its associated index file are opened. The Id field is used to tie the two databases together, and the SEEK command is used to find the first match. The DO WHILE loop processes each record of the secondary database until the end-of-file marker is reached or until the value of the Id field changes, which indicates there are no more matches.

You also use the DO WHILE loop to process a section of code until some condition is met, as shown here:

```
LOCAL x := 0            // initialize variable called x
DO WHILE x < 10
   * do something
   x++                  // add 1 to the x variable
ENDDO
```

The DO WHILE in this example continues for as long as the condition (x < 10) is evaluated to be TRUE. The condition used can be anything imaginable. However, the condition must be TRUE at some point or some other escape mechanism must be present within the DO WHILE loop, or the program will run forever.

The FOR/NEXT construct is used to process a section of code a specific number of times. A variable is initialized with a lower boundary value, and the loop continues until some upper boundary is reached, as illustrated here:

```
FOR x := 1 TO 100
    ? "Hello"
NEXT
```

The x control variable is used as a counter and is initialized with a lower boundary value (1) the first time the FOR statement is executed. The number following the TO statement (100) determines the upper boundary. The value of x is incremented by 1 each time through the FOR/NEXT loop, and this continues until the upper boundary is reached.

The STEP clause sets the value of the increment or decrement. The default is to add 1 to the control variable if the STEP clause is not included as part of the statement. The program could cause the control variable to increase or decrease by any amount each time through the loop, as this example shows.

```
FOR x := 100 TO 1 STEP -1
    ? "Hello"
NEXT
```

In this example, the initial value of the control variable is set to 100 and the upper boundary is set to 1. The STEP clause causes the x variable to be decremented each time through the loop. The loop terminates when the upper boundary (1) is reached.

The FOR/NEXT loop is useful when transversing the elements of an array, as in this example:

```
m_len = LEN(m_array)        // get length of array
FOR i = 1 to m_len
    ? m_array[i]            // display array element
NEXT
```

This transverses the array called *m_array* and displays the value of each element. The control variable called *i* is initialized to 1 and the upper boundary is set to the length of the array, using the Clipper LEN()

function. The control variable is used in brackets to access the various elements in the array.

There are two Clipper functions that provide a hidden looping mechanism. The Clipper AEVAL() function sequences through each element of an array and performs a block of code on that array element. The Clipper DBEVAL() sequences through each record in a database and performs a block of code on each record. The AEVAL() and DBEVAL() functions are covered in greater detail in the section "Storing Functions to Array Elements" later in this chapter.

The main rule when creating loops is to always include a way of getting out of the loop. This way out may be a condition to be met (such as reaching the end of the file). Another way out may be an EXIT or RETURN statement to be executed within the loop when a particular event occurs. Sometimes the way out is achieved by calling another program that contains a QUIT statement. This method of exiting is quite common when certain housekeeping chores (such as closing databases and updating configuration files) must take place before the program is finished. You can provide a function that would perform housekeeping chores and terminate the application in the event a critical error occurs. An example of a critical error would be a missing database file.

Relational Operators

You use relational operators to compare various data types. Some of these operators were presented in the program examples in Chapters 4, 5, and 6. You should be aware of all the relational operators available in order to take full advantage of the Clipper language. They are listed here:

Operator	Purpose
<	Less than
>	Greater than
=	Equal to
<>,#,or !=	Not equal to
<=	Less than or equal to
>=	Greater than or equal to

Operator	Purpose
==	Exactly equal to
$	Is contained within the string

As an example, the less-than relational operator (<) could be used on date type variables, as shown here:

```
var1 := CTOD("11/27/89")
IF var1 < DATE() + 365
   * perform statements
ENDIF
```

You can use relational operators on all data types to control the flow of logic within a program by checking one value against another or to determine if a search string is located in another string.

Reviewing the Data Types and How to Use Them

Clipper supports several data types. With the exception of the array type, they reflect the types supported by .DBF files. These are character string, numeric, logic, date, and memo. All the various data types are actually stored as character types in the database, but they are converted to the appropriate type while the program is running.

Character String Operations

Recall from Chapter 4 that you use character variables to store strings of characters such as a person's name, address, and city. Character variables can accommodate very large strings or may only be a single character. You might use character strings to display text on the screen or to allow data input from the user. Clipper provides the ability to manipulate strings in a wide variety of ways. The following section describes those methods.

Combining Strings

Concatenation is the process of combining two or more strings to create a new string, as shown here:

```
var := "Joe "+"Blow"
```

The + string operator combines the two character strings on the right side of the equation and creates a single character string called *var*. Character variables can be combined in the same way, as shown here:

```
l_name := "Joe "
var := l_name + "Blow"
```

The contents of the variable *l_name* and "Blow" are combined and stored in the variable called *var*.

Searching for Patterns

Clipper provides several functions that allow a pattern of characters to be located within a character string. The Clipper AT() function returns the starting position of a pattern of characters within a character string. The first parameter is the search pattern, and the second parameter is the character string to be searched, as shown here:

```
var := AT("c","abcde")
```

The first parameter (c) is searched for within the second parameter (abcde) and returns a value of 3 because it is the third character in the list. If the pattern is not found, a value of zero is returned as the value of the function.

The RAT() function performs the same process but returns the relative position from the end of the string instead of the start of the string.

The $ operator is similar to the AT() function, but it returns a logical value rather than the relative position within the string, as shown in this example:

```
var := "abc" $ "defabcghi"  // var will be .T.
```

The string "abc" is searched for within the string "defabcghi" and returns a logical value to the *var* variable. A TRUE value will be stored in the *var* variable since the pattern was found within the character string.

Extracting Portions of Strings

Use the SUBSTR() function to extract specific subsets of strings, as shown here:

```
var := SUBSTR("defghi",1,3) // var will equal "def"
```

The first parameter (defghi) is the string you want to extract a subset of. The second parameter (1) is the starting position within the string. The third parameter (3) is the number of characters you want to extract. The result of the function is returned as the value of the function and stored in the *var* variable.

The LEFT() and RIGHT() functions are similar to the SUBSTR() function, but they extract a specified number of characters from either the right or left of a string. The RIGHT() function extracts a specified number of characters from the right of a string. The LEFT() function extracts a specified number of characters from the left of a string.

Comparing Strings

You can use the various relational operators to compare strings, but be careful in choosing the equality operator. The = is used to determine if two strings are alike—meaning that they must have the same characters. You must use the == operator to determine if two strings are *exactly* equal—meaning that all the characters must be the same *and* the strings must be the same length. The order of the expressions can be important, as shown here:

```
var1 := "abcdef" = "abc"      // var1 = .T.
var2 := "abc" = "abcdef"      // var2 = .F.
```

The first statement results in a TRUE value being stored in the variable *var1* since the value on the right determines the number of characters that are compared to determine if the expressions are equal. If the expressions are switched, as in the second example, a FALSE value results. You should always use the == operator if you need to know whether there is an exact match, as shown here:

```
var1 := "abcdef" == "abc"      // var1 = .F.
```

The value is FALSE since the entire strings must match up, character for character, in order for the statement to be TRUE.

The ISALPHA() function detects whether or not the leftmost character in a string is alphabetic. A logical value is returned by the function, as demonstrated here:

```
ISALPHA("ABC")      // returns .T.
ISALPHA("2ABC")     // returns .F.
```

The first example would return a TRUE value since "A" is alphabetic. The second example would return a FALSE value since "2" is numeric.

The ISDIGIT() function detects if the leftmost character in a string is a digit. A digit is a character from zero to 9. A logical value is returned by the function, as demonstrated here:

```
ISDIGIT("ABC")      // returns .F.
ISDIGIT("2ABC")     // returns .T.
ISDIGIT(".123")     // returns .F.
```

The first example returns a FALSE value since "A" is not a digit. The second example returns a TRUE value since "2" is a digit. The third value returns a FALSE value since "." is not a digit.

The ISLOWER() function checks the first character of a character string and returns a logical value of TRUE if the character is lowercase and FALSE if the character is uppercase. The ISUPPER() function checks the first character of a character string and returns a logical value of FALSE if the character is lowercase and TRUE if the character is uppercase.

Character String Conversions

There are many conversion functions that act on strings. These may involve converting the character string from lower- to uppercase, converting it from upper- to lowercase, or actually changing the variable type of the string.

You can use the STRTRAN() function to search and replace characters within a character string or a memo field. The following example demonstrates the use of the STRTRAN() function:

```
var := "ABCABC"
var := STRTRAN(var,"AB","XY")
```

The first line of this example initializes the value of the *var* variable to ABCABC. The variable is passed as the first parameter of the STRTRAN() function. The second parameter is the string you are searching for. The third parameter is the string you want to replace the search string with. The variable *var* would contain a value of XYCXYC upon completion of the STRTRAN() conversion.

The STUFF() function can serve many purposes when you adjust its parameters to suit your needs. The first parameter is the character string you want to manipulate. The second parameter is the position number within the string where you want to make changes. The third parameter is the number of characters that are to be affected by the change. The fourth parameter is the new string to be inserted into the string. To use the STUFF() function to insert characters in a string, pass a zero as the third parameter, as shown here:

```
var := STUFF("ABCDEF",4,0,"abc")
```

This inserts the characters abc starting at the fourth position within the string. The variable *var* is assigned a new value of ABCabcDEF.

You can use the STUFF() function to replace characters. The same number of characters should be specified in the third parameter as are going to be inserted. The following example demonstrates the STUFF() function's replace ability:

```
var := STUFF("ABCDEF",4,3,"abc")
```

This removes the three characters starting at the fourth position and inserts the new characters in their place, resulting in a new value of ABCabc.

You can use the STUFF() function to delete characters in a string simply by passing a blank string to insert, as the following example illustrates:

```
var := STUFF("ABCDEF",4,3,"")
```

This removes the string of three characters starting at the fourth position and inserts nothing in its place. The resulting value stored in the *var* variable is ABC.

The PADC(), PADL(), and PADR() functions discussed in Chapter 6 allow easy padding of spaces to the beginning or end of a string to make it a specified length. The PADC() function accepts a string and the string length as parameters and centers text in the returned string. The PADL() function pads blank characters to the beginning of a string to make it the desired string length. The PADR() function pads blank characters to the end of a string to make it the desired string length.

Use the SPACE() function to return a string of spaces with a specified length. This function is very useful when you are initializing variables and printing blank space on a report.

The REPLICATE() function is similar to the SPACE() function, but it allows you to specify the character to be used in addition to the number of characters to be returned, as in the following example:

```
var := REPLICATE("A",10)
```

This example stores the character string "AAAAAAAAAA" to the variable called *var*.

You use the RTRIM(), LTRIM(), and ALLTRIM() functions discussed in Chapter 6 to trim leading and trailing spaces from a string.

Use the LOWER() function to convert a character string from upper- to lowercase, as this example shows.

```
var := LOWER("ABC")     // var will be assigned "abc"
```

The UPPER() function converts a string from lower- to uppercase, as shown here:

```
var := UPPER("abc")     // var will be assigned "ABC"
```

The CTOD() function converts a character string to a date type, as shown here:

```
var := CTOD("12/12/99")    // var will be a date type
```

The character string must consist of numbers representing the month, day, and year, separated by some character other than a number. The CTOD() function is useful when you want to initialize a date variable, specify a date to be used in date arithmetic, specify a literal to be used in date comparisons, or replace date fields with a literal date string. A null value will result from using the CTOD() function on an invalid date.

You can also convert a character string to a numeric value by using the VAL() function. VAL() evaluates a character expression until a second decimal point is reached or a nonnumeric character is reached. Here are some examples of the VAL() function in use:

```
var := VAL("123.45")       // result of var is 123.45
var := VAL("A")            // result of var is 0.00
var := VAL("123.45.55")    // result of var is 123.45
```

The first example converts the character value passed as a parameter to its corresponding numeric value and stores the result in the *var* variable. The second returns a value of zero since the evaluation stops at the first nonnumeric character. The third expression stops at the second decimal point and returns a value of 123.45.

There is no Clipper function that will convert a character type to a logical type. There may be many times when you want the user to enter a Y or N value to a question and convert the answer to a logical value to be used throughout the program. It is necessary to use comparison and use the result as the assignment:

```
var2 := IF(var1=="Y",.T.,.F.)
```

Here, the immediate IF() function converts the value of *var1* to a logical value. If the first parameter is TRUE, the second parameter (.T.) is returned as the value of the function. If the value of the first parameter is FALSE, the third parameter (.F.) is returned as the value of the function.

The ASC() function returns the ASCII value of the leftmost character in a character string. Each character is assigned a numeric value. For example, an uppercase "A" is assigned a numeric value of 65, while a lowercase "a" is assigned a numeric value of 97. Use the ASC() function when you want to perform numeric calculations on the ASCII values of characters.

You use the SOUNDEX() function to index and search for sound-alike phonetic matches. This function is useful when there is a good chance the user will misspell names. The SOUNDEX() function will bring sound-alike names such as "Smith" and "Smyth" together so that they have the same key value.

Combining String Operations

You can combine the various string operations to perform many useful tasks. The following example replaces every first name field in a database with the first character uppercase and the rest lowercase:

```
REPLACE ALL Fname WITH UPPER(SUBSTR(Fname,1,1))+;
                 LOWER(SUBSTR(Fname,2,19))
```

Note that a combination of the UPPER(), LOWER(), and SUBSTR() functions is used along with the + string operator in this example. The UPPER() function converts the first character to uppercase. The first character was extracted using the SUBSTR() function. The remaining characters are extracted using the SUBSTR() function and are converted to lowercase using the LOWER() function.

Numeric Operations

Recall from Chapter 4 that numeric variables are used to store numbers. Use numeric variables to store a piece of data if you expect to perform mathematical calculations on that data.

Numeric Conversions

You should have at least a working knowledge of integers versus real numbers. The function INT() converts a real number into an integer. An *integer* is a number without a decimal point. When you use the INT()

function, you are losing the noninteger part of a number, as in the following example:

```
var := INT(12.5)            // 12 will be stored to var
```

The INT() function truncates the decimal places and leaves the whole number. You should make sure you want to lose the decimal portion of a number before you use the INT() function.

The ROUND() function returns a value rounded to a specified number of decimal places. The first parameter of the function is the number to be rounded. The second parameter is the number of decimal places the returned value is to contain. The following examples demonstrate the ROUND() function:

```
var := ROUND(12.567,2)     //  12.57 will be stored in var
var := ROUND(12.564,2)     //  12.56 will be stored in var
```

The number will be rounded up or down depending on the values to the right of the decimal position indicated in the second parameter.

The PICTURE clause discussed in Chapter 5 is very useful for displaying numeric data. Using the PICTURE clause to format data may cause problems if the PICTURE template does not match up with the actual number you are attempting to display. The following example demonstrates this problem:

```
var := "12345.678"
@ 10,10 SAY var PICTURE "999,999"
```

This example displays "12,346" on the screen. You lose the decimal portion of the number because your PICTURE template did not handle the complete number. You must make sure the PICTURE template will handle the entire number to be displayed.

You can use the STR() function discussed in Chapter 4 to convert numeric values to string values. Recall that the STR() function accepts the number to be converted as the first parameter and the length of the string as the second parameter. The optional third parameter accepts the number of decimal positions desired in the returned string.

You can also use the TRANSFORM() function to convert numbers to strings. It works in much the same way as the PICTURE clause in @ SAY and @ GET commands. TRANSFORM() functions or TRANSFORM() templates can be passed as parameters to format character, date, logical, or numeric values. TRANSFORM functions, as shown in the following table, work the same way as PICTURE functions, discussed in Chapter 5:

Function	Action
B	Displays numbers left justified
D	Displays date in SET DATE format
E	Displays date in British format
Z	Displays zeros as blanks
!	Converts alphabetic characters to uppercase

Use the @ character to indicate that a TRANSFORM() function is to follow, as shown here:

```
? TRANSFORM("abc","@!")
```

The value to be transformed (abc) is passed as the first parameter. The TRANSFORM() function (@!) or template is passed as the second parameter. In the preceding example, "ABC" is displayed on the screen since the @! converts the value passed to uppercase.

TRANSFORM() templates, illustrated in the following table, work in much the same way as the PICTURE templates discussed in Chapter 5 since they operate on a character-by-character basis rather than on an entire string.

Template	Action
A,N,X,9,#	Displays digits for any data type
L	Displays logical values as "T" or "F"
Y	Displays logical values as "Y" or "N"
!	Converts value to uppercase
$	Displays dollar sign in place of leading space in a numeric value
.	Specifies a decimal position

A TRANSFORM() template is especially useful in formatting numeric data, as shown here:

```
? TRANSFORM(71628,"$99,999")
```

This example formats the numeric value passed as the first parameter (71628) into the string "$71,628". Include the decimal template to display the appropriate decimal positions desired, as shown here:

```
? TRANSFORM(71628.45,"$99,999.99")
```

This results in the string "$71,628.45".

There are many functions available in Clipper that perform useful arithmetic operations. The SQRT() function returns the square root of a positive number. A zero is returned for a negative number.

Numeric Comparisons

The MIN() and MAX() functions determine either the larger or smaller of two numbers. Both functions accept two numbers as parameters and return one of the values. The MIN() function returns the value of the smaller of the two numbers. The MAX() function returns the value of the larger of the two numbers.

Numeric Formatting

The SET DECIMALS command determines the number of decimal places to be displayed in the results of numeric functions or calculations, as shown here:

```
var := 2/4
SET DECIMALS TO 2
? var                // 0.50 will be displayed
SET DECIMALS TO 4
? var                // 0.5000 will be displayed
```

The SET FIXED ON/OFF command determines whether or not the SET DECIMALS assignment is in effect. Keep in mind that the internal representation of the number does not actually change. This only affects the way in which the number is displayed.

Problem Areas

You can run into problems with numeric variable types as a result of not allowing enough room in database fields to store the amounts. An example would be if you attempted to store a value of 999 to a database field that was defined as a two-digit long numeric field. A run-time error would result, and ** would be placed into the field prior to termination of the program, indicating an overflow value.

When converting numbers, make sure the PICTURE template in the TRANSFORM() function or the length parameter in the STR() function is large enough to handle the number. Be aware that when you use the ROUND() or INT() function, there is the possibility of losing part of the number in the process.

Logic Operations

Recall from Chapter 4 that logical variables can be either TRUE or FALSE. You can use logical variables to control the logic within a program or to keep track of certain conditions within the program. Clipper assumes that the logic type can only be TRUE or FALSE, represented by .T. and .F.

You can use the "Y" PICTURE function to display a logical value as either a "Y" or an "N," as shown here:

```
@ 10,10 SAY var PICTURE "Y"
```

Logic variables are often used in databases as flags. If there is a logic field called Paid, the database can be processed like this:

```
TOTAL ON Amount TO var FOR Paid
? "Total amount paid = ",var
```

A logic variable can be created as the result of an expression:

```
goodguy := "JOE" $ "JOE:JANE:TOM:MARGE:BOSS"
IF .NOT. goodguy
   QUIT
ENDIF
```

In this example, the $ relational operator is used to locate the string "JOE" in the list of names. A logical variable is returned by the expression, depending on the results of the search.

Date Operations

Recall from Chapter 4 that date variables are used to store dates such as a person's birthdate or a transaction date. Date fields are very useful for putting information into chronological order, stamping date of entry, triggering past-due conditions, and, assuming the computer's system clock is working correctly, triggering processing events such as end-of-month processing.

Date Conversions

You use the DTOC() function to convert a date type to a character type. The CTOD() function converts a character type into a date type. Both the DTOC() and CTOD() functions use the form *mm/dd/yy* in their conversions. The DTOS() (date to string) function returns a slightly different format, as shown here:

```
var := DTOS("11/27/89")
```

This example would return 19891127 to the *var* variable. The form *yyyymmdd* is used to format the returned string. Use the DTOS() function when creating index expressions since the string is independent of the various Clipper settings such as SET DATE and SET CENTURY.

Extracting Date Information

Recall from Chapter 4 that the DATE() function obtains the current date from the system clock of your computer. Keep in mind that this date is only as accurate as the date on your system clock. If the battery goes out, the DATE() function will not return a correct value. Most programs should display the current system date returned from the DATE() function to allow the user to verify that it is correct and modify it if necessary.

You can use the DAY(), MONTH(), and YEAR() functions to pull the numeric value of the day, month, or year from a date type variable or field. A date is passed as the parameter to all three functions and an integer is returned as the value of the function.

The DOW() function returns a number indicating the day of the week. A date type value is passed as the parameter to the function. The number zero is returned if the date value is empty. Numbers 1 through 7 are returned depending on the day of the week, with 1 corresponding to Sunday and 7 corresponding to Saturday.

The CDOW() function converts a date value into a string representing the day of the week, such as "Sunday" or "Monday". The first letter is uppercase and the remaining letters are lowercase.

The CMONTH() function converts a date value to a string representing the month of the year, such as "January" or "December".

The combined use of the various date functions enables you to format dates for display in reports and screens, as in the following example:

```
l_date := CTOD("03/27/88")
? CMONTH(l_date) + " " + ALLTRIM(STR(DAY(l_date)))
```

This would result in the following output on the screen:

```
March 27
```

Date Arithmetic

Clipper date values can be manipulated as if they were numbers, as in this example:

```
var := DATE()+30    // var = 30 days from today
```

The number 30 is added to the current system date. This would result in a date value of 30 days past the current date getting stored in the *var* variable. Days can also be subtracted, as this example demonstrates.

```
var := DATE()-365 // var = a year ago
```

This would subtract 365 days from the current system date and store that value into the *var* variable.

Date Formatting

The SET CENTURY ON/OFF command toggles the entry and display of dates to force display and input of the century. When SET CENTURY ON has been issued, the user will be required to enter the entire year (including the century). Any date that is displayed would include the century, as this example shows.

```
l_date := CTOD("03/27/88")
SET CENTURY OFF
? l_date                    // will display 03/27/88
SET CENTURY ON
? l_date                    // will display 03/27/1988
```

It is not necessary to use SET CENTURY ON in most cases since Clipper will assume the century correctly based on the SET EPOCH command. The SET EPOCH command establishes a date marker from which all two-digit year dates are to be calculated. The default date marker is the year 1900. If your application requires dates in the year 2000 and beyond, you adjust the date marker accordingly. The following example demonstrates the use of the SET EPOCH command:

```
SET EPOCH TO 1960
? CTOD("11/27/58")      // equals 11/27/1958
? CTOD("12/11/61")      // equals 12/11/1961
```

The date marker is set to the year 1960. Any year that is 60 or greater will be considered to be in the 20th century. Anything less will be considered to be in the 21st century. This is an important concept if your application performs calculations based on various dates in the system.

You use the SET DATE command to format date output. The default format is in the format *mm/dd/yy*. Here are the possible formats:

AMERICAN	mm/dd/yy
ANSI	yy.mm.dd
BRITISH	dd/mm/yy

FRENCH   dd/mm/yy

GERMAN   dd.mm.yy

ITALIAN   dd-mm-yy

JAPAN   yy/mm/dd

USA   mm-dd-yy

You can change the format in this way:

```
SET DATE TO FRENCH
```

This changes the format of the date to *dd/mm/yy*. You can also specify the format method by using the SET DATE FORMAT command, as shown here:

```
SET DATE FORMAT TO "yyyy-mm-dd"
```

which causes the entire year to be displayed followed by the month and day.

Memo Functions and Commands

As discussed in Chapter 4, Clipper handles memo fields differently than other fields. Normally, all of the data is stored in a file with a .DBF extension. When you add a memo field to a database, a separate file with a .DBT extension is created. Any time you edit a memo field, the data is stored in the .DBT file and a connection is established between the .DBT and .DBF files. Although the memo field is represented as a ten-character field in the structure of the .DBF file, it is in fact merely holding the address of memos assigned to that record and held in the .DBT file. This allows the .DBT file to hold a variable-length string associated with that record.

The additional file required to use memo fields can tangle things up if you decide to copy the lead database to another location and forget to take the .DBT file as well. In a large database, the size of the .DBT file can grow enormously. The reason for this is that if the user puts one character into a memo field, a large block of characters is reserved, and when that block is used and you go over the edge of the block by one character, another large block is reserved. Thus, most .DBT files are usually three-quarters empty. Before creating a memo field in your database, you should consider how much data is going into it. It may suffice to create an 80-character comment field instead. An alternative solution, if you are unsure of how much data the users will enter, is to create an 80-character comment field and a memo field. If the data goes longer than 80 characters, you can empty the comment field and leave a one-character marker indicating the data has been moved to the memo field. In 90 percent of the cases, the 80-character field will suffice and the .DBT file will grow gradually instead of in leaps and bounds.

Since a memo is treated somewhat differently, it requires support functions to operate properly. Clipper provides a mini word processor called MEMOEDIT() to edit memo fields. If you had a database with a memo field called Notes, the Notes field could be edited in the following manner:

```
REPLACE Notes WITH MEMOEDIT(Notes,2,2,20,77)
```

The Notes field is passed as the first parameter of the MEMOEDIT() function. The remaining parameters are the screen coordinates where you want the editing to be performed. The MEMOEDIT() function returns the new string as its value.

The user can use the cursor keys to move around the memo field and various other keys to perform other operations. The following table lists some of the other operations available to the user:

Key	Purpose
UP ARROW	Moves up one line
DOWN ARROW	Moves down one line
LEFT ARROW	Moves one character to the left
RIGHT ARROW	Moves one character to the right
HOME	Moves to the beginning of a line
END	Moves to the end of a line
CTRL-Y	Deletes the current line
CTRL-W	Saves the memo and exits
ESC	Aborts the edit and exits

When word wrap is used, the MEMOEDIT() function places a soft carriage return/line feed at the end of each line within the edit window. It is necessary to convert the memo by using the HARDCR() function before printing, as this example shows.

```
? HARDCR(Notes)
```

This converts all of the soft carriage returns to hard carriage returns to allow the memo field to be displayed.

It is possible to read and write text files resident on the disk by using MEMOREAD(), MEMOEDIT(), and MEMOWRIT():

```
var := MEMOREAD("Sample.txt")
var := MEMOEDIT(var)
IF .NOT. MEMOWRIT("Sample.txt",var)
   ? "Problem writing out Sample.txt"
ENDIF
```

The first line of this example reads in a text file called SAMPLE.TXT into a variable called *var* by using the MEMOREAD() function. The second line calls on the MEMOEDIT() function to allow the user to edit the document. The third line writes the *var* variable back to the SAMPLE.TXT text file by using the MEMOWRIT() function.

Memo fields should be used whenever you need to store very large character strings such as letters. You can use all the various string functions and operators on memo fields. In addition, Clipper provides other functions specifically for memos. The MEMOLINE() function, for example, will present a line of text within the memo. In conjunction with MLCOUNT(), you can use it to print out a memo in a controlled fashion. Here they are in action:

```
Use Customer
* edit notes and post changes to database
REPLACE Notes WITH MEMOEDIT(Notes,5,5,20,75)
SET PRINT ON
? "Here is the contents of notes"
? HARDCR(Notes)
? "Here it is again"

maxlines := MLCOUNT(Notes)
```

```
FOR linecount :=1 to maxlines
    ? MEMOLINE(Notes,,linecount)
NEXT
?
? "Now to print only the second line"
? MLPOS(Notes,,2)
?
? "Now to print the autoexec.bat file"
? MEMOREAD("C:\Autoexec.bat")
?
? "Now to change the autoexec.bat file"
string := MEMOREAD("C:\Autoexec.bat")
string :=  string+CHR(13)+"dir"+CHR(13)
? string
?
MEMOWRIT("C:\Autoexec.bat",string)
? "now to present autoexec.bat without carriage returns"
? MEMOTRAN(string," ")
SET PRINT OFF
```

Array Operations

Recall from Chapter 4 that an array is a collection of variables with the same name. In the C language, a Clipper array would be described as a structure since arrays in C must be of the same type. In Clipper, each element within an array can be any of the possible variable types. The first element of an array could be another array, the second element could be a date, and the third element could be numeric, or they can be any combination required.

This tremendous flexibility allows you to build structures with a considerable degree of sophistication. These structures can then become the key elements in the internal organization of a program. It is possible to store a function's name as an array element and still be able to activate it. Arrays provide the ability to store both data and functions. This is very close to object-oriented programming (OOP). It is possible to build objects by using Clipper's array system.

Inside and outside of Nantucket, several resourceful programmers have been using these array-handling functions to produce object-oriented shells. Object-oriented programming is mentioned at this point to emphasize the importance of learning array handling well. Arrays in Clipper are very useful for many types of problem solving. Learning to use arrays in the form of sophisticated data structures will give you a tremendous boost in your programming endeavors. Time spent on array manipulation is time well spent.

Creating Arrays

There are several ways to create arrays. You can create an array as part of the DECLARE statement, as shown here:

```
DECLARE var[10]
```

This creates an array containing ten elements. You can also create an array as part of a variable declaration statement, as the following examples demonstrate.

```
PUBLIC var[10]
PRIVATE var[10]
LOCAL var[10]
STATIC var[10]
```

Each of these declarations creates an array containing ten elements. You can also use the ARRAY() function to create arrays, as the following example shows.

```
LOCAL var := ARRAY(10,20)
```

Another method for creating arrays is simply to assign literal values, as in the following example:

```
var := {1, 2, 3}
```

This creates a one-dimensional array that contains three elements. Note that the { and } characters are used to enclose the values to be assigned to the array. You can create multidimensional arrays in the same way by placing a series of values in braces, as shown here:

```
var := {1, 2, 3}, {4, 5, 6}, {"hello", .T., 0}
```

This example creates a 3x3 dimensional array that contains the values indicated within the brackets.

The ACLONE() function makes a copy of an existing array. The new array will contain the same number of elements as the source array.

The ACOPY() function copies the contents of one array into another. Both arrays must exist prior to calling on the ACOPY() function. You should use the ACLONE() function to create a new target array and copy the contents at the same time.

Storing Information to Arrays

You can assign data to a one-dimensional array element by enclosing the element number in brackets, as shown here:

```
var[3] := "Jack"
```

This assigns the third element of the array to a character string containing "Jack".

You can assign data to a multidimensional array element by enclosing the element numbers of the row and column in brackets, as shown here:

```
var[1][1] := "Jack"
var[1][5] := "Mary"
var[5][5] :=  144
```

This example is taken from Chapter 4, in which the two-dimensional array called *var* was created containing five rows and five columns. The two-dimensional array contains 25 slots to store data. The row is accessed by the first number in brackets and the column is accessed by the second number in brackets.

The AFILL() function fills an array with a specified value, as in AFILL(myarray,"hello"), which fills every element with the character string "hello". Normally, you will want to initialize an array with some value prior to processing, as in the following example:

```
var := ARRAY(10)
AFILL(var,0)
```

This example creates an array called *var* that has ten elements. The AFILL() function initializes all ten elements to a value of zero. You can fill arrays partially by passing the starting position and the number of elements to fill, as in AFILL(myarray,"hello",5,3), which fills the next three elements, starting from the fifth element.

Changing the Size of an Array

An array's dimensions can change dynamically. This means that an array may start off as a single-dimension array and end up as a multidimensional array if you assign an array as one of the elements of the initial array. You can delete array elements by using the ADEL() function. You can insert new elements by using the AADD() and AINS() functions.

Sorting an Array

The ASORT() function sorts the items in an array in ascending order. All the elements in the array must be of the same data type. The starting position and the number of elements to sort can be passed as optional parameters.

Searching for Patterns Within Arrays

You can use the ASCAN() function to scan an array for a specific search value. The function returns the number of the first array element in which the search value was found. You can optionally pass the desired starting element and the number of elements to search. You can search an entire array by adjusting the starting element after each match is found.

Storing Functions to Array Elements

The interesting thing about arrays is that they can store functions as well as variables. Thus, it is possible to get close to object-oriented programming, where an object has both the data and the code necessary to perform a specific action.

You can store macros to array elements and evaluate them by using the & macro operator discussed in Chapter 1. The following example demonstrates the use of the macro:

```
var = "DATE()"
? var          // will print the word DATE()
? &var         // will print todays date
```

The first line stores the Clipper DATE() function to a variable called *var*. The second statement simply displays the contents of the string. The third statement uses the macro operator to evaluate the contents of the *var* variable. The result is that the current date is displayed.

You can store an expression in an array element in the same manner and evaluate it by using the macro operator, as shown here:

```
var := ARRAY(3)
var[1] := "DATE()"
? &var[1]
```

The first line creates an array called *var* that contains three elements. The second line stores the DATE() function to the first element of the array. The third line evaluates the contents of the array element, using the macro operator.

The other way of running a function within an array is with code blocks. Some argue that a code block is another type of variable. It is similar to a macro except that you can pass parameters to it. It must also be evaluated by one of three functions, called AEVAL(), DBEVAL(), and EVAL(). The following example assigns a code block to a variable:

```
var := {|data|UPPER(data)}
? EVAL(var,"abc")   // will print "ABC"
```

The entire code block is enclosed in the brace characters {}, and the | | characters enclose any parameters. In the preceding example, the variable called *data* is the parameter of the code block. The action taken by the code block is defined after the second | character. The code block is passed as the first parameter of the EVAL() function. The second parameter is the parameter to be passed to the code block. In this example, "abc" matches up to the parameter called *data*, and the UPPER() function converts the data to uppercase. Code blocks are explained in more detail in Chapter 10.

The DATE() function used as part of the macro operator example can also be assigned to a code block in the following way:

```
var := {||DATE()}
? EVAL(var)  // will print todays date
```

This performs the same function as storing the DATE() function to the variable and using the macro operator to evaluate its contents. Code blocks are more efficient than macros. This is because the program has no idea what is inside a character string before it runs. The statement has to be parsed at run time, prior to executing the commands contained in the macro expression. The compiler is told of the contents of a code block prior to execution of the program.

The AEVAL() and DBEVAL() functions are similar to the EVAL() function except that they operate on groups of items rather than on a single item. The AEVAL() function evaluates a code block for each element of an array. The DBEVAL() function evaluates each record in a database that matches a scope and condition passed as parameters to the function.

Checking Contents of Variables

The EMPTY() function checks all type of variables for the "no value" condition. A string is considered empty if it is all spaces or "". A numeric value is considered empty if it has a value of zero. A date is considered empty if a date value has not been entered. When a date is first initialized by using CTOD(" / / "),it is considered to be empty.

The TYPE() function tests the data type of a variable. The TYPE() function can only be used on public and private variables and uses macro evaluation to arrive at a result. The VALTYPE() function is more flexible since it will evaluate the type of local and static variables as well as user-defined functions.

Here are the different types:

A	Array
B	Block
C	Character
D	Date
L	Logical
M	Memo
N	Numeric
O	Object
U	NIL and local or static using TYPE()
UE	Error syntactical
UI	Error indeterminate

You can use VALTYPE() to check if a function or procedure actually exists, as this example shows.

```
IF VALTYPE(myfunc) == NIL
   ? "the myfunc function does not exist"
ENDIF
```

TYPE() and VALTYPE() can be very useful in creating generic functions. Suppose you want to write a function that calculates the age of a person. You could set up the function so that either a date or character type could be passed to the function. The function would determine the variable type and make the conversion to a date type if necessary.

Database Functions and Commands

Clipper provides a wealth of commands and functions used for database manipulation. These are crucial elements to a programmer's knowledge since being able to store information and retrieve it at a later time are important aspects of a database management system.

Opening, Closing, and Selecting Databases

The functions and commands described in this section are used to open and close databases and to acquire information about the various work areas. As discussed in Chapter 4, each database requires an area in which to operate, called a work area. More than one database can be open at a single time, but each must be in its own work area.

Recall from Chapter 4 that the USE command opens a database. You can open various databases at the same time by opening each in a different work area. You can move the databases between the different work areas by using the SELECT statement or the SELECT() function. The desired work area or the alias of the file opened in that work area is included as part of the SELECT statement, as the following example illustrates.

```
SELECT 1
USE Customer
SELECT 2
USE Trans
SELECT Customer
```

The first line of this example uses the SELECT statement to go to work area 1. The Customer database is then opened. The third line uses the SELECT statement to switch to work area 2, where the Trans database is then opened. Clipper uses the filename of a database as its alias. You can also use the alias to select a work area instead of the actual work area number. The last line of the example demonstrates selecting a work area by using the alias. You can use the statement

```
SELECT 0
```

to find the first unused work area. You can use the SELECT() function for the same purpose, but it also returns the number of the current work area prior to changing to the new work area. This is useful when you want your function to remember what the current work area was when the function started. This enables that same work area to be restored prior to the end of the function, as shown here:

```
l_holdsel := SELECT(0)
USE Customer
*  process customer database
SELECT(l_holdsel)
```

The SELECT statement accepts the desired work area as its parameter. If zero is passed, the first available work area is selected. The function returns the current work area prior to selecting the new work area. The preceding example stores the current work area to a variable called *l_holdsel* and then moves to the first available work area. The Customer database is then opened and processing done. The last line of the example selects the original work area, which had been stored in the *l_holdsel* variable.

There is an additional clause to the USE statement that allows you to assign an alias to the work area. Recall that the name of the database becomes the alias if the ALIAS clause is not included in the USE statement. Here is an example of the use of the ALIAS clause:

```
SELECT 1
USE Contact ALIAS Ct
SELECT 2
? Ct->Lname
SELECT Ct
```

The first line of this example selects the first unused work area. The second line opens a database called Contact and assigns an alias of Ct. You can use the alias followed by the -> symbol to access fields in a different work area even if you are not currently in that work area. The last line of the example uses the alias to return to the work area in which the Contact database had been opened.

The ALIAS() function returns the name of the current work area if no number is passed to it; otherwise, it returns the name of the referenced work area. In the preceding example, the ALIAS() function would return Ct as the alias for Contact.

The SELECT() and ALIAS() functions are useful in determining your current database environment, such as which files are opened and in what work areas.

When opening more than one database, make sure you change work areas after opening each one by using either the SELECT statement or the SELECT() function. If there is already a database opened in a work area and you attempt to open a second one, the first one will be closed prior to the second one's being opened. The following example closes the first database when it opens the second, which may not be what you intended.

```
USE Names
USE Contacts
```

Here is how to do it by using the SELECT statement:

```
SELECT 0
USE Names
SELECT 0
USE Customers
```

SELECT 0 was used instead of SELECT 1 and SELECT 2 because SELECT 0 automatically gives you the next available work area. The USE statement also has a NEW clause that causes the database to be opened in the first available work area, as shown in this example:

```
USE Names NEW
USE Customers NEW
```

This opens the two databases called Names and Customers in the first two available work areas. This ensures that there are no databases opened in the same work area where you are attempting to open a database.

The USED() function determines if a file is in use. By default, it checks the current work area to see if a file is currently open. It can be made to check other work areas, as shown here:

```
? Names->(USED())
```

The alias of the database followed by the -> symbol points to the work area you want information about. A TRUE or a FALSE is returned as the value of the USED() function.

The CLOSE statement closes the currently selected database and has several variations. The CLOSE DATABASES statement closes *all* databases, indexes, and associated memo files in all the work areas. The

CLOSE <alias> statement closes the specific file and its associated files, such as index files and memo files, in the work area designated by the alias clause. The CLOSE INDEXES statement closes all indexes open in the current work area. The SET INDEX statement is used to open a new index or change the current index. You must first select a work area in which a database is open or open a database prior to issuing this command, as shown here:

```
USE Names NEW
SET INDEX TO Id
```

Positioning and Motion Within the Database

Recall from Chapter 4 that Clipper maintains a record pointer for each database you have open. The Clipper functions and procedures in this section are used to move the record pointer and search for data within a database.

A database consists of a series of records. You move through the database by issuing various requests to move the record pointer. A record pointer, in this case, is an address of a record. Because the system knows the length of a record, it knows to add that number to the record pointer when you issue a command such as SKIP. When a database is opened, the position of the first record and the last record are known. If an index file has been opened, the record pointer points to the location of the first logical record for that index, which does not necessarily correspond to the first physical record.

The command GO TOP tells the record pointer to position itself at the first logical record in the database. The command GO BOTTOM instructs it to go to the last logical record. The statement GO 27 moves the pointer to record number 27.

The SKIP command moves the record pointer either forward or backward. Using the SKIP statement by itself moves the record pointer to the next record. Keep in mind that there are several Clipper SET commands that affect what is considered to be the next record. If the SET DELETE ON setting is in effect, the SKIP command ignores any records that have been marked for deletion. If a database filter has been set using the SET

FILTER TO command, then those records not matching the filter are ignored. The SKIP command also accepts an additional clause indicating the number of records to skip and the direction to skip, as demonstrated in the following examples:

```
USE Customer
SKIP
SKIP 5
SKIP -5
```

The first line opens a database called Customer. The record pointer is positioned at the first record of the database. The second line advances the record pointer one record. The third line advances the record pointer five records. The last line causes the record pointer to move five records backward rather than forward since the number 5 is preceded with the – symbol.

When you request data from a record, the information in the record would be loaded into a record buffer from the disk as one read action. Any subsequent requests concerning this record would access the buffer. If the power to the computer were switched off when you were editing the data in this buffer, the changes would be lost. The SKIP 0 command writes the data in the buffer to the hard disk and can be used to avoid losing data in the event of a system halt. You can use the COMMIT command to write the information contained in the buffers for all the open databases to the hard disk.

The LOCATE FOR command searches for the first record that meets some criterion, as shown here:

```
USE Customer
LOCATE FOR l_fname == Fname
```

The condition to be evaluated follows the LOCATE FOR command. In this case, *l_fname* is a variable containing the name you wish to locate and Fname is the name of the field in the Customer database. The LOCATE FOR command evaluates each record in the database until it finds a match or until the end-of-file marker is reached.

The FOUND() function determines if any matches were found, as in this example:

```
USE Customer
LOCATE FOR l_fname == Fname
IF FOUND()
    ? l_fname+" was located in record "+LTRIM(STR(RECNO()))
ENDIF
```

The database called Customer is opened using the USE statement. The LOCATE FOR statement is used to find a matching name to the variable *l_fname*. The FOUND() function returns a logical value indicating whether the name was found. If the FOUND() function returned a FALSE value, the record pointer would be at the end-of-file marker. If the FOUND() function returned a TRUE value, a match was found and the record pointer will point to the matching record. Subsequent records can be found by using the CONTINUE command, which continues the search from the point of the last found record. Keep in mind that the LOCATE FOR command processes each record in the database and may take a long time—especially on large databases.

A faster way to locate information is to build an index on a specific field and then use the SEEK command, as described in Chapter 4. The SEEK command takes advantage of the sort order of the database to evaluate any matches in a split second. Here is an example of the use of the SEEK command:

```
USE Customer NEW
INDEX ON Lname+Fname TO Customer
SEEK l_name
IF FOUND()
    ? l_name+" already exists."
ENDIF
```

The SEEKing is actually being done inside the CUSTOMER.NTX index file. The inside of this file looks something like the roots of a tree. It races through these roots the way people play the game 20 questions. (Is it bigger than an elephant, smaller than a shoe box?) It then returns the record number of the correct record if the item was found. It normally takes less than a second to make this search. This is a much faster method than skipping through every record for a match.

The LOCATE FOR and CONTINUE commands are seldom used. However, it is sometimes better to use the LOCATE FOR command in a database of less than 100 records than to bother to build and maintain an index.

General Database Status

This section covers the functions used to obtain general information and status information about databases.

The DBFILTER() function returns the current filter, which would have been set using the SET FILTER TO command.

The functions DBRELATION() and DBSELECT() work together to get information on relationships. You can relate two or more databases to each other by using the SET RELATION TO command, as shown in this example:

```
USE Customer INDEX Customer NEW
USE Trans INDEX Trans NEW
SET RELATION TO Id INTO Trans
? DBRELATION(1)      // will display "Id"
? DBRSELECT(1)       // will display 2
```

Chapter 5 discusses the connection of a primary database to a secondary database through a field value. In Chapter 5, the SEEK command was used to find matches in the secondary database. You can use the SET RELATION command to make the connection automatically. Each time the record pointer in the primary record is changed, the record pointer of the secondary record is automatically adjusted, depending on the value of the field connecting the two databases. This eliminates the need to perform a SEEK command to adjust the record pointer in the secondary database.

Once two databases have been tied together using the SET RELATION TO command, the DBRELATION() function can be used to return the field name that ties the two databases together. The DBRSELECT() function is used to return the work area of the secondary database. In the preceding example, the Customer database was opened in the first available work area (1) and the Trans database was opened in the next available work area, which was work area 2.

DBSTRUCT() creates a multidimensional array containing the structure of a database. There is a row in the array for each field in the database. The first column contains the name of the field. The second column contains the type of the field. The third column contains the length of the field. The fourth column contains the number of decimal positions in the field. Here is an example of the use of the DBSTRUCT() function:

```
var := Customer->(DBSTRUCT())
? var[1][1]      // will display "LNAME"
? var[1][2]      // will display "C"
? var[1][3]      // will display length of Lname
? var[1][4]      // will display decimals if any
? var[2][1]      // will display "FNAME"
```

The FCOUNT() function returns the number of fields in the current database. FIELD() returns the name of the field pointed to by the integer passed as a parameter, as shown here:

```
var := FIELD(1)    /// will display "LNAME"
```

You can use the HEADER() function to return the number of bytes used by the header of a database. The *header* is the first part of a database that is used to store information on how many records are in the database, the size and names of the fields, and so forth.

The RECSIZE() function may be used to return the record length of the database in the current work area. A value of 0 is returned from the function if there is not a database open.

The total number of records in a database is returned by the LASTREC() function. The SET DELETE ON and SET FILTER commands have no effect on the number returned.

The current record number is returned by the RECNO() function. If there are no records in a database, a value of 1 is returned from the function.

The LUPDATE() function returns the last modification date of the database.

The DELETED() function returns a logical value indicating whether the record has been marked for deletion by using the DELETE command.

Clipper enables you to use dBASE III-compatible indexes with Clipper databases. Clipper indexes normally have an extension of .NTX, and dBASE III indexes have an .NDX extension. INDEXEXT() returns a character string representing the currently used extension. Keep in mind that the Clipper method of indexing is more efficient than the dBASE III format, and you should use it whenever possible.

INDEXKEY() returns the current index expression of the currently selected database as a character string. Since a database may have more than one index file opened, the ordinal position of the desired index file is passed as a parameter to the INDEXKEY() function, as shown here:

```
USE Customer INDEX Customer,City NEW
? INDEXORD()     // returns 1
SET ORDER TO 2   // Making City the controlling index
? INDEXORD()     // returns 2
```

This example opens a database called Customer and two index files called CUSTOMER and CITY. The order in which the index files are placed in the USE statement indicates the original order of the index files. The INDEXORD() function returns a value of 1 until the controlling index is changed by using the SET ORDER TO command.

Network Considerations

Sooner or later you will have to deal with networks. *Networks* allow two or more computers to share data and access various peripheral devices such as printers. The network software must allow more than one user to access databases at the same time. When users want to share the same database, they usually do so one record at a time. A record that a user is working on should be protected until that user is finished. The mechanism for protecting a record so that another user may not tamper with it is the RLOCK() function. This function locks the record for exclusive use by the user and locks anyone else out from making changes to the record until the lock is turned off. Other users can access the data for viewing purposes only. The RLOCK() function returns a TRUE value if the lock was successful. A FALSE value is returned if the lock was unsuccessful. This would happen if someone else already has the record locked when the RLOCK() function was called.

You should use the FLOCK() function if it is necessary to make a database-wide change. The FLOCK() function locks all other users from making changes to the database. The NETERR() function is used to detect if there has been a network error locking a file.

There are two ways of opening databases, exclusively and shared. Normally, a database such as Customer.dbf would be opened in shared mode, like this:

```
USE Customer SHARED NEW
IF NETERR()
   ? "Unable to open file - file is locked by another"
ENDIF
```

You would open a file in exclusive mode when reindexing the file or updating all the records. Here is an example program that would open a file in exclusive mode:

```
USE Customer EXCLUSIVE NEW
IF NETERR()
   ? "Cannot lock file - in use by others"
ENDIF
```

The EXCLUSIVE clause is used as part of the USE statement to lock all other users from opening the file. This USE EXCLUSIVE statement will fail if any other users have already opened the database, in either shared or exclusive mode.

Any time you want to change the data in a record, you must lock the record prior to performing any REPLACE commands. Since a record lock or file lock may be unsuccessful the first time, you must attempt to lock repeatedly until the lock is successful. The following function demonstrates this idea:

```
FUNCTION rec_lock()
DO WHILE .NOT. RLOCK()
   l_ans := .T.
   @ 24,0
   @ 24,0 SAY "Unable to lock record RETRY Y/N " ;
        GET l_ans PICTURE "Y"
   READ
   @ 24,0
```

```
      IF .NOT. l_ans
         RETURN .F.
      ENDIF
ENDDO
RETURN .T.
```

The DO WHILE looping structure repeats the loop over and over until the RLOCK() function is successful. If the RLOCK() function fails, the user is asked whether he or she wants to retry. The rec_lock() function continues to try to lock the record until the user decides to terminate the process. The rec_lock() function returns a TRUE logical value if the record lock was successful and FALSE if it failed.

This function merely attempts to lock the record over and over. You can rewrite it so that it tries multiple times with a short pause between tries. The INKEY(1) function could be used to pause one second between tries. You may wish to add a parameter for the number of attempts to make at locking the record before terminating.

The call to the rec_lock() function would look like this:

```
IF .NOT. rec_lock()
   RETURN .F.
ENDIF
* process the record
```

In this example, the control of the program returns to the calling program if the attempt to lock the record was unsuccessful. If it was successful, the program would continue on to the statement following the ENDIF statement.

A locked record is automatically unlocked when you move the record pointer to another record. The UNLOCK command unlocks a record or a file that was previously locked by using the RLOCK() or FLOCK() function.

The APPEND BLANK command may not be successful because of a network error. At a minimum, the NETERR() function should be checked right after the APPEND BLANK to ensure the record was added to the database, as shown here:

```
APPEND BLANK
IF NETERR()
   @ 24,0 SAY "Failed to add a record - file locked or other "+;
            "user using record"
```

```
    RETURN .F.
ENDIF
```

The first line of this example attempts to add a new record to the database. The NETERR() function is used to determine if a network error occurred. If an error did occur, the user is notified and the program is terminated. You could write a function similar to the rec_lock() function to make numerous attempts to add a record until successful.

The NETNAME() function returns a workstation identification as a character string of up to 15 characters.

The SET EXCLUSIVE OFF command at the top of your program lets everyone share databases. Dealing with networks can be a relatively simple process if you write various functions to lock records, open files, and add new records.

Make sure your program locks all users except for one when performing maintenance on a file, such as reindexing or performing file-wide operations like month-end processing. This is one of the biggest differences between working on a single-user system and working on a networked system. It is best to save this kind of work until after everyone's gone home.

Adding, Changing, and Deleting Records

In order to add records to a database, you need to issue the APPEND BLANK command. Records are always added to the end of a database. After you issue the APPEND BLANK command, the record is added and available for use by commands such as REPLACE. The APPEND FROM command adds records from another database. This command can append all the records of a database, as shown here:

```
USE Customer
APPEND FROM Trans
```

In this example, Clipper will add one record to the Customer database for each record in the Trans database. Only data for fields with the same name (ID) are copied. All the other fields of the appended records will be empty since there are no more field matches.

DBU allows you to modify the *names* of the fields in the database to be appended so the field names will match the fields of the database receiving the data. You also want to ensure that the field types are identical for fields with the same names. If the City field in the Customer database is shorter than the City field in the database you are appending from, you will lose characters in the process.

The APPEND FROM command can specify specific fields in the database to be appended, using the FIELDS clause:

```
APPEND FROM Newbase FIELDS City,State,Zip
```

This example copies only the data in the City, State, and Zip fields from the database called Newbase.

You may also wish to extract only those records that meet a certain condition, as shown here:

```
APPEND FROM Newbase FOR City=="Sacramento"
```

This example copies only the records from the Newbase database that match the specified condition. You can specify any condition to determine the records to be appended.

You can add the WHILE statement to specify records to be appended while a condition is TRUE. The APPEND FROM statement copies records until the condition is no longer TRUE. At that point, the program resumes with the statement following the APPEND FROM statement.

Quite often it is necessary to bring a text file into a database. You do this by using the SDF clause of the APPEND FROM statement. Each record in the text file should end with a carriage return. A database record will be created for each line in the text file. When you are bringing in this kind of structure, it is often best to create an intermediate database with a single 80-character field and append into that structure. Then you can extract the data out of this intermediate database and into your target database, depending on patterns or lengths within the 80-character field. You could use the AT() function to search these patterns and extract them by using the SUBSTR() function. A field in the intermediate database could be called Line80. The contents would look like this after appending the data from the ASCII file:

"Beverly Hills, CA 90210"
"Chicago, IL 60600"

The program used to extract the various data fields would look something like this:

```
APPEND FROM "address.txt" TO Newbase
USE Newbase NEW
DO WHILE .NOT. EOF()
   l_pos := AT(", ",Line80)
   IF l_pos <> 0        // match found
      l_city  := SUBSTR(Line80,1,l_pos-1)
      l_state := SUBSTR(Line80,l_pos+2,2)
      l_zip   := SUBSTR(Line80,l_pos+5,5)
      SELECT Customer
      APPEND BLANK
      REPLACE City WITH l_city, State WITH l_state,;
              Zip WITH l_zip
      SELECT Newbase
   ENDIF
   SKIP
ENDDO
```

This example pulls the data from the ADDRESS.TXT ASCII file into a database called Newbase. The program will process the Newbase database record by record by looking for a specific pattern (", "). If the pattern is found, a new record is appended to the Customer database and the data is moved.

Usually, when you import data, it will come from another product like a word processor or a different database program. They will usually separate the fields within a record by using a comma and enclose character strings in quotes, as shown here:

"Beverly Hills","CA","90210"

This structure can easily be imported by Clipper, using the DELIMITED clause of the USE statement:

```
APPEND FROM Newfile DELIMITED
```

This command appends the data from the ASCII file called Newfile. Each value separated by a comma will be matched up with the fields in the database.

The Clipper DELETE command marks the current record for deletion. The DELETE command does not actually remove the record. If the SET DELETE ON command has been set, the records marked for deletion will not be visible to most Clipper commands. You can physically remove the records by using the PACK command. Use the PACK command only when absolutely necessary. You should attempt to reclaim records that have been deleted, as demonstrated by the sample application developed in Chapter 5.

The COPY TO command copies records to a target database. Only records that have not been marked as deleted will be copied. You can use the FOR and WHILE clauses with the COPY TO command.

You can also use the FOR and WHILE clauses with the DELETE command. Here are variations of the DELETE command:

```
DELETE NEXT 100
DELETE FOR City="Sacramento"
DELETE WHILE City="Sacramento"
DELETE WHILE City="Sacramento" FOR SUBSTR(Zip,1,2)=="92"
```

The first line deletes 100 records in the current database, starting at the current record. The second example causes all records where the city is equal to "Sacramento" to be deleted. The third statement continues deleting records until the city is no longer equal to "Sacramento". The last statement combines the WHILE and FOR clauses. Records are checked until the city no longer is equal to "Sacramento" and any records found with the first two characters of the ZIP code equal to "92" are deleted.

The RECALL command is the opposite of the DELETE command and has the same options. It is used to "unmark" records that had previously been marked for deletion, as shown here:

```
RECALL ALL    // will undelete all deleted records
RECALL        // will undelete the current record
```

The REPLACE command replaces the contents of a database field with new data, as shown here:

```
REPLACE City WITH l_city
```

This example replaces the value in the City field with the value contained in the *l_city* variable. You can use the REPLACE command to operate on entire databases by using the same *scoping commands* (FOR, WHILE) as the DELETE command. Each REPLACE command invokes a single disk write. By contrast, other methods manipulate the data in a memory buffer until the record pointer is moved by using the SKIP or GO command or by issuing a COMMIT statement. Consequently, you should replace several fields at once as opposed to performing a REPLACE statement for each field, as these examples demonstrate.

```
REPLACE City WITH l_city, State WITH l_state, Zip WITH l_zip
```

```
REPLACE City WITH l_city
REPLACE State WITH l_state
REPLACE Zip WITH l_zip
```

The first example will be much faster than the second example since it performs a single disk write instead of three.

Treating the Database As a Single Unit

This section describes the functions and commands used to manipulate an entire Clipper database. The COPY FILE command is the same as the DOS COPY command except that the words FILE and TO are added, as in this example:

```
COPY FILE oldfile.dbf TO newfile.dbf
```

This makes an exact duplicate of the file called OLDFILE.DBF, including the records and data. The COPY STRUCTURE command copies only the structure of a database file to a new database file. The old file may have records but the new file will be empty. Here is a sample:

```
USE Customer
COPY STRUCTURE TO Newcust
```

The Newcust database will have an identical structure to the Customer database but will not contain any records. The COPY STRUCTURE command is very often used when a temporary file must be created. As an example, suppose you have a database called Labels that has a structure suitable for storing label information. You might wish to create a copy of the structure to a temporary database. This would be a valid mechanism in a network environment where several people may wish to run labels using different parameters. Anyone can make a copy of the Labels structure and use the copy to do their processing. In a network situation where everybody has a C drive on his or her local machine, you could use these commands:

```
SELECT Labels
COPY STRUCTURE TO C:Labels
USE C:Labels NEW
* process the Labels database
```

This example creates a new database called Labels on the C drive that has the same structure as the Labels file located on the network disk drive. The user could use the Labels database on the C drive without the worry of running into problems with other users attempting to lock records or lock the file.

You can delete the temporary file by using the DELETE FILE command, as shown here:

```
DELETE FILE C:Labels.dbf
```

or by using the ERASE command, as shown here:

```
ERASE C:Labels.dbf
```

You must remember to close the file before attempting to delete it or you will get an error message.

The Clipper RENAME command is also similar to its DOS counterpart. The syntax is shown here:

```
RENAME Old.dbf TO New.dbf
```

The TO must be inserted between the two file names. The file must be closed before you issue the RENAME statement. Any associated memo files (.DBT extension) must also be renamed or there will be unpredictable results.

It is also a good idea to check that there is not a file with the target name before renaming. You would do this by using the FILE() function, as in this example:

```
IF .NOT. FILE("New.dbf")
    RENAME Old.dbf TO New.dbf
ENDIF
```

You can use the commands CREATE, CREATE FROM, and COPY STRUCTURE EXTENDED and the function DBCREATE() to create a new database where one did not exist before. This is a very important capability. If a database does not exist, the program would have to terminate unless the program could go ahead and create a new one with the proper structure. There are two ways to do this. Here is the first:

```
CREATE Temp
APPEND BLANK
REPLACE Field_name WITH "Fname", Field_type WITH "C",;
      Field_len WITH 30
APPEND BLANK
REPLACE Field_name WITH "Total", Field_type WITH "N",;
      Field_len WITH 10, Field_dec WITH 2
USE
CREATE New FROM Temp
```

This CREATE command creates a database with four fields called Field_name, Field_type, Field_len, and Field_dec. Records are added to it and filled with the specifications of the target structure. Once the specifications have been added, the database is closed and the CREATE FROM command is issued to create the New database containing the field structure defined in the Temp database.

Here is the other method:

```
newstruc := {}
AADD(newstruc, { "Fname","C",30,0})
```

```
AADD(newstruc, { "Total","N",10,0})
DBCREATE("New",newstruc)
```

In this case, an array is initialized and the AADD() function is used to add field structures to it. The DBCREATE() function is then used to create the New database.

The second example is quicker than the first since it does not have to create a temporary file on the disk. Once the new file is created, there is no temporary file sitting on the disk that may need to be deleted. You can use the CREATE FROM command by itself to create new files from existing structure files.

The COPY STRUCTURE EXTENDED command allows you to make a snapshot of a database structure. You might use this in the creation of a data dictionary where all the field structures would be documented in one place. The database that the command creates looks like a filled version of the database made by the CREATE command with Field_name, Field_type, Field_len, and Field_dec. You could also use this command to create two structure databases from two normal databases, combine them, and create a third normal database with a combined structure. Here is the syntax:

```
USE Customer
COPY STRUCTURE EXTENDED TO Abc
USE Trans
COPY STRUCTURE EXTENDED TO Def
USE Abc
LOCATE FOR Field_name="Id"
IF FOUND()
    DELETE
    PACK
ENDIF
APPEND FROM Def
USE
CREATE Abcdef FROM Abc
```

There is a duplicate field in the Customer and Trans databases called Id. It should be deleted prior to creating the combined database called Abcdef. If you wanted to build a data dictionary, you would do this:

```
CREATE Temp
COPY STRUCTURE EXTENDED TO Temp2
USE Temp2
APPEND BLANK
REPLACE Field_name WITH "Filename", Field_type WITH "C",;
        Field_len  WITH 8
USE
CREATE Dic FROM Temp2
```

This creates a structure that has Filename, Field_name, and so on. You could then add the structures of Customer and Trans like this:

```
USE Dic
APPEND FROM Abc      // Structure of Customer
REPLACE ALL Filename WITH "Customer"
APPEND FROM Def      // Structure of Trans
LOCATE FOR Filename == SPACE(8)
REPLACE Filename WITH "Trans" WHILE .NOT. EOF()
LIST TO PRINT
```

As you can see, you can do lots of different things with these database structure manipulation commands. These commands and functions are not used very often but you should know how to use them in the event you need them.

Setting Database Environment Conditions

The SET statements described here are used to affect the way in which a database is viewed.

The SET DELETED ON command tells Clipper to respect the deleted flag. The deleted flag is a byte associated with each record. The record becomes invisible to most Clipper commands if the SET DELETED ON statement has been issued. Only the PACK command or a COPY TO command of the complete database with the SET DELETED ON command in place would cause the records to be physically removed. If you want your program to be able to "see" the deleted records, issue a SET DELETED OFF statement. This is useful when attempting to reclaim records that have been deleted, as discussed in Chapter 4.

The SET FILTER command tells Clipper to view only a portion of the database meeting a specified condition, as shown here:

```
SET FILTER TO City="Sacramento"
```

This example would make the database appear as if those records matching the condition (City="Sacramento") were the only records in the database. Only records that meet the condition specified will be seen by such commands as COPY and SEEK. Keep in mind that the database is still the same size as before. When your program sequences through the database, all of the records will be processed to determine if they meet the specified condition. You should turn off the filter when the task is completed by issuing a SET FILTER TO statement without a condition.

The SET INDEX command opens and associates index files with a database, as shown here:

```
SET INDEX TO City,Id
```

This opens the index files called CITY and ID. The City index would be considered the active index since it was the first in the list. Any modification to the database would update the currently open indexes if necessary. You would create a potential problem if you forgot to open one of the index files associated with a database. If you made changes to the database, the unopened index file would not get the necessary changes made to it.

The SET RELATION command connects two databases when the second database has an active index. When the pointer is moved in the lead database, the pointer will automatically be moved to the appropriate position in the secondary database. (See the discussion on DBRELA-TION() in the section "General Database Status" earlier in this chapter for an example.) You can choose to SET RELATION between databases or to use the SEEK command to perform the same thing. Using the SEEK command gives you a little more control over the logic in the program, but the SET RELATION command does a lot of the work for you.

The SET SOFTSEEK ON command positions the record pointer to the next higher value if a SEEK fails. Normally, a failed SEEK positions the record pointer at the end of the file. With SET SOFTSEEK ON, the next possible item is found. This is a good idea when you want to have the user enter part of the key to a database and move to the closest record if there is not an exact match.

Changing the Physical Database or Index File

You use the functions and commands described in this section to change the actual physical makeup of a database by clearing out records, sorting the records, recreating the index files, and copying and merging databases.

The SORT command copies records from the current work area to a new database. Records matching the criteria specified by the FOR clause are copied in the order specified by the ON clause, as shown in this example:

```
SORT TO Newfile ON Id FOR City="Sacramento"
```

In this example, the database is sorted in ID order to a new database called Newfile. Records are copied to the new database only if the City field is equal to "Sacramento".

The ZAP command deletes the contents of the database while leaving the structure intact. This is a potentially damaging command and great care must be taken when using it. The ZAP command physically removes all the records from a database. Make sure that you really intend to wipe out the contents of a database. It may even be a good idea to make a backup of the database file prior to performing the ZAP command.

The INDEX command builds an index file that stores the records of a database in the order requested. The purpose of the index file is to allow rapid access to the database. If a database is indexed on the field Lname (last name), the SEEK command can rapidly find a last name by checking in the index file for the location of the record. Here is the INDEX command:

```
USE Customer
INDEX ON Lname+Fname to Customer
SEEK "Bloggs           Fred"
```

The first line of this example opens a database called Customer. The second line creates an index on the combination of the Lname and Fname fields. The third line of the example performs a SEEK command to quickly locate a customer. If the customer's name is found, the record pointer will point at the appropriate record. If it is not found, the record pointer will point at the end-of-file marker.

Use the REINDEX command to reindex a database when an index has already been created. You would use it only if there were a suspicion of a corrupted index.

The PACK command removes all records that have been marked for deletion using the DELETE command.

The JOIN command creates a new database from the contents of two other databases. It processes every record in the support database for every record in the lead database. You should avoid this command if at all possible because it is very slow. Here is an example of the JOIN command:

```
USE Trans NEW
USE Customer NEW
JOIN WITH Trans TO Newbase FOR Id==Trans->Id
```

The two databases called Trans and Customer are opened in different work areas. The JOIN statement joins the database in the current work area with a database currently open in a different work area. You can specify a condition, as in the example, by using the FOR clause.

The COPY TO command copies from one database file to another or from a database file out to a text file. Here is a sample:

```
USE Customer
COPY TO Newbase FOR State="CA" SDF
```

This sample creates a text file in *system data format (SDF)*, where each record has a fixed length ending in a carriage return. The FOR condition declares that only customers resident in California are to be exported. COPY TO can also use the WHILE clause. The DELIMITED clause can instruct Clipper to create an ASCII file delimited with quotes and commas. The FIELDS clause means that only certain fields should be copied, as in this example:

```
COPY TO Newbase FIELDS Lname, Fname, City
```

This creates a new database called Newbase containing only the Lname, Fname, and City fields. A corresponding record is created for each record in the current database.

You use the DESCEND() function in conjunction with the INDEX command to create a descending index, as in this example:

```
INDEX ON DESCEND(Lname) TO Upsidedn
```

The resulting index will be in the opposite order, as expected. This means that the name "Zarofonetis" will be before "Adams" in the logical order of the database. You must use the DESCEND() function as part of the SEEK command in order to find anything, as shown here:

```
SEEK DESCEND("Bloggs")
```

This performs a seek of the index file that has been created in descending order. If you leave off the DESCEND() function, the name will not be found when using the SEEK command.

Processing the Entire Database

The commands and functions described in this section process an entire database either to come up with a total or an average or to display or list values in the database.

You use the SUM command to sum amounts in numeric fields and store the result in a specified variable, as shown here:

```
USE Trans
SUM Quantity*Cost to l_total
```

This example opens the database called Trans and sums up the values of the Quantity field multiplied by the Cost field. You can use the WHILE and FOR scoping clauses with the SUM command.

The TOTAL command creates a new database with a series of records containing totals from the processed database. The TOTAL command must be processed on an indexed database and must reference the proper key. The following example totals up the activity for all accounts within the Trans database:

```
USE Trans
TOTAL ON Id FIELDS Quantity TO Result
```

The Result database will have records with the same structure as Trans, but with only one record per unique ID number; however, the Quantity field will contain a total of each ID that matched. This works in Trans when there are multiple instances of the same ID number. You can use the WHILE and FOR scoping clauses with the TOTAL command.

The AVERAGE command averages a specific field and places the results in a variable, as shown in this example:

```
AVERAGE Quantity TO l_avequan
```

This stores the average quantity in the variable called *l_avequan*. Clipper keeps track of the total number of records and the sum of all of the Quantity fields in order to calculate the average. You can use the WHILE and FOR scoping clauses with the AVERAGE command.

The COUNT command counts the number of records that meet a certain criterion. You can optionally use the FOR and WHILE scoping clauses, as this example demonstrates.

```
COUNT TO l_bigbucks FOR Quantity > 3
```

The entire database will be processed and the total number of records that meet the criteria specified after the FOR clause will be stored in the variable called *l_bigbucks*.

DBEVAL() is a special function that processes each record in a database against a code block. (Code blocks are discussed in detail in Chapter 10.)

The DISPLAY and LIST commands are very similar. They are a "quick and dirty" way to dump data to the screen or printer. DISPLAY is identical to LIST except that its default scope is the current record rather than all the records. Here are some examples:

```
DISPLAY Lname,Fname TO PRINTER FOR State=="NY"
LIST Lname,Fname,Quantity*Cost TO FILE Temp.doc ;
        FOR SUBSTR(Zip,1,5)=="90210"
```

The first example displays the Lname and Fname fields to the printer for all records that have a state code of NY. The FOR clause specifies the records that are to be processed. The second example lists the Lname and Fname fields and the value of the Quantity*Cost field to a file called TEMP.DOC. Recall that the ; character is used to continue the statement on the next line. The FOR clause specifies that only records that match the criteria specified after the FOR word will be included in the listing. The LIST and DISPLAY commands are seldom used since the formatting is imprecise. However, they can be used for "quick and dirty" listings.

User Interface Functions and Commands

Clipper provides a rich language for displaying and printing information and for handling keyboard input.

Allowing User Input

The functions and commands described in this section make up the user interface. Chapters 4, 5 and 6 demonstrate the use of many of these items. There are three types of interfaces involved. They are the menu system, the scrolling window, and the individual entry point. These three systems work together to form a unified user interface.

You can handle the menu system by using the PROMPT/MENU TO command, as explained in Chapter 4. Here is a brief example of the PROMPT/MENU TO command:

```
@ 10,10 PROMPT "Red  "  MESSAGE "The color red"
@ 11,10 PROMPT "Blue "  MESSAGE "The color blue"
@ 12,10 PROMPT "White"  MESSAGE "The color white"
MENU TO l_ans
```

The user selects a choice by using the arrow keys to move the cursor bar up and down among the items in the menu. The ENTER key is used to make the choice. The user can press ESC to escape the menu without selecting one of the items. The number of the menu item is stored in the variable specified right after the MENU TO command. In this example, if the Blue item is selected, the number 2 will be stored in the *l_ans* variable. You can assign a message to be displayed while the user is positioned at the various menu items. You accomplish this by specifying the message after the MESSAGE clause of the PROMPT statement. The environment command SET MESSAGE TO 24 CENTER activates the display of the message on line 24 and causes the text to be centered. As you move up and down the menu, the appropriate message is echoed on the 24th line of the screen.

The SET WRAP ON command indicates that if the DOWN ARROW key was pressed and the last element had been reached, the cursor bar would jump to the first element. Pressing the UP ARROW key when the cursor bar is positioned on the top element would cause the cursor bar to jump to the last element.

Chapter 5 discusses the use of the PROMPT/MENU TO command to present secondary database records to the user for selection. There are other alternatives available to you, such as the ACHOICE() and BROWSE() functions and the TBROWSE object. The ACHOICE() function accepts the coordinates of a menu and an array containing the menu choices. The advantage of ACHOICE() over the PROMPT/MENU TO alternative is that there can be more choices than what will display on the screen at one time. ACHOICE() scrolls the selections in the window in order to display all the items. The BROWSE() function presents the user with a table-oriented browser and editor for records in a database. The TBROWSE object is discussed in more detail in Chapter 10.

The @ SAY/GET command is probably the most widely used command in the Clipper language. You perform data entry in Clipper by using one or more @ SAY/GET commands followed by a READ statement. Nothing happens until the READ statement is issued. At that point, the user is given the ability to move freely among the pending GETs. The pending GETs are those @ GET commands encountered since the last READ or CLEAR GETS command. Chapters 4, 5, and 6 demonstrate the use of the @ SAY/GET command in greater detail. The CLEAR GETS command clears all pending GETs. The UPDATED() function determines whether any data was changed by the user during a full-screen data entry session.

The MEMOEDIT() is another user-interface function. It presents the user with a mini word processor to allow the edit of memo fields and is discussed earlier in this chapter.

Keyboard Handling

You use the functions and commands in this section to process keystrokes entered by the user or to manipulate the keyboard buffer.

When the user types on the keyboard, the keystrokes are stored in a keyboard buffer. This contains a fixed-length string of character codes. You can adjust the length of the buffer by using the SET TYPEAHEAD statement. The characters are removed as they are processed by Clipper. The LASTKEY() function tells you the value of the last key pressed, as in this example:

```
@ 10,10 SAY "City " GET City
READ
IF LASTKEY() == K_PGDN
   * jump to next screen
ENDIF
```

The keystroke is removed from the keyboard buffer when the function is called. This example uses the LASTKEY() function to determine how the user exited the data entry screen.

NEXTKEY() is similar to LASTKEY(), but it does not remove the keystroke from the keyboard buffer. The CLEAR TYPEAHEAD command clears the buffer of all keystrokes. INKEY() removes keystrokes from the buffer but also accepts an additional parameter that will cause it to delay until another key is pressed or for a specified amount of time, as shown in these examples:

```
@ 24,0 SAY "No help available"
INKEY(0)    // wait until a key is pressed
```

The zero passed as a parameter causes the program to wait until the user presses any key.

In the next example, the number 10 indicates the number of seconds the program should wait before resuming:

```
@ 24,0 SAY "Shutting down network in 10 seconds"
INKEY(10)               // wait 10 seconds
```

The INKEY() function with no parameters immediately checks the keyboard buffer for keystrokes. If there are any keystrokes, the numeric value of the keys are returned by the function. Otherwise, a zero is returned.

The following DO WHILE loop will continue as long as the value of the INKEY() function is equal to zero:

```
DO WHILE INKEY() == 0   // wait for a keystroke from the user
ENDDO
```

The INKEY() function will return zero as long as no keys have been pressed. Once a key is pressed, the numeric value of the key is returned as the value of the function. You can set up a loop to wait for a specific key, as shown here:

```
DO WHILE .NOT. INKEY(0) == K_ESC  // wait for the escape key
ENDDO
```

This DO WHILE loop continues until the user presses ESC.

You can use the KEYBOARD statement to simulate keystrokes entered by the user. Chapter 5 demonstrates the use of the KEYBOARD command by "stuffing" a PGDN key into the keyboard buffer from a user-defined function. The PGDN key causes the PROMPT/MENU TO selection list to terminate.

Saving and Restoring the Screen

You use the SAVE SCREEN command to save a screen. Clipper allows you to save and restore a single screen by using just the SAVE SCREEN and RESTORE SCREEN commands, as shown here:

```
SAVE SCREEN
* do something
RESTORE SCREEN
```

The first line of this example saves the screen. You can then do anything to the screen and then use the RESTORE SCREEN command to restore the contents of the screen. This is a "quick and dirty" way to preserve the screen. You can also use a variable as a buffer to hold the screen. This allows more than one screen to be saved at a single time. Here is an example of how to use the commands with a variable:

```
SAVE SCREEN TO l_buffer
* do something
RESTORE SCREEN FROM l_buffer
```

The SAVESCREEN() and RESTSCREEN() functions also enable you to save and restore the screen but provide more flexibility than the SAVE SCREEN and RESTORE SCREEN commands. The coordinates of the screen to be saved are passed to the SAVESCREEN() function, and the screen image returned from the function can be stored to a variable. This allows a portion of the screen to be saved, which is quicker and uses less memory. The same coordinates and the variable used to store the screen image can be passed to the RESTSCREEN() function to restore the same portion of the screen, as shown here:

```
l_buffer := SAVESCREEN(1,1,5,10)
* do something
RESTSCREEN(1,1,5,10,l_buffer)
```

This stores an image of the screen starting at row 1, column 1 and ending at row 5, column 10 into a variable called *l_buffer*. The same coordinates are passed to the RESTSCREEN() function. The variable that was used to store the screen image is passed as the fifth parameter.

The nice thing about being able to specify the screen coordinates when restoring the screen is that the image can be restored to a different portion of the screen, as shown here:

```
l_buffer := SAVESCREEN(1,1,5,10)
* do something
RESTSCREEN(6,6,10,15,l_buffer)
```

When restoring the image to a different location, you must make sure you restore the same amount of screen as you saved. You may end up with a lot of strange characters on the screen if you attempt to restore a larger screen area than you saved using the SAVESCREEN() function.

Clearing the Screen

You can clear all or a portion of the screen by using the CLEAR, @ CLEAR, and CLEAR SCREEN commands. You should use the CLEAR SCREEN command to clear an entire screen since the CLEAR command also releases any pending GETs and positions the cursor at the upper-left corner. You can include screen coordinates as part of the @ CLEAR statement to clear a rectangular portion of the screen, as shown here:

```
@ 5,5 CLEAR TO 15,40
```

This example clears the section of screen from row 5, column 5 to row 15, column 40.

You can clear all or part of a line in this manner:

```
@ 24,0
```

This clears line 24. The column could have been adjusted to clear only a portion of the line.

Cursor Positioning

The SETPOS() function moves the cursor to a different screen location. The ROW() function returns the current row position of the cursor. The COL() function returns the current column position of the cursor.

Drawing Boxes

Most of the routines used to draw boxes require a string of eight line-draw characters to be used for the border and a fill character to be used to fill in the middle of the box. A Clipper header file called box.ch includes some manifest constants that you can use rather than defining your own. You can have the include file in your program, as shown here:

```
#include "Box.ch"
```

By including this file in your program, you make the following constants available for use:

B_SINGLE	Single-line box
B_DOUBLE	Double-line box
B_SINGLE_DOUBLE	Single-line top with double-line sides
B_DOUBLE_SINGLE	Double-line top with single-line sides

The DISPBOX() function accepts the screen coordinates and one of the preceding constants as parameters. The desired color of the box can also be passed as a parameter to the function. There is an @ BOX command that will perform basically the same task. Here are examples of the DISPBOX() function and the @ BOX command that would perform the same task:

```
#include "Box.ch"

DISPBOX(5,5,15,40,B_SINGLE)
@ 5,5,15,40 BOX B_SINGLE
```

Both the DISPBOX() function and the @ BOX command allow the desired color to be passed as an option. Keep in mind that a function can be used as part of a code block or stored in an array. This makes the function much more flexible.

You can use the @ TO command when you want to draw a box without disturbing the text in the middle of the box. This example demonstrates how to use the @ TO command:

```
@ 5,5 TO 15,40
```

This draws a box from row 5, column 5 to row 15, column 40. The screen contents within the box will remain. The box is drawn using a single line. You can add the word "DOUBLE" to the end of the command to draw a box with a double line.

Writing to the Screen

The @ SAY command is the primary method used for displaying text on the screen. It accepts the row and column and a text string that is to be displayed. You can add the GET clause, which adds data entry items to the pending GET list.

You can also use the ? and ?? statements to display information on the screen or printer. Each is followed by the expression to be printed, as shown here:

```
? "HI THERE"
```

The single question mark performs a line feed prior to printing the expression. The double question mark displays the text at the current position.

The @ SAY and ?/?? commands allow expressions to be combined on the same statement by using the + operator, as shown here:

```
? "HI THERE" + " " + "JAKE"
```

The + operator simply combines the various expressions. In this case, "HI THERE" is combined with a single space and "JAKE". Variables, Clipper functions, and user-defined functions can also be displayed as part of the @ SAY and ?/?? commands, as shown here:

```
? "TODAY'S DATE IS " + DTOC(DATE())
```

This example uses the Clipper DATE() function to display the current system date. Since the DATE() function returns a date type, it must be converted to character type before it is displayed using the ? command; you do this by using the Clipper DTOC() function.

You can also use the QOUT() and QQOUT() functions to dump information to the screen. The ? command is synonymous with the QOUT() function. Both issue a carriage return/line feed prior to printing the text. The QOUT() function is designed to be used within code blocks, which are discussed in Chapter 10. These two examples would perform the same task:

```
QOUT("Hi there folks")
? "Hi there folks"
```

The ?? command and QQOUT() function output data the same way but do *not* send a carriage return/line feed to the screen or printer. They are normally used to send printer codes to the printer. These codes usually take the form of the ESC character combined with a number, as in CHR(27)+CHR(18). The codes control behavior like font size, compressed mode, landscape, and portrait on laser printers and so forth.

The SCROLL() function allows a specified portion of the screen to be scrolled, meaning that the lines will be moved either up or down, depending on the parameters passed to the function.

Printer Control

The SETPRC() function is the printer version of SETPOS(). It positions the printer cursor at a specific location. The desired row and column are passed as parameters, as in this example:

```
SETPRC(10,10)
```

This positions the printhead of the printer to row 10, column 10 even if it has to go to the next page to do it. Remember than you cannot go backward when printing.

The SET PRINT ON command echoes screen output to the printer. This statement is usually issued before the first line of a report is printed. Once the report has been completed, echo to the printer can be turned off by the SET PRINT OFF command.

Making Noise

There are two ways to alert the user that a process such as a report has completed or that an error has occurred. You can issue the following statement:

```
?? CHR(7)
```

This "displays" a beep.

A better method is to use the TONE() function, in which the frequency and duration of the sound can be defined, as shown in this example:

```
TONE(100,3)
```

This calls the Clipper TONE() function to sound the speaker tone for a frequency of 100 and a duration of 3/18 of a second. Various frequencies and duration could be used to indicate different types of warnings or messages.

Global Settings

The following functions and commands provide the ability to make changes to the Clipper environment to affect the way everything works together. You can use the SET() function as an alternative to many of the following items. SET() is a system-level function that allows you to inspect or change any of the SET environment commands. This is a very important command as it allows global setting and resetting of the environment. See the set.ch file for the list of constants to be used with this command.

Data Entry Settings

You use the READEXIT() function to determine whether or not the UP ARROW and DOWN ARROW keys can be used to exit a full-screen data entry session. Setting READEXIT() to TRUE, as in READEXIT(.T.), enables the arrow keys.

The READINSERT() function can be used to switch the INS key on and off. READINSERT(.T.) causes the program to act as if the user had pressed INS. READINSERT() also returns the current state of the INS key.

The SET CONFIRM ON/OFF command forces the user to use an exit key such as ENTER in order to leave a GET field. This may be useful where a data entry person is going so fast that he or she zips past fields without properly entering the data. By using SET CONFIRM ON, you can force the person to stop and confirm each entry with the ENTER key.

The SET ESCAPE ON/OFF command toggles the ability of the ESC key to exit from a full-screen data entry session.

The SET BELL ON command enables a bell to be sounded if the last character of a GET is reached or an invalid data type is entered, as in entering characters into a number field. SET BELL OFF disables the bell sound for any of these operations.

The SET DELIMITERS command delimits the entry points. You would use this command if you could not use color or shade to define the entry points. SET DELIMITERS TO ":." forces the GET command to display a colon before the GET and a period after the GET of each field.

The SET INTENSITY ON/OFF command enables/disables the intensity of GETs. The intensity determines whether a GET field is displayed in the standard color setting or in the enhanced color setting. When the command SET INTENSITY OFF has been issued, the intensity of the SAYs and GETs is the same.

The SET SCOREBOARD ON/OFF command allows/disallows information concerning READs and MEMOEDIT to be displayed on line zero of the screen. When SET SCOREBOARD ON has been issued, various error messages, abort messages, and the current status of the INS key are displayed in the upper-right corner of the screen.

Color

The SETCOLOR() function detects the current color setting and can assign a color setting.

The five groups to be set are listed here:

Standard	All screen output commands and functions
Enhanced	GETs and selection highlights
Border	Border color, not supported by EGA and VGA
Background	Not supported
Unselected	Unselected GETs

The colors can be assigned in this form:

```
SETCOLOR(Standard,Enhanced,Border,Background,Unselected)
```

The actual symbols representing the colors are passed as a character string:

```
SETCOLOR("W/N,BG+/B,,,W/N")
```

Here are the codes for color:

Black	N,Space
Blue	B
Green	G
Cyan	BG
Red	R
Magenta	RB
Brown	GR
White	W
Gray	N+
Bright blue	B+
Bright green	G+
Bright cyan	BG+
Bright red	R+
Bright magenta	RB+
Yellow	GR+
Bright white	W+
Black	U
Inverse video	I
Blank	X

The SETCOLOR() function returns the current color setting prior to setting the new color. This makes it easy to restore the original color; you store the color to a variable and later restore the color, as in this example:

```
l_holdcol := SETCOLOR("W/N,BG+/B,,,W/N")
* do something
SETCOLOR(l_holdcol)
```

The first line of this example calls on the SETCOLOR() function to change the current color. SETCOLOR() changes the color and returns the original color to the *l_holdcol* variable. Once the program has done its processing, the SETCOLOR() function is called again with the variable as a parameter to return to the original color.

Keep in mind that certain color mixtures may appear as one shade on some monochrome monitors. This prevents the user from reading anything on the screen. You should test your color scheme on all types of monitors to ensure that the user will be able to see everything. You may want to provide the ability to change color schemes in your application.

Cursor Control

The SETCURSOR() function allows you to change the shape of the cursor, as in SETCURSOR(2). Here are the possible values:

0	None
1	Underline
2	Lower half block
3	Full block
4	Upper half block

The function also returns the current cursor shape. This value can be stored to a variable in order to restore the cursor to its original state. You may want to turn the cursor off temporarily when displaying messages; use the SETCURSOR() function for this purpose.

Screen or Printer Output

Use the SET CONSOLE ON/OFF command to toggle output to the screen. It is most often used when running reports. The console would be switched off while printing.

Use the SET MARGIN TO command to define the margin in printer output.

The SET PRINTER ON/OFF/TO command is mostly used to switch output to the printer. The TO file variation allows output to a DOS text file. The SET PRINTER TO LPT1/LPT2/LPT3 parallel ports or the COM1/COM2 serial ports allow the printer output to be directed to the appropriate port. The @ SAY commands will not be sent to the printer. The SET DEVICE command should be used to direct @ SAY commands to the printer.

The SET ALTERNATE command redirects output to a file that would normally go to the screen or report. SET ALTERNATE is actually three commands that work as a team. Here is an example:

```
SET ALTERNATE TO output.txt
SET ALTERNATE ON
LIST Name,City,State
SET ALTERNATE TO
```

The first line of this example sets up a file called OUTPUT.TXT to accept output that would normally go to the screen or printer. The LIST command is used to list the Name, City, and State fields to the file. The last command closes the file OUTPUT.TXT.

The SET DEVICE command directs output to the screen or printer. This command accepts output from the @ SAY command, as shown here:

```
SET DEVICE TO PRINTER
@ 10,10 SAY "Hello"
SET DEVICE TO SCREEN
```

The first line sets the device to the printer. All output will be directed to the printer until the SET DEVICE command is issued again.

You can use the DEVPOS() function to determine the starting row and column of the printer.

Hot Keys

The SET FUNCTION command assigns a character string to a function key. When the assigned function key is pressed, the string is stuffed into the keyboard buffer. You can use this to perform unusual navigation techniques. A good example of the use of this function would be to set up a function key for use when entering the customer information on a data entry screen. A function key could be set up with the default city, state, and zip code of the user's location. Any time the user presses the function key, the keyboard would be stuffed with the value of the city, state, and zip code.

The SET KEY command assigns a key or key combination to a function. When that key is pressed, the program jumps to the referenced function immediately. Three parameters are automatically passed, indicating the name of the current procedure or function, the line number, and the variable active at that moment. Here is an example:

```
SET KEY F1 TO help
*do stuff
FUNCTION help(l_proc,l_line,l_var)
@ 24,0 SAY "You hit the F1 key in procedure "+l_proc+;
" line "+LTRIM(STR(l_line))+" variable "+l_var
* help based on procedure or variable here
RETURN .T.
```

The SETKEY() function associates a code block with an assigned key in the same way that SET KEY associates a function with an assigned key. (Code blocks are covered in more detail in Chapter 10.)

Keyboard Control

Use the SET TYPEAHEAD command to define how large the keyboard buffer is to be. The limit is 4096 characters and the minimum is 16.

Directory Information

You use the SET DEFAULT command to declare the default subdirectory and/or drive where databases are to be found or created. This command allows you to have the programs in one location and the databases in another.

The SET PATH command defines where Clipper will find databases to be used. This differs slightly from the SET DEFAULT command, which allows creating of databases as well.

You can use the DIRECTORY() function to store an image of the current directory as a multidimensional array. The created array will contain five columns corresponding to name, size, date, time, and attribute. The include file directory.ch has constants representing the positions in the array: F_NAME, F_SIZE, F_DATE, F_TIME, and F_ATT. You can narrow the list of selected files by passing the file attribute as a parameter to the function. Here are the single characters that can be passed to indicate various file attributes:

H = Hidden files
S = System files
D = Include directories
V = Search for the DOS volume label and exclude all other files

Here is an example of the DIRECTORY() function:

```
dirarray := DIRECTORY("*.PRG","D")
```

This returns an array containing information of all of the files with a .PRG extension. The file mask (*.PRG) is passed as the first parameter. The desired file attribute (D) is passed as the second parameter.

Error Handling

You can use the ALTD() function to invoke the Clipper debugger menu if you are running the program within the Clipper debugger. You might use it in an error-handling function that would invoke the debugger when an error occurred.

The ERRORBLOCK() function is part of the error object mechanism covered in Chapter 10.

You can use the ERRORLEVEL() function to set or inspect a DOS-level error. As an example, you could use the ERRORLEVEL() function to indicate that the application program had crashed. A batch file in DOS could then detect the ERRORLEVEL condition and take appropriate actions.

The NETERR() function returns a TRUE value if some kind of network error occurred during an attempt to open or update a database.

The DOSERROR() function returns the last DOS error number. Your program would use this to determine various DOS errors, such as a missing file.

DOS-level File Handling

Clipper provides many functions that allow you to read and write files at the DOS level. When a database file is opened with the USE command, a lot of things happen. Not only is the file opened, but information about the file is loaded into a structure. This information is used to calculate how many records there are, the length of records, the names of fields, and so on.

The FOPEN() function opens a DOS text file in one of three modes: read only, write only, or read/write. The FOPEN() function returns a value of –1 if the attempt to open the file was unsuccessful. The FERROR() function evaluates errors while performing low-level file operations, as shown here:

```
#include "Fileio.ch"
handle := FOPEN("myfile.txt",FO_READWRITE)
IF FERROR() != 0      // not equal (!=)
   ? "Cannot open myfile.txt, DOS error ",FERROR()
ENDIF
```

The Clipper constant definition file called Fileio.ch is included since it contains useful constant definitions. Study this file if you intend to use these low-level DOS functions. Notice that the FOPEN() function assigns its value to the variable handle. This returned value is called a file handle, and it will be used by the other functions in this group. A file handle is actually a number between zero and 65,535. The FERROR() function checks to make sure the FOPEN() function was successful.

The next action would be to read data from this file. The FREAD() function reads data into a buffer. The buffer must first be created, as in this example:

```
buffer := SPACE(256)
IF FREAD(handle,@buffer,256) <> 256
   ? "Error reading file"
ENDIF
```

The handle is passed as the first parameter of the FREAD() function. The variable buffer is passed as the second parameter and will receive the characters read. The third parameter indicates how many bytes you want to read from the file. The FREAD() function returns the actual bytes read. If the number of actual bytes read is not equal to the number of bytes expected, it means an error occurred. You can manipulate the variable buffer by using the various string functions and commands.

A variation of the FREAD() command is FREADSTR(), which reads characters up to a null character CHR(0), whereas FREAD() will read any characters, including the null character. Here is an example of FREADSTR():

```
string := FREADSTR(handle,50)
```

You use the FSEEK() command to move around within a DOS text file. The start position can be the beginning of the file, the end-of-file marker, or the current position of the file pointer.

If a file does not exist, you can create it by using FCREATE(). This function allows files to be created in four modes: normal, read only, hidden, and system. You can also use the FCREATE() function to overwrite any existing file, as shown here:

```
#include "Fileio.ch"
handle := FCREATE("myfile.txt",FC_NORMAL)
IF handle == -1
   ? "Error creating file - DOS error ",FERROR()
ENDIF
```

The first line makes the constants in the include file called Fileio.ch available. The second line creates a file called MYFILE.TXT in normal mode (defined by the constant FC_NORMAL). The handle is returned to the variable called *handle*. The FCREATE function returns a –1 if the operaton was not successful. The FERROR() function is used to display why the operation was unsuccessful.

Use the FWRITE() function to write data to a file, as shown here:

```
IF FWRITE(handle,"Hello there") <> 11 // bytes in string
   ? "Error while writing to file "
ENDIF
```

This example writes the character string "Hello there" to the file opened and assigned the file handle called *handle*.

The FCLOSE() function closes the DOS text file. The function returns a FALSE value if an error occurred.

You can use the RENAME() function to rename a file, as in this example:

```
IF FRENAME("old.txt","new.txt") == -1
   ? "Error",FERROR()," while renaming"
ENDIF
```

The file must be closed before being renamed. You can erase a closed file by using the FERASE() function. Here is an example:

```
IF FERASE("badfile.txt") == -1
   ? "Error erasing file"
ENDIF
```

You can check the existence of a file by using the FILE() function, as shown here:

```
IF FILE("mytext.txt")
   result :=  FOPEN("myfile.txt")
ENDIF
```

The DOSERROR() function returns the DOS error code associated with a failed action. In the low-level DOS functions mentioned earlier, this is the same code as returned by FERROR().

Here is a list of the FERROR() codes:

0	Successful
2	File not found
3	Path not found
4	Too many files open

5	Access denied
6	Invalid handle
8	Insufficient memory
15	Invalid drive specified
19	Attempted to write to a write-protected disk
21	Drive not ready
23	Data CRC error
29	Write fault
30	Read fault
32	Sharing violation
33	Lock violation

These functions are seldom used in normal day-to-day programming, but you will need to know how to use them in circumstances where you are reading or writing text files, such as modifying AUTOEXEC.BAT or CONFIG.SYS or extracting data from other files. The only things to note are to always check FERROR() after an action and to remember that the pointer is moving inside the text file every time you use FREAD(), FWRITE(), FSEEK(), and FREADSTR().

Examining the Clipper Environment

The following functions are a way for your program to look around at the current state of affairs and respond accordingly.

Accessing the System Clock

You can access the clock in your computer by using the DATE(), TIME(), and SECONDS() functions. Keep in mind that these are only as accurate as the date and time on your system clock. If the battery goes out, these functions will not return correct values.

The DATE() function returns the date from the system clock in date format. The TIME() function returns the current time from the system clock in character format. The SECONDS() function returns the number of seconds since midnight.

Operating System Information

The OS() function returns the name of the operating system, such as DOS 3.3. An example of when this might be used is to ensure there are enough file handles available to run your application. DOS version 3.1 allows a maximum of 20 file handles. If your application uses more than 20, you should check the DOS version to make sure the system is running on a version after 3.1.

Computer System Information

You can find the amount of disk space available on the drive by using the DISKSPACE() function. A numeric value is returned indicating the number of bytes remaining. This is useful when you are copying or adding to files to ensure there is enough space prior to executing the command.

The MEMORY() function tells you how much memory is available for use. Memory should not be a problem since Clipper implements a memory manager that switches out blocks of memory to disk as necessary. Use MEMORY(0) with a zero as a parameter to return available space. Clipper allocates a different amount of memory for the running of external programs using the RUN/! command. You can check this by passing 2 to the MEMORY() function, as in MEMORY(2).

You could use the MEMORY(2) function to ensure you have enough memory to execute DOS programs from within a Clipper application, as the following example demonstrates.

```
IF MEMORY(2) < 100
    ? "Not enough memory to run editor"
ENDIF
```

The current path can be detected by using the CURDIR() function. Here is an example:

```
IF .NOT. CURDIR("C:") == "CLIPPER5\SOURCE"
   RUN CD \CLIPPER5\SOURCE
ENDIF
```

The ISCOLOR() function detects if there is a color video card in the computer. This would be used to set up color schemes. Monochrome screens may show various colors as the same shade, and it is best to stick to black and white or blue and white under these circumstances. ISCOLOR() returns a value of TRUE if the color video board exists.

The ISPRINTER() function checks to see if the printer is online. This is very useful in printer operations where printers run out of paper or are not switched on. The function returns a TRUE value if the printer is ready to print.

Checking DOS Environment Settings

The GETENV() function is the last of the specifically DOS environment functions. Its purpose is to return the contents of a DOS environment variable. One such variable is *PATH*, which tells DOS where to search for programs. You can check this variable like this:

```
pathstring := GETENV("PATH")
```

If you create an application, you may wish to set up your program different ways for different users by using something like this at the DOS prompt:

```
SET USER=Jane
```

Then your program could check the contents of the *USER* variable, and if it contained "Jane", you could run the program differently for Jane (such as in a different color set).

High-resolution monitors and video cards allow more lines and columns on the screen than 25x80. You can use the MAXROW() and MAXCOL() functions to determine the current set values.

Function and Procedure Information

As your application runs, Clipper keeps track of information such as which program is currently running, the line number that is being processed, and the number of parameters that may have been passed to a function. The PROCNAME() function returns the name of the currently running function or procedure. The PROCLINE() function returns the current line number within the function or procedure. PCOUNT() detects how many parameters were actually passed to a function.

Memory Variable Handling

Clipper performs the memory management required in most applications. There may be times when you want to control memory a little bit more, save the contents of variables to disk files, or restore those that had been saved. You can use the CLEAR MEMORY command to clear all variables from memory. You can use the RELEASE ALL LIKE command to release variables that match a specified pattern, as in this example:

```
RELEASE ALL LIKE g_*
```

This releases all variables that have a name that starts with g_. If you plan on using this syntax, it would be a good idea to select a variable-naming convention that would allow you to release only a group of variables at a time. It is fairly common practice to create public variables for use in data entry and then release them once the operation has been completed. The variables are made public so that they are available to various editing routines in your application.

You can save memory variables to memory files that have a .MEM extension by using the SAVE TO command, as shown here:

```
l_var := 23
x_var := 56
```

```
z_var := "hello"
SAVE ALL LIKE l* TO myvar     // * wildcard symbol saves all
```

This example creates three variables called *l_var*, *x_var*, and *z_var*. The SAVE TO command saves all the variables that have a first character of l to a file called MYVAR.

You could modify the SAVE TO command to save all the variables currently in memory by leaving off the LIKE clause, as shown here:

```
SAVE ALL TO myvar
```

You can use the EXCEPT clause to save all variables except the ones specified, as shown here:

```
SAVE ALL EXCEPT x* TO myvar  // excludes those starting with x
```

This saves all the existing variables except those with a first character of "x" to the MYVAR.MEM file.

The RESTORE FROM command restores variables that were saved to a .MEM file, as this example shows.

```
CLEAR MEMORY                  // clears ALL variables from memory
RESTORE FROM myvar
? l_var,x_var,z_var           // prints  23,56,"hello"
```

The first line clears all variables from memory. The RESTORE FROM command restores variables from the MYVAR.MEM file. The values of the variables are also preserved in the memory.

Running External Programs

You can use the RUN or ! command to call DOS commands while within a Clipper application. The MEMORY() function should be used to ensure there is enough memory to run the program. Keep in mind that the Clipper application takes up a considerable amount of memory and you will not be able to run programs that take a lot of memory.

Terminating the Clipper Application

A RETURN statement issued always returns to the procedure or function that called the current procedure or function. If the calling program was DOS, a RETURN statement causes the Clipper application to terminate.

You can use the QUIT statement to cause an immediate termination of the Clipper application. Clipper closes any open database and index files prior to returning to DOS.

Key Points

Exiting Looping Structures

Always include a way of getting out of the loop. This may be a condition to be met (such as end-of-file marker) or an EXIT or RETURN statement executed within the looping construct.

Numeric Problems

Programmers usually run into problems with numeric variable types as a result of not allowing enough room in database fields to store the amounts. Be aware that when you use the ROUND() or INT() function, there is the possibility of losing part of the number in the process.

Memo Field Considerations

Before creating a memo field in your database, you should consider how much data is going into it. It may suffice to create an 80-character comment field instead.

continues . . .

Array Flexibility

It is possible to store a function's name as an array element and still be able to activate it. Arrays provide the ability to store both data and functions in an array. This is very close to object-oriented programming.

Generic Functions with the Type Functions

TYPE() and VALTYPE() can be very useful in creating generic functions. A function could be set up so that any data type can be passed to it as a parameter. The function could use the TYPE() or VALTYPE() function to determine the type and make the necessary conversion to process the data.

Writing Buffers

Be aware that data is not always written to the disk drive. It may be stored in a record buffer temporarily. You can use the SKIP 0 and COMMIT commands to write the information contained in the buffers to the hard disk.

dBASE Index Files

Clipper provides the ability to use dBASE III format index files. Keep in mind that the Clipper method of indexing is more efficient than the dBASE III format and should be used whenever possible.

continues . . .

Zapping Databases

The ZAP command deletes the contents of the database while leaving the structure intact. This is a potentially damaging command and great care must be taken when using it. The ZAP command physically removes all the records from a database.

System Clock

You can access the clock in your computer by using the DATE(), TIME(), and SECONDS() functions. Keep in mind that these are only as accurate as the date and time on your system clock. If the battery goes out, these functions will not return correct values.

File Handles and DOS 3.1 or Below

MS DOS versions 3.1 and below limit the number of file handles your program can access. The OS() function returns the name of the operating system and can be used to determine if this is a potential problem for your program.

CHAPTER

Special Tools and Features

This chapter concentrates on the fine-tuning of an application. You accomplish this fine-tuning through memory management, data-driven techniques, compile and link options, and the use of various programming techniques.

The MAKE utility is discussed as a way to make the compile and link cycle trouble free. The use of the Clipper debugger is discussed as a way to find problems in programs quickly.

Memory Considerations

Recall from Chapter 2 that computer memory is a temporary, high-speed storage area where data and programs reside while they are being processed. Storage is temporary since anything residing in memory is lost whenever you shut off the computer.

Memory can be a problem when your application becomes very large or when the machine you are attempting to run your application on has very little memory to begin with. As a result of the original INTEL 8086 architecture, memory may only be mapped up to 655,535 bytes (referred to as 640K). All programs must fit into this space in order to run.

A part of this 640K is used up by the operating system. In addition, network software such as IPX.COM and NETn.COM (where n indicates the DOS version) can occupy a portion of this 640K. Any other memory-resident software, such as menus, popup calculators, and clocks also take up an additional portion of this base 640K. The remaining amount of memory can be used by your application.

There have been many schemes developed to overcome this boundary. One is the ability to load part of the operating system and other memory-resident software into *extended memory* (memory beyond the 640K limit), thereby leaving a greater portion of the 640K for your applications. However, these schemes may not always be available on the machines where your application will be run. For that reason you still need to watch the memory requirements of your application.

Watching Your Memory

Upon successful completion of the linking of your Clipper program, the linker will return the load size, as shown here:

```
C:\CUST>rtlink file cust
.RTLink for Clipper Dynamic Overlay Linker/Pre-Linker Version 3.13
(C) Copyright Pocket Soft Inc., 1988-1991. All Rights Reserved.

246K
```

The 246K indicates the amount of memory required to load the program into memory, even though the size of the file may be larger. As you add more code to your program, the load size will increase. You can also use the Clipper MEMORY() function to watch the memory in your application. While you are developing your application, you can place the MEMORY() function at strategic places throughout the program to watch the memory. MEMORY(0) will return the amount of memory available for character values. MEMORY(2) will return the amount of memory allocated for the RUN/! command.

You want to watch memory so you can catch and correct potential memory problems before sending the application to your client. If you have a good idea of the memory requirements of your clients, you can predict problems by watching memory on your own machine.

You can modify the SET CLIPPER statement to reduce the memory available on your own machine to simulate the memory available on your client's machines. You do this by using the X switch of the SET CLIPPER statement, as shown here:

SET CLIPPER=F:59;X:64

In this example, the F switch sets the number of file handles available to 59. The X switch reduces the available memory on your machine by 64K. This number can be adjusted up or down while you are testing your application.

Memory Management

Imagine your job is to valet park 1000 cars. Your main car park has room for 640 cars. The restaurant staff uses up 55 spots, so you have 585 spots left. Fortunately, you have another parking lot across a busy street. The restaurant's customers are not going to park their cars there and cross the busy street; that is your job. This other parking lot has room for 360 cars. A football team drives up in 20 cars. They want all the cars parked together. At first you park the cars in the main parking lot. Then the team's supporters show up in 200 buses, and each bus takes up two spots. Your available space drops to 165 spots in the main parking lot. Now the opposing team's fans show up and require 175 spots—all together, of course. You figure the original football team will be in there for a while, so you move their 20 cars across the street, put a little marker on the board to remind you they are there, and then park the 175 vehicles of the opposing team. When you see the original team preparing to come back outside, you rush across the street with 20 other cars from the main lot and rush back with the 20 cars belonging to the team and put them in the main lot. This juggling and switching back and forth is what *memory managers* do.

The Clipper memory manager performs the juggling and swapping of program variables and code. Ideally, you would like your entire application to be loaded into memory. Since this is not possible most of the time, the Clipper memory manager uses overlays, disk swapping, and extended memory to get around the problem.

Overlays

Overlays allow very large applications to run in a limited amount of memory. Normally, all of a program loads into memory at once. If the program was 400K and it used 200K of memory variables and buffers, the program would terminate with an "out of memory" error. To solve this problem, a scheme called *overlaying* was developed. Instead of all 400K of the program loading into memory, only a portion of it is loaded.

The Clipper *overlay manager* controls the loading in and swapping of code sections while the application is running. The memory manager keeps track of which code is currently loaded in memory. When a new section of code is called, the overlay manager checks to see if it is already in memory. If it is not, the memory manager discards a low-use section of code currently in memory in order to load the new section of code.

Many programs today use overlay technology to allow them to run applications larger than 1 megabyte in 640K of memory. The main problem is encountered when there is not enough memory to keep enough of the program in memory at the same time. The application may slow to a crawl while sections of code are swapped in and out of memory repeatedly.

Extended Memory

Another mechanism for handling this memory problem is to use extended memory, or memory beyond the 640K barrier. Most 286 and above machines are shipped with at least 1 megabyte of memory. Clipper will take advantage of this additional memory. The area between 640K and one megabyte is called *high memory.* The area beyond 1 megabyte is called *expanded memory* and is different from high memory because special software must be used to access it.

A large portion of DOS 5 can be placed into high memory. Network software and other memory-resident programs can also be loaded into high memory. This frees up more of the initial 640K to be used by your application.

Memory Variable Swapping

In low-memory situations, the Clipper memory manager will attempt to swap memory variables either to extended memory or to a temporary disk file if extended memory is not available. This stored information is later pulled into main memory as needed.

Memory Considerations in Programming

You should always be aware of memory. You will not always be able to dictate the hardware that your application will be run on. The user may have memory requirements you are not aware of. Suppose the user is running a DOS version prior to 5 on a network. The user has requirements for numerous memory-resident programs. By the time your monster Clipper program is loaded into memory, there is very little memory remaining. Because you are running the Clipper program on the network, and because all of the Clipper executable file will not fit in available memory, Clipper is having to swap to disk—a disk that is at the other end of a network cable. Your application slows down drastically as it loads and unloads sections of code.

Overlaying Code

Recall from Chapter 2 that RTLINK.EXE is a dynamic overlay linker. Dynamic overlays allow programs larger than available memory to run by swapping sections of code in and out of memory as needed. Instead of leaving it up to Clipper to swap functions in and out of memory, you can specify which sections of code will remain in memory at all times.

Certain routines that are called over and over by your application should remain in memory at all times. This process could be applied to the sample application developed in Chapters 4, 5, and 6. There is really no need to keep the report programs in memory while you are entering transactions. The same goes for the system maintenance functions. If you are making backups, the code for data entry and reports does not have to be in memory.

RTLINK allows you to specify the modules that will reside in memory continuously or be handled dynamically. The term *dynamic* indicates that the program will be swapped in and out of memory as needed. The term *resident* indicates that the program will reside in memory at all times. In the sample application, you could specify that certain functions, such as the menu programs and the dialog box, remain in memory at all times. You could do this by combining those routines in a single file called MYLIB.PRG. You can pass the files and libraries to be linked to RTLINK by using the following DOS command:

RTLINK FILE CUST MYLIB SCREENS REPORTS SYS

At some point, you will want to split up your application into many files. The menu, report, and system utilities should be split into separate files. You will need to compile each file separately, using CLIPPER.EXE. You could continue to call RTLINK from the command line by using this command:

RTLINK @CUST

The @ symbol tells the linker to use the link script file following the symbol. The link script file, called CUST.LNK, which is used in the preceding command, is created by you, the programmer, and contains the following statements:

```
RESIDENT
FILE cust,mylib
DYNAMIC
FILE screens,reports,sys
```

The files are listed using the FILE statement. The RESIDENT keyword causes any subsequent Clipper-compiled modules (cust,mylib) to be loaded into the root section of the executable file. When the executable file is run, that code will remain in memory at all times. The DYNAMIC keyword causes any subsequent Clipper-compiled modules (screens,reports,sys) to be loaded into the overlay area of the executable file. A more detailed description of RTLINK options follows in the section "Clipper Link Options" later in this chapter.

Memory Variables

Recall from Chapter 5 that you should use constants whenever possible. Variable names take up system memory since variables must reside in a symbol table. The symbol table is a list in memory of all the variable names and function names. Using constants conserves memory because constants do not occupy space in the symbol table.

You should use static and local variables in favor of public and private variables whenever possible. Each public and private variable uses 20 bytes of memory in the symbol table, in addition to the bytes required for the actual value of the variable.

Using Databases for Other Tasks

It is common practice to store information used by your program in databases rather than hardcoding it into the program itself. This allows you to change items easily by simply making changes to the database. A common example is to store the color scheme used by a program in a database.

You can also save the data as memory variables to a .MEM file, using the SAVE ALL LIKE command. You can save the data as a very long character string to a text file by using Clipper's low-level file functions, such as FOPEN() and FWRITE(). These methods involve a great deal more work than storing information into database files.

It is possible to make a whole application data driven. Screen layouts, menu choices, messages, and even database structures could be stored in databases. Some applications provide all the capabilities to develop systems without ever having to compile and link programs. A design module allows the user to design a system, with that design stored in databases. A run module runs the design. No code is generated or needed, and the system is very easy to change.

Storing Color Scheme to a Database

It is fairly common to store the color schemes used in a program in a database. Recall that the SETCOLOR() function accepts a color string as a parameter, as in the following examples.

The line

```
SETCOLOR("W/R")
```

sets the color to white characters on a red background. The color string can also be stored to a variable and used in the SETCOLOR() function, as shown here:

```
l_errcolor := "W/R"
SETCOLOR(l_errcolor)
```

It is a good idea to declare different color variables for different uses. As an example, white characters on a red background might be used for error messages or warnings. White characters on a blue background might be used for normal text display. Your program could initialize these variables at program startup. The problem is that you have to recompile and relink your program in order to change the colors. A better method is to store the character strings used for the various colors in a database. A database called Colors might have the following format:

Field Name	Field Type	Field Length
Program	C	10
Says	C	10
Gets	C	10
Border	C	10
Error	C	10

Each field would contain a character string indicating the color associated with each purpose. At the beginning of your program, the Colors database would be opened and the color strings stored to public variables that can be used throughout the application. In this way, the color settings for the program are embedded in data (databases) rather than in code. That section of code becomes *data driven* instead of *code driven*.

Lookup Tables

Another common use of the data-driven technique is to store lists in databases. You might have a list of states referenced when data is entered into the State field, a list of customer types, a list of part names, a list of ZIP codes and tax rates, or a list of shoe sizes. This type of information would occupy considerable memory if stored in arrays.

The advantage of storing the data in a database rather than hardcoding the data in your program is that the data is easily changed. Suppose you used a database to store a list of state codes and their associated tax rates. If the tax rates change, you could simply go into the database and make the changes. If the tax rates had been hardcoded into the application program, you would need to recompile and relink the program. Also, you would have to send the user a new copy of the executable file.

Help Information

Probably the most common use of data-driven methods is for implementing a help system. In this case, the name of the entry field or menu item the user requires help with is stored in a database along with the help message. If the user presses a hot key, the function associated with the hot key could handle the help message. Recall from Chapter 5 that functions can be assigned to certain keys. These are called hot keys because when the key is pressed, the function is immediately executed. The function could determine where the key was pressed and look in the database to get the appropriate help information.

Programming on a Network

Chapter 7 discussed the mechanics of networking, such as record and file locking and network error checking. What was not covered is how networks can affect your programming activities.

Since all the users on a network are usually accessing the same hard disk, the failure of that hard disk or some network component within the system will affect all the users on the network. As an example, a bad network card may appear to work fine except when a very large file is indexed. The user (or your program) may not even know that something went wrong while the file was being indexed. As another example, suppose the electronic mail system takes priority over data transfers on the network system. The user may wait a long time waiting for his or her changes to be updated on the network disk drive.

The normal reason for having a network is to use common databases and to share peripherals such as printers and modems. Consequently, there is usually a lot of traffic coming and going on the network. *Traffic* is the data transferred to and from the file server. The *file server* is the computer that contains the network operating system and the common storage area for shared files. There is a limited amount of traffic that the file server can handle at a given time. In this melee, you may be searching for records in a shared database, extracting data, posting data, and possibly indexing over a network. The speed at which the data is transferred over the network cable is limited. An increase in the number of users on a network may increase the traffic to an unacceptable level. The users may have to wait for the software while their data transfers take place.

You can take steps to minimize the amount of traffic that will take place among the various work stations on a network. It is a good idea to think carefully about where to store data and when to process data off-line (on your local machine), such as indexing a database, and to structure your programs so they grab a block of data, go offline, process the data, and then go back online to post it.

Certain actions, such as normal data entry, will require records to be locked while the user is working on the record. Other actions should be reviewed carefully to expose data as little as possible to the vagaries of network systems. It is a good idea to reduce traffic as much as possible when there are many users on the system. An example of this would be to "print" a report to a file on a local hard disk. The output does not have to travel through the network since it is stored on a local drive. At the end of the day, the file can be printed on the network printer. In this way, the traffic caused by the report is eliminated during peak hours, which improves the speed at which other work stations can perform data transfers.

Index files are usually the first victims of network problems. Indexes can become corrupted for many reasons. For example, perhaps a work station had a power failure during an update operation. It may not be obvious that an index file has been corrupted. The user may indicate that certain customers or transactions are "missing" from the system.

Routines used to index the files in your application should always be included as part of the system utilities. It is a good idea to keep track of how long it takes to reindex files. If you should have to reindex during peak business hours, you can notify all users that you have to take the system down temporarily and give them an idea of how long it is going to take. The users may not be happy that they are being taken off the system. If at all possible, wait until the end of the day to perform anything that requires all activity to stop.

Clipper Compiler Options

You specify the compiler options by typing a forward slash followed by the letter for each option, as shown here:

clipper cust /L

This would compile a program called Cust using the L switch. The L switch indicates that line numbers will not be embedded in the resulting object file. Clipper automatically inserts line numbers so a line number can be displayed in the event of a run-time error. If you remove the line number information, the resultant .OBJ file can be reduced in size by 3 bytes per line. However, you will not be able to use the debugger on programs that were compiled using the /L option. In addition, run-time errors occurring in those modules will return a line number of zero. It may be difficult to determine exactly where in the program the run-time error occurred. Table 8-1 gives a list of the available compiler switches.

You must use the /B switch if you plan to run your program under the Clipper debugger. This makes the program bigger, and it should be removed from the compile statement if the resulting executable file will be sent to the end user.

It is possible to compile only certain parts of your code by using the #ifdef and #end statements, like this:

```
#ifdef DEMO
* code for demo in here
#end
```

By setting up various sections of code in this manner, you can control the code that is actually compiled by using the /D switch of the compiler. In the preceding example, the section of code between the #ifdef DEMO and #end statements will compile only if the DEMO identifier is defined as part of the compile statement, as shown here:

clipper myprog /DDEMO

TABLE 8-1 Compiler Switches

Switch	Parameter	Action
/A		Performs automatic declaration of public and private variables.
/B		Includes debugging information.
/D	*identifier*[=*text*]	Defines an identifier to the preprocessor. Used when you want to specify conditional compilation directives.
/I	*pathname*	Expands the include directory search list.
/L		Suppresses line numbers.
/M		Compiles only the current .PRG file.
/N		Suppresses automatic main procedure.
/O	*objfile*	Compiles to a specified object name.
/P		Produces a preprocessed output listing.
/Q		Suppresses line number display.
/R	*libfile*	Tells the linker where to search for unresolved externals.
/S		Checks syntax only. An object file is not created.
/T	*pathname*	Specifies the location of temporary files.
/U	*headerfile*	Preprocesses with an alternate header file.
/V		Treats all ambiguous variable references as dynamic variables.
/W		Generates warning messages for ambiguous variable references.

This compiles the demo code. If the /DDEMO part of the statement is removed, the demo code would not be compiled. You can also use the #else statement to specify an alternate section of code to be compiled if the identifier directive is not included.

You can use the /U compiler option to create your own Clipper commands. You can make a copy of the file called std.ch in the Clipper include directory. You can add or modify the commands as described in Chapter 10. You would use the /U option to force the new file to be the de facto definitions, as in this example:

CLIPPER myprog /Umystyle.ch

This would force the mystyle.ch definition file to override any declarations contained in the std.ch file.

You use the /W switch to identify *ambiguous variables* in programs— that is, when a field and a variable share the same name—and the compiler wants to know which one to use. The default is to treat ambiguous names as fields. /V forces the compiler to cause ambiguous names to default to variables. The compiler will generate a warning message for undeclared or unaliased variable references. This /W switch tightens up your code by finding and explicitily declaring variables to be of a certain type.

The /V switch forces the compiler to assume that all undeclared or unaliased variables are public or private variables.

The first program in an application normally is not specifically declared as a procedure or a function. If you want to explicitly name a procedure and function at the top of the program, such as FUNCTION main, you must use the /N option. This tells Clipper that the first procedure or function that it comes across is the main procedure.

Normally, Clipper will compile not only the program mentioned on the compile line, but also any other programs mentioned within that program if they are present in the same directory. You use the /M option to compile only the program you specify.

If you were working on one program within a group and wanted to quickly check the syntax of the program, you could use /M and /S in combination, as in this example:

CLIPPER myprog /M /S

If your program has many errors, the error listing might scroll past too quickly for you to determine what you need to fix. You could use the DOS redirection command to redirect the output of the Clipper compiler to a text file, as shown here:

CLIPPER myprog /M /S > ERRLIST

The > redirection symbol sends any screen output from the compiler to the text file called ERRLIST. You could view this file to determine if any errors exist.

Clipper Link Options

The linker, RTLINK, also has options for linking programs together. You can perform many tasks with this linker. You can link a file on the command line, like this:

RTLINK FILE myprog

If you have several programs, the link command would look like this:

RTLINK FILE myprog, prog2, prog3

and RTLINK will not only link them but will also link the support programs as dynamic. This means the support programs will be swapped in and out of memory as needed.

Another way RTLINK works is to process a link script file, as discussed in the section "Overlaying Code" earlier in this chapter. Here is an example of a link script file called MYLINK.LNK:

```
RESIDENT
FILE myprog
DYNAMIC
FILE prog2, prog3
```

Recall that RTLINK allows you to specify files to be placed in resident or dynamic memory. "Dynamic" indicates that the program will be swapped in and out of memory as needed. "Resident" indicates that the program will reside in memory at all times. In this example, MYPROG will remain in memory at all times, and PROG2 and PROG3 will have their functions swapped in and out of memory as needed.

Prelink Libraries

You can also *prelink* files. This means you can create a library of functions that can be used by one or more executable files. The prelink file (which has an extension of .PLL) is distributed with the executable file and contains portions of the code required to run the executable file. The code contained in a prelink library is usually code that is very rarely modified. This includes code found in CLIPPER.LIB and EXTEND.LIB, as well as in your own library of functions that do not change very often.

Advantages of Prelink Files

The prelink library is a Clipper feature that should not be overlooked. The prelink library has three distinct advantages, as described here.

Increased Link Speed The speed of the linking process increases since the code contained in the prelink file has already been linked. The amount of time saved varies, depending on the code you choose to include in the prelink library.

Decreased Size of the Executable File The size of the executable file is usually considerably smaller when a prelink library is used. The overall size of the code is not reduced and may actually be increased in some cases. Once the .PLL file has been sent to the client, it does not need to be sent again unless changes are made to the code within it. Since this is rarely done, the only code that needs to be sent is the executable file.

Prelink libraries are very important if you send application updates over a modem. For example, you could fix a bug and send the executable file over the modem. The time it takes to send the executable file would be considerably less.

Reduced Disk Space   You can use a prelink library for more than one executable file. If you had more than one Clipper application, the total disk space required to store the applications would be decreased. As an example, suppose you had three applications written in Clipper and each application was approximately 500K. The total disk space required would be 1.5 megabytes. If you used a prelink library, the resulting executable files would be approximately 200K each and the prelink library would be approximately 350K. Thus, the overall disk space required would be reduced by 550K.

Using and Creating Prelink Libraries

If you have successfully installed Clipper 5, a directory called \CLIPPER5\PLL has been created. Three files, called BASE50.LNK, BASE50.PLL, and BASE50.PLT, should reside in that directory. BASE50.LNK is a link script file used to create the prelink files called BASE50.PLT and BASE50.PLL. The prelinked transfer file (.PLT) is needed when you link your application using a prelink library. This file contains information about addresses and segments within the .PLL file. If an application has been linked using the prelinked library option, the associated .PLL file must be available when your application program is run.

Using the Standard Prelink Library   You can take advantage of the prelink library option by adding the following line to your link file:

```
/PLL:BASE50
```

This tells the linker to use the prelink library when linking your application. The resultant executable file will be considerably smaller than the original. However, the file called BASE50.PLL must accompany the executable file in order for it to run.

Here is a complete link file used previously, with the addition of the prelink library option:

```
/PLL:BASE50
RESIDENT
FILE myprog
```

```
DYNAMIC
FILE prog2, prog3
```

The BASE50.PLT file must be accessible when linking the preceding link script file. The file can be in the same directory where the linking is taking place. If not, the PLL environment statement should be set up in the following manner:

```
SET PLL=C:\CLIPPER5\PLL;
```

Place this statement in your AUTOEXEC.BAT file so the linker will always be able to find the BASE50.PLL file.

Creating Your Own Prelink Library   At some point, you may want to add your own functions and procedures to the prelink library. Keep in mind that you do not want to include routines that are likely to change. If you have to make changes to any of the programs contained in the prelink library, a new .PLL file must be distributed with your application.

The BASE50.LNK file is a good starting point for creating your own prelink libraries. Here is what the unmodified BASE50.LNK file looks like:

```
prelink

output base50

lib clipper, extend, terminal, dbfntx

refer _VOPS, _VMACRO, _VDB, _VDBF, _VDBFNTX
refer _VTERM, _VPICT, _VGETSYS
refer _VDBG

exclude ERRORSYS
```

The PRELINK statement in the first line of the link script file indicates that a prelink library should be created. The OUTPUT statement indicates the desired name of the .PLL and .PLT files. The LIB statement indicates which libraries should be linked to the prelink library. The REFER statement forces the linking of the referenced modules into the resultant prelink library. The EXCLUDE statement indicates files that should not be linked into the prelink library.

Suppose you had a routine you wanted to include in the prelink library called PROG2.PRG, as shown here:

```
? "this is prog2"
```

You would first compile the program, as shown here:

CLIPPER prog2

This creates the object file called PROG2.OBJ, assuming the compile was successful. At this point you can include the file in the BASE50.LNK, as shown here:

```
prelink
file prog2
output base50

lib clipper, extend, terminal, dbfntx

refer _VOPS, _VMACRO, _VDB, _VDBF, _VDBFNTX
refer _VTERM, _VPICT, _VGETSYS
refer _VDBG

exclude ERRORSYS
```

The only thing different with this link file is that the FILE statement was used to indicate that the PROG2 program should be included in the prelink library. You could include any number of your programs in the same manner.

You then create the prelink library by typing the following command at the DOS prompt:

RTLINK @BASE50

This creates two files called BASE50.PLL and BASE50.PLT. The prelink library (including PROG2) is now available for use.

You will not want to include any programs that are likely to change in the prelink library. Suppose your system contained two files called MYPROG.PRG and PROG1.PRG, as shown here:

```
* prog1.prg

? "this is prog1"

* myprog.prg

? "This is myprog"
prog1()
prog2()
```

myprog.prg simply displays a message and calls the two procedures called prog1 and prog2. Recall that prog2 was included in the prelink library. You would compile the preceding programs by typing the following commands at the DOS prompt:

CLIPPER prog1
CLIPPER myprog

This creates two object files called prog1.obj and myprog.obj, assuming the compile was successful. The following link script file would be used to link myprog and prog1 using the prelink library developed earlier in this section:

```
FILE myprog
FILE prog1
OUTPUT myprog
/PLL:BASE50
```

The FILE statement indicates the files that should be linked (myprog and prog1) in order to create the executable file. The OUTPUT statement indicates the desired name of the executable file. The /PLL:BASE50 statement tells the linker that the resultant executable file should use the prelink library called BASE50.PLL.

There is a considerable difference in the size of the executable file. myprog.exe created without the prelink library would be 146,432 bytes. myprog.exe created by using the prelink library would be 5120 bytes. The BASE50.PLL would have to accompany the executable file but would have to be sent to your client only the first time.

Clipper Make Options

RMAKE.EXE is a program that manages the assembly of your program. You could create a file with an .RMK extension and invoke it using this format:

rmake mymake

The make file called MYMAKE.RMK would include information such as the files included in the application and the compile and link instructions. The RMAKE program compares the creation date and time of the .PRG file with the date and time of the .OBJ file to determine if the program needs to be recompiled. If you were working on a large application that required you to edit code in 5 separate programs out of a possible 20, you would have to remember which files to recompile or else recompile them all. RMAKE compiles only the programs that have changed since the last time you compiled. Here is an example of an .RMK file:

```
.prg.obj:
    clipper $< /m

.obj.exe:
    set rtlinkcmd=/posi
    rtlink $**, $@ ;

rlfront.obj:    rlfront.prg
rlback.obj:     rlback.prg
rldialg.obj:    rldialg.prg

rl.exe:         rlfront.obj  rlback.obj  rldialg.obj
```

This is used by Clipper to compile and link the report and label writer program included with Clipper 5. The lines

```
.prg.obj:
    clipper $< /m
```

are the *dependency rules* for .PRG and .OBJ files. RMAKE compares the date of the item on the left to the date of the item on the right. If the item on the left has a more recent date, the action is performed. These two lines go hand in hand with the *dependency statements,* as shown here:

```
rlfront.obj:    rlfront.prg
rlback.obj:     rlback.prg
rldialg.obj:    rldialg.prg
```

Each of the lines is evaluated using the dependency rules in the following manner:

```
If (date/time of rlfront.obj) < (date/time of rlfront.prg)
   clipper rlfront /m
```

RMAKE uses the dependency rule and makes the appropriate substitutions in order to determine if the action (clipper $< /m) needs to be performed.

The dependency rules for the executable file are set up in a similar way, as shown here:

```
.obj.exe:
    set rtlinkcmd=/posi
    rtlink $**, $@ ;
```

This defines the commands to perform if any of the object files have a more recent date and time than the executable file. It goes hand in hand with the dependency statement shown here:

```
rl.exe:         rlfront.obj  rlback.obj  rldialg.obj
```

RMAKE checks the date/time stamps on all the object files listed. If any have a date/time stamp more recent than the date/time stamp on the executable file, the dependency actions will be taken. The set rtlinkcmd=/posi will be executed followed by the RTLINK command.

The RTLINK command includes a *MAKE macro* that allows you to access dependency information from the last dependency statement encountered. Following is a complete list of the predefined MAKE macros:

Macro	Purpose
$*	Expands to target filename without path or extension
$@	Expands to target filename with path and extension
$**	Expands to complete list of dependency filenames
$<	Expands to full name of dependency file that triggered the rule
$?	Expands to list of dependencies that have a more recent date/time stamp than the target file

In the dependency rule for the executable file, the $** expands to a complete list of the full dependency filenames. The $@ expands to the target filename, including the path and extension. The resulting statement would look like this:

RTLINK RLFRONT RLBACK RLDIALG, RL.EXE

It would create the desired executable file.

Finding Bugs Quickly Using the Clipper Debugger

Your program will inevitably have bugs. There are just too many variables to possibly get everything right the first time. Some of the bugs will be easy to fix. Other bugs may make your life very difficult. The first task when tracking down a bug is to duplicate it. This may not be easy to do since the problem may occur only during unusual circumstances. Once you are able to duplicate the problem, the next task is to fix it.

Clipper 5 comes with a debugger you can use to track down bugs and test code on a line-by-line basis. A *debugger* is a program that helps you look at your Clipper application in much the same way as a microscope is used to look at blood cells. The debugger lets you look at the contents of your variables and tells you which databases are open and which program is currently active. It allows you to step through the lines of your code one line at a time if desired. In this way, you can run through the logic of your program and determine why it is not working correctly.

You load the debugger by typing **cld** followed by the name of the executable file. CLD.EXE is loaded into memory first. Then CLD loads your program into memory. Since both are loaded at the same time, the overall memory available to your program is reduced. The line

cld cust

loads the debugger and an executable file called CUST.EXE.

Provided you have compiled your programs with the /B compile switch, a debugger screen similar to the one shown in Figure 8-1 is presented to you. The startup code of your program is shown in the middle of the screen. The ALT key submenu items are displayed at the top of the screen. By pressing any of the ALT key combinations, you can access various options within the debugger.

The debugger does not do anything until you instruct it to begin. You can use the menu to access the various debugger options, or you can press F5 to start your program. Clipper also provides single keystrokes that you can press instead. For example, you could press ALT-R to pull up the Run submenu and then press the G (go) key to start the program. Another alternative is to press F5. Either way begins execution of your application program. Suppose you were attempting to debug this sample program:

```
m_age := "20"
DO func1
? "Jack is " + m_age + " years old"

PROCEDURE func1
m_age := "30"
? "Jill is " + m_age + " years old"
RETURN
```

This example was taken from Chapter 4. You have discovered that the program is not displaying Jack's age correctly. (This is a very simple example, but it demonstrates the use of the debugger.) The file is loaded into the debugger and the screen shown in Figure 8-2 is displayed. The first line of your program is highlighted. The debugger waits for you to perform some action. You could press F5 to start the program. This would run the program just as if you had run it from the DOS prompt. You can

FIGURE 8-1

Initial Clipper debugger screen

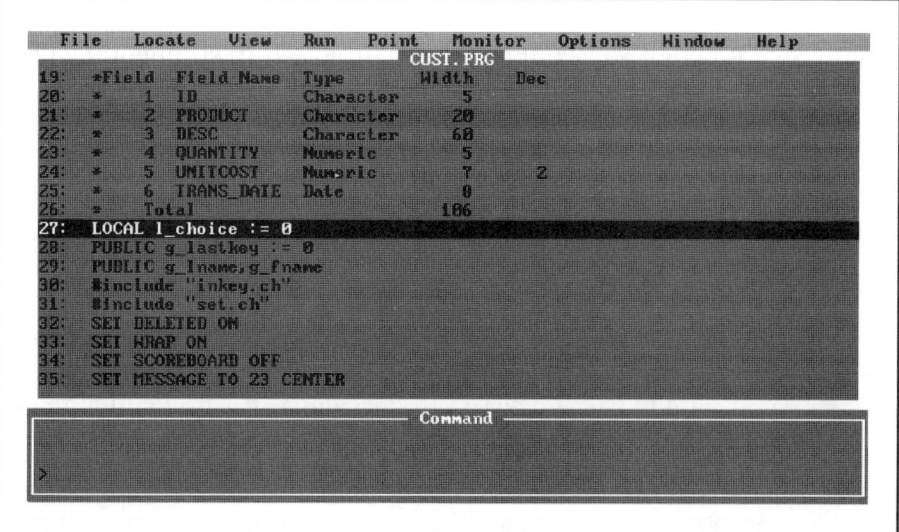

```
  File   Locate   View   Run   Point   Monitor   Options   Window   Help
                              CUST.PRG
19:   *Field   Field_Name   Type        Width   Dec
20:   *     1   ID           Character     5
21:   *     2   PRODUCT      Character    20
22:   *     3   DESC         Character    60
23:   *     4   QUANTITY     Numeric       5
24:   *     5   UNITCOST     Numeric       7      2
25:   *     6   TRANS_DATE   Date          8
26:   *    Total                         106
27:   LOCAL l_choice := 0
28:   PUBLIC g_lastkey := 0
29:   PUBLIC g_lname,g_fname
30:   #include "inkey.ch"
31:   #include "set.ch"
32:   SET DELETED ON
33:   SET WRAP ON
34:   SET SCOREBOARD OFF
35:   SET MESSAGE TO 23 CENTER
                           Command
>
```

FIGURE 8-2

Initial debugger screen—test program

```
  File   Locate   View   Run   Point   Monitor   Options   Window   Help
                              TEST.PRG
1:    m_age := '20'
2:    DO func1
3:    ? "Jack is " + m_age + " years old"
4:
5:    PROCEDURE func1
6:    m_age := '30'
7:    ? "Jill is " + + m_age + " years old"
8:    RETURN
9:    →
10:
11:
12:
13:
14:
15:
16:
17:
                           Command
>
```

press ALT-D while the program is running to halt execution and cause the Debugger menu to be presented.

A better way would be to pull up the Run submenu by pressing ALT-R. The Run submenu options shown in Figure 8-3 are displayed. You can use UP ARROW and the DOWN ARROW to get to the desired item or press the highlighted letter corresponding to the action you want to take. In this case, you want to press the letter S, which causes the debugger to step through a single line of your program. You could accomplish the same thing by pressing F8.

When you press F8, the debugger executes one line of code. The highlighted bar moves to the next statement in your program, as shown in Figure 8-4. Since the variable *m_age* is not getting printed correctly, you want to keep an eye on that variable. The first statement should have initialized the variable to 20.

There are a couple of ways you can check the value of the *m_age* variable. You can check the contents of *m_age* by pressing ALT-M to pull up the Monitor submenu shown in Figure 8-5. You are presented with the various variable visibility types; public, private, static, and local. By selecting the highlighted character, you can cause a watch window to be opened that contains the variables of the selected type.

Since the *m_age* variable was not declared, it will be defined as a private type variable by Clipper. If you press V while in the Monitor submenu, a watch window is opened containing a list of variables, as shown in Figure 8-6. Each line contains the variable's name, visibility, type, and value. In this case, the value is 20.

Another way to display the value of *m_age* would be to execute a command in the Command window. You could type **? m_age**, and the answer would be displayed on the next line, as shown in the Command window at the very bottom of Figure 8-7.

You can press F8 repeatedly to continue stepping through the program while keeping an eye on the *m_age* variable. Notice in Figure 8-8 that the *m_age* value is no longer displayed in the Monitor window (at the top of the screen) while the program is executing the func1 procedure. The *m_age* variable displayed in the Command window remains from the previous action. This tells you the variable is external to the procedure currently running. You can still display the value of *m_age* in the Command window as before.

FIGURE 8-3   The Run submenu

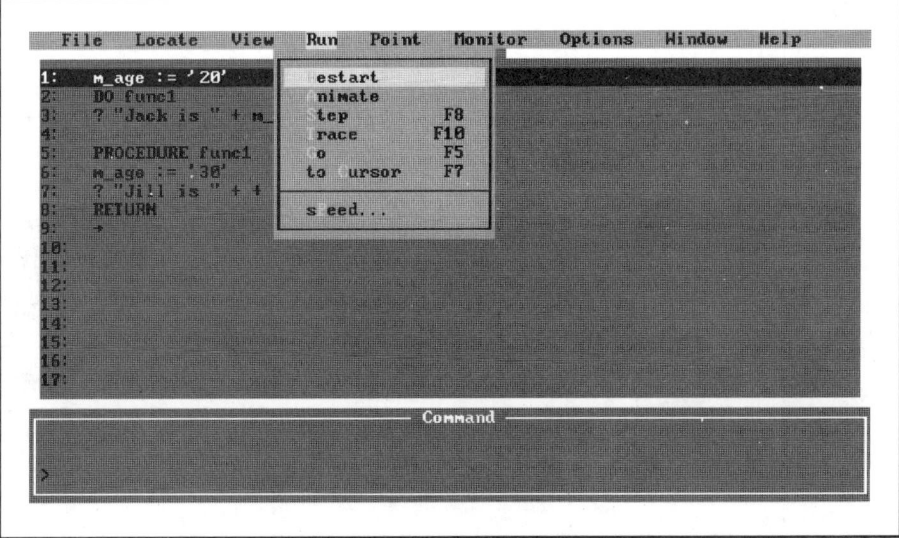

FIGURE 8-4   Stepping through the test program—the second line

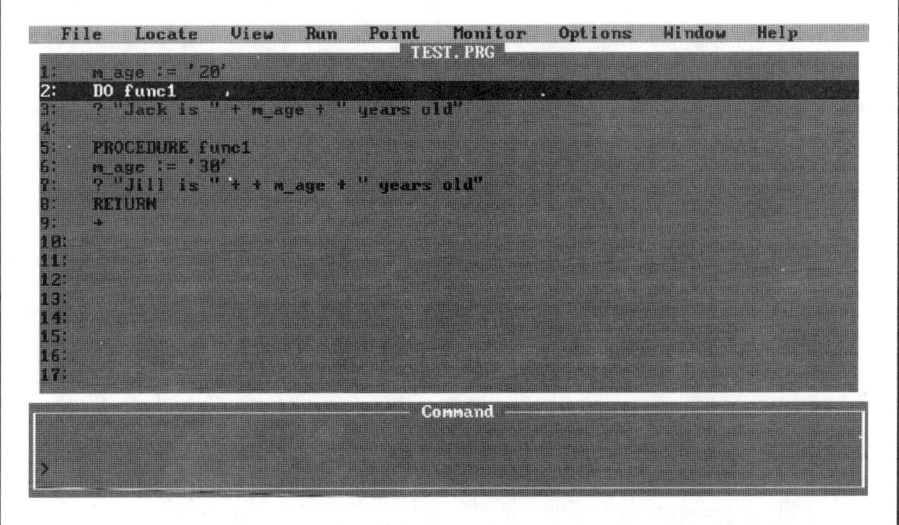

FIGURE 8-5   The Monitor submenu

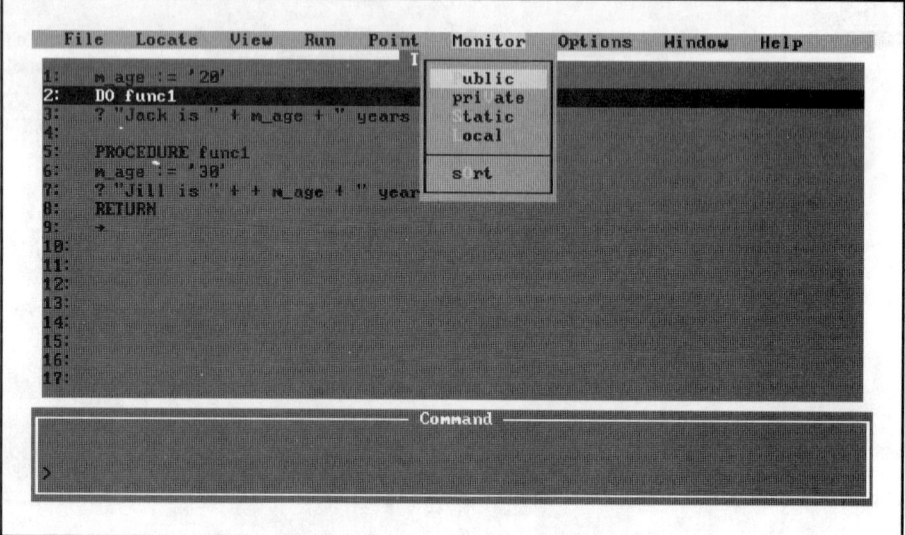

FIGURE 8-6   Monitor window showing the m_age variable

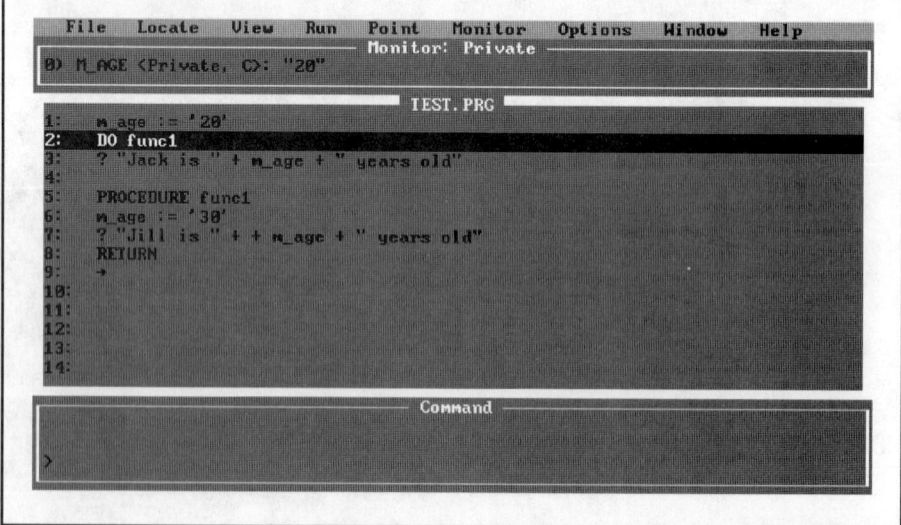

FIGURE 8-7 Command window showing the m_age variable

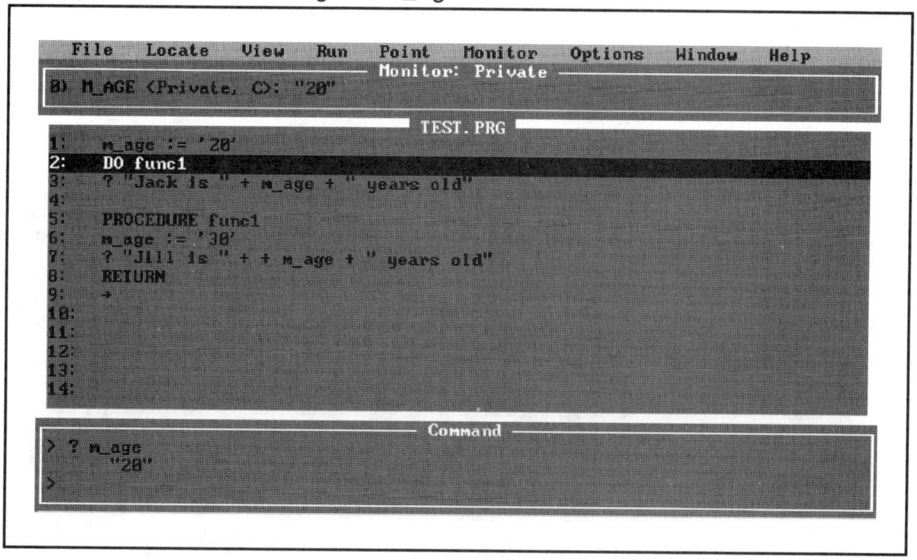

FIGURE 8-8 Stepping through the test program—the func1 procedure

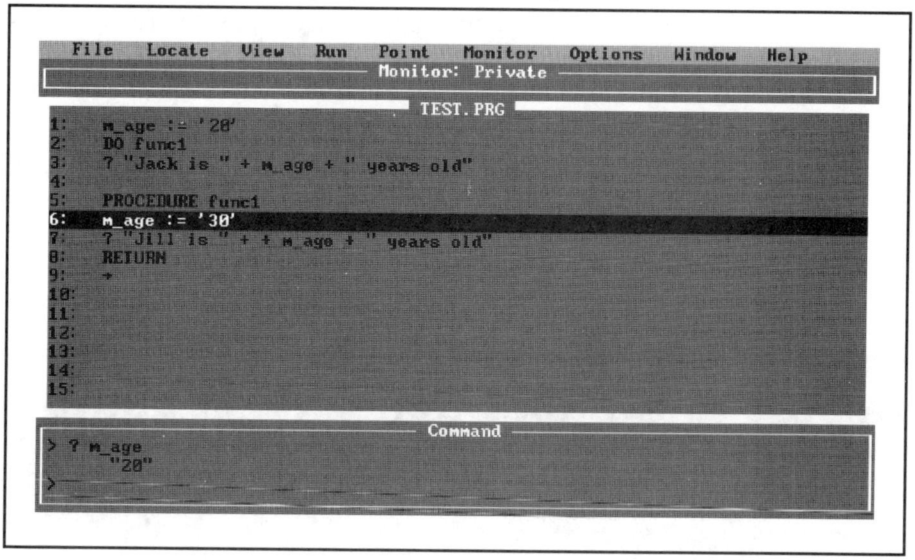

FIGURE
8-9

Stepping through the test program—the print statement

Once you step through the func1 procedure, the highlight bar is positioned at the print statement. At that point you can see that the value of the *m_age* variable has changed to 30 as shown in Figure 8-9. This is a very simple example, but the same technique applies to applications of any size.

The idea is to zero in on the section of code where you think the error might be. If necessary, start with the very first line of your program and step through the code one line at a time. While stepping through the code, continue to monitor the environment, such as the values of variables and the currently open databases. The best way to learn the debugger is to use it. The extra effort required initially will pay off later when you are able to fix bugs quickly. Refer to the Clipper 5 debugger manual for a detailed description of all of the options available.

Report and Label Generation using RL

Clipper has a report and label generator program called RL.EXE. The progam is actually written in Clipper, and the Clipper installation program places it under the SOURCE subdirectory. A report generator is designed to ask you questions about which databases to use and how you would like the information laid out on the printed form. Labels are even simpler since they are basically a report with very few options.

When you start up RL by typing **RL** at the DOS prompt, you are presented with the choices REPORT, LABEL, and QUIT. If you choose REPORT, you are asked to create or open an .FRM file. An .FRM file is used to hold the configuration data that defines the report. You are then asked to define columns for the report. The Contents field is where you enter the name of a field from a database or an expression that is to be printed. Then you are prompted to define a header for that column. You continue filling in questions left, right, and center until you have all the information needed for the report. Once you have saved the data, the report can be used in your program, as shown here:

```
USE Customer INDEX Customer NEW
REPORT FORM myreport TO PRINTER
```

You create labels in much the same way. Label configuration files are created with an .LBL extension. You can create standard labels one, two, or three across. To run the designed and saved .LBL file, enter this code:

```
USE Customer INDEX Customer NEW
LABEL FORM mylabel TO PRINTER
```

The report and label generator program is useful for "quick and dirty" reports, but you should get comfortable writing your own reports. You will have a lot more flexibility in the reports you write yourself.

Online Help Using Norton Guides

Clipper comes with an online help system that explains all the commands, functions, and various utilities in Clipper. The program can be loaded in memory and referenced while you are writing programs. The online help is supplied via the Norton Instant Access Engine, which is placed in the \NG subdirectory during the Clipper installation process. To access the online help system, make sure the \NG directory is included as part of the PATH statement. Type **NG** at the DOS prompt to load the Norton Guides into memory. Once the program has been loaded into memory, you can activate it by pressing SHIFT-F1. Keep in mind that it is a memory-resident program that will take approximately 65K of memory.

Popups, Shadows, and Hot Keys

Once you are comfortable with the basics of Clipper programming, you will wish to enhance your applications with more sophisticated interfaces and user interaction. An example of this would be to provide pick lists. Chapter 5 demonstrated the use of a pick list to allow the user to select a secondary transaction.

A common use of pick lists is to provide answers to data entry fields when the user may not know what to enter. An example would be to provide a pick list of the state codes available to fill in the state code field. The user presses ALT-H to call up a help window. A scrolling list of all of the states is presented to the user.

A nice effect is to display a shadow of the box to produce the illusion that the window is floating above the surface of the screen. Within the shadow, the characters of the previous screen can be barely seen. The user scrolls to Alaska and presses ENTER. The window disappears and the screen looks the same as before except that the letters "AK" have been inserted into the State field.

The same techniques used to produce a pick list for state codes could be applied to other fields such as ZIP codes, general ledger account numbers, employee types, and so on. Following are the basic steps involved.

First, the size of the box on the screen must be decided. You determine the size of the shadow box by adding an extra row and column to the size of the popup window. The shadow area is the area of the screen that must be saved. Once this has been done, here is the sequence of actions:

1. Assign the ALT-H hot key to a specific function before allowing the user to enter data into the screen.
2. Create the function being invoked by the hot key.

3. Create a DO CASE within the function to branch to a specific action, depending on the name of the current field.

4. Create the function that supports the State field.

5. Save the screen section where the box will be painted.

6. Save the screen section where the shadow will be painted.

7. Save the color of the current screen.

8. Change the color to gray text on black.

9. Restore the shadow section onto the screen.

10. Change the screen to a pleasing color.

11. Paint a box on the screen.

12. Invoke ACHOICE with an array containing the names of the states.

13. Get the user's selection and store it in a variable.

14. Restore the original screen color.

15. Restore the shadow screen and the box screen.

16. Stuff the keyboard buffer with the code for the state.

17. Return to the calling program.

The data entry would be initiated in this way:

```
#INCLUDE "inkey.ch"
SET KEY K_CTRL_H TO help
* says and gets
@ 10,10 SAY "State " GET State
* more says and gets
READ
RETURN .T.
```

The CTRL-K key would be assigned to the help function. The pending GETs are initialized and activated by the READ statement. Any time CTRL-K is pressed, the program execution automatically jumps to the help() function shown here:

```
FUNCTION help()
l_var := READVAR()
DO CASE
   CASE l_var == "STATE"
```

```
      statehelp()
   CASE l_var == otherstuff
ENDCASE
RETURN .T.
```

This help() function is set up to handle multiple fields. The READVAR() function returns the variable name of the field the user was on when CTRL-H was pressed. The CASE statement branches to the appropriate function, which handles the pick list. If the user presses CTRL-H while at the State field, the following function is called:

```
FUNCTION statehelp()
l_boxscr := SAVESCREEN(10,10,20,30)
l_shadscr := SAVESCREEN(11,11,21,31)
l_oldcolor := SETCOLOR(g_shadow)
RESTSCREEN(11,11,21,31,l_shadscr))
SETCOLOR(g_nice)
@ 10,10,20,30 BOX g_boxstrng
l_statepos := ACHOICE(11,11,19,29,g_states)
SETCOLOR(l_oldcolor)
RESTSCREEN(11,11,21,31,l_shadscr)
RESTSCREEN(10,10,20,30,l_boxscr)
KEYBOARD g_abbrev[l_statepos]
RETURN .T.
```

The first SAVESCREEN() function saves the area of the screen where the pick list window will be placed. The second SAVESCREEN() statement saves the area of the screen where the shadow area will be displayed. A variable initialized earlier in the program, called *g_shadow*, contains the color that will be used to display the shaded portion of the screen. The character string can be set to W/B,W/B, or you can experiment with other color combinations.

Two arrays, called *g_states* and *g_abbrev*, would have been created near the beginning of the program. The *g_states* array would contain the names of the states. The *g_abbrev* array would contain corresponding abbreviations for those states. The ACHOICE() function displays the pick list, with the resulting state code returned to the *l_statepos* variable. This will contain the element number of the array item selected. The screens are restored as they were before the function was called. The state code is stuffed into the keyboard buffer by using the KEYBOARD() function.

Program execution returns to the data entry screen with the state code filled in.

As you can see, this it not a complicated program, but it adds a great deal of sophistication to the completed data entry screen.

Key Points

Watching Memory

You can determine the memory use required by your application by using the MEMORY() function within the application or by viewing the load size displayed by the linker.

Memory Management

The Clipper memory uses overlays, disk swapping, and extended memory to get around the problem of limited memory.

Overlays

Overlays allow very large applications to run in a limited amount of memory. The Clipper overlay manager controls the loading in and swapping of code sections while the application is running.

continues . . .

Variable Swapping

In low-memory situations, the Clipper memory manager will attempt to swap memory variables either to extended memory or to a temporary disk file. This stored information is later pulled into main memory as needed.

Dynamic and Resident Modules

The Clipper linker allows you to specify the modules that will reside in memory continuously (resident) or be swapped in and out of memory as needed (dynamic).

Data-driven Techniques

You can store screen layouts, menu information, database structures, and report layouts in databases rather than hardcoding them in an application. This allows changes to be made to the system without the need to recompile and relink the program.

Network Traffic

One of the main goals when programming on a network is to reduce as much traffic as possible. Traffic is the data transferred to and from the file server.

continues . . .

Key Points
(continued)

MAKE Utility

You use the Clipper MAKE utility to assist you in maintaining applications.

Debugging Programs

You use the Clipper debugger to track down bugs and to test code on a line-by-line basis.

CHAPTER

Expanding Your Skills

There are many skills that go hand in hand with developing success-ful applications. Many of these have nothing to do with the knowl-edge of the language itself. This chapter discusses the qualities required to be a professional programmer and the importance of communication.

This chapter also discusses the problems and challenges associated with presenting the application to the user and the ongoing maintenance and development of the application. This discussion includes techniques to avoid problems in the first place and ways to handle problems and new developments when they do arise.

Professionalism

Writing hundreds of lines of code per day does not guarantee success in a project. Writing quality code does. You are usually hired to solve a problem. Very often, the user becomes so involved in telling you what code to write that you no longer look carefully at the problem he or she is *really* trying to solve. Sometimes it is best to step back from the system and try to gain or regain the big picture. You may have to mentally unhook yourself from the current task list and put yourself in the user's shoes. Very often, a bolt of lightning strikes, and you go back to the office and write the precise code required to solve the problem—or tell the user how to solve the problem if it does not require programming.

Simply because "programmer" is your job title doesn't mean you have to restrict yourself to those tasks. There are times when an approach that does not even involve your programming abilities may be the best solution. Maybe it is a suggestion to the boss to do things in the office a little differently. It is better to think of yourself as an analyst who is attempting to bring together the overall system, not just the programming aspect of it.

The image you get of a professional is one of a competent problem solver. A professional car mechanic *will* get the car running. A dentist *will* fix your teeth. An airline pilot *will* control the plane correctly. Your job as a programmer is to ensure that the program *will* work correctly. This may take a little longer to achieve in the beginning. As your skill improves, so will your ability to solve problems and your confidence in your abilities. This confidence should be projected to the customer. Clients want to know that you are capable—a professional in your field.

They do not want to hire someone who *might* be able to do the project. They want to hire someone who is confident that the project will be completed correctly and in a satisfactory amount of time.

All professionals study even when they have mastered their immediate profession. There is a continuous stream of new developments and technology. This is especially true in the computer field. As a professional programmer, it is your job to keep on top of all the new information—a very difficult task.

At the very least, you have to know more than your client in the area you are supposed to be the expert in. As an example, it would look bad if you told the client "No! That can't be done; there is not enough memory," only to have your client come back with "I thought the latest version of DOS handles that." Your client is going to wonder about your expertise and perhaps start thinking about finding someone who really knows what he or she is doing.

The ability to keep a mastery of your field involves an ongoing commitment to read all the computer magazines and newspapers you can get your hands on. Get on CompuServe and dial into the Nantucket Forum. Attend programmer user group meetings. You must continue to study if you intend to be a professional in this field.

Knowledge is greatly undervalued in this day and age. One programmer can spend all day struggling to solve a problem, and another programmer may come along and solve the problem in ten seconds. Does the second programmer get paid the day's wages of the first for the ten seconds' worth of work? No! But the second programmer may have spent ten years building up a knowledge base that allows the ten-second solution to happen. This is why experts are usually paid more. Most of the time they do the same work as the rest of us. But once or twice a day the synapses click and a brilliant solution appears.

Professionalism also occurs in the way you do business. This might mean staying at the client site all night long attempting to fix a problem so the client's business will be able to run smoothly the next morning. Professionals can be depended on to pull through no matter what because their own pride and ethics play a large part in seeing that the job is done right. If you did work all night, don't be afraid to tell your client; it will assure them that their business is utmost in your mind.

The computer industry includes numerous professionals—system programmers, application programmers, system analysts, hardware specialists, and networking specialists. There are brilliant system-level programmers who make rotten application programmers. There are brilliant hardware specialists who cannot write programs. You are learning to be an applications programmer. As an applications programmer, you should know at least a limited amount about these other fields. The main thing is that you be aware of the solutions and expertise available and be able to tap into the expertise whenever necessary. Your main goal as a problem solver is not necessarily to always have the answer in your head. It is to be able to get the correct answer when required.

Communicating with the Customer

In order to succeed as a programmer, you need to master the art of communication. There are two parts to communication that must be done effectively in order for a project to succeed. The first part is listening and understanding what the other person is attempting to say. The other part is telling the other person what you want to say and providing him or her with an understanding of what you are saying. In the programming world, the quality of communication can make or break a project.

Suppose a programmer is hired to work on an application. The programmer knows how to program and the client knows how to operate a business. Unfortunately, the programmer does not know the business and the client does not know how to program. The client outlines the type of system required and goes back to the business of running a business. The programmer goes back with the specifications and tries to figure out how to implement the system. Since the client is always too busy or too impatient to answer questions, the programmer avoids communicating with the client after numerous attempts and, instead, has to fill in the missing pieces.

When the system is presented to the client, the client becomes upset that the system is not what was agreed upon. Since money has been spent and contracts signed, the programmer goes back with a set of modifications to be done. The programmer may have bid the job at a fixed price and has to perform a lot of extra unpaid work.

This essentially boils down to a lack of ability to communicate. You must force the communication to take place when the customer is unwilling. Even when the client is willing, the ability to communicate may be lacking. Clients who have had little experience with computers and software may have a difficult time understanding the concepts. In this case, you must go to great lengths to improve the communication. Visual aids such as diagrams or graphs may succeed where verbal communication does not.

If your communication skills are lacking, it is an area you will want to improve. There are many books, workshops, and seminars available on the subject.

Estimating Work

Contracts are an important part of working as an independent programmer. When you make an estimation on a programming job, you had better be exceptional at estimating your ability to produce the specific results in the time you estimate. Nine times out of ten, there is a miscalculation in how long it takes to deliver an application; it always seems to take longer.

When clients make changes to the original request, make sure they know it is going to cost extra. In that way, they will not be shocked when you present the bill at the end of the project. In addition, attaching a cost to items causes the client to think twice about what modifications are really important. Even if you are working as a salaried programmer, you would do well to assign time estimates to programming requests. In this way, your supervisor can more accurately gauge the value of the work.

Whether you are salaried or independent, you may find that a great many requests fall by the wayside when a time or money value is attached to it. In addition, this ensures that you work on the requests that are considered valuable. The tasks you do accomplish add substance to the completed application.

Presenting the Application to the User

When you finally complete your application and deliver it to the clients, don't be surprised if they present you with a list of changes. The user may not realize what is really important or needed until using the application for a while. If you do a good job up front, you can reduce this problem to a minimum.

The development usually takes on a broad focus in the beginning. At this level, the programmer and the customer are concerned with the big issues. You might ask questions such as "Is this a customer tracking system?" and "Is this a billing system?" You will also want to know who is going to use the system during its lifetime, what modules will be added in the future, and what industry changes are likely to affect the future of the application.

Design is probably one of the most neglected areas of custom programming. Customers want to see results as soon as possible and often do not want to pay for the design part of the project. The programmer has to cut corners unless he or she wants to spend their own time on design. Thus, the programmer and the customer rush headlong into the eternal patching of a badly designed system. The programmer must convince the customer that the design of a system is money well spent.

Once an overall design has been developed, it is possible to provide the customer with a portion of the application. This initial version may include only basic data entry and one or two reports. By doing this, you satisfy the customer's need to see something immediately while giving yourself the time to develop the application properly.

The task then becomes one of modifying the existing application. You do this by adding additional data entry fields, enhancing the data entry with error checking and pick lists, and expanding the reports. This is how the first version of Clipper was implemented. A basic set of commands was provided in the beginning. This allowed the basic set to be tested while additional options and commands were being developed. Feedback from the user is available right from the start. This feedback ensures that the development is progressing in the right direction.

This technique could be applied to the sample application developed in Chapters 4, 5, and 6. The initial design determines that the completed application will track customers and their transactions and produce various reports to pull out this information. The basic program is developed that allows the user to enter information about customers and transactions and provides a simple report to list the customers and the products they bought. The basic program is submitted to the user. The programmer may then add more detail to the data entry screens and reports a little bit at a time.

Prepare to Throw One Away

The first three attempts at creating the Clipper program were thrown away. It takes a certain level of courage to throw away code that you slaved to create. More often, code is held close to the heart as the development continues. Sometimes you are going down a programming path and realize it is a dead end. You realize the design may never work—or it will work for a month and then blow itself to bits. Perhaps the system could not be supported properly once installed or there isn't room for future growth.

You should attempt to salvage as much as possible if you decide to scrap a project. This may be screen layouts, some of the database design, and some of the generic functions. Throw the rest out the window. There are two ways to handle a system that is not going to work. The first approach is to admit you made a mistake and accept the heat while there is still time to make the system right. You are either fired or allowed to continue. If you continue, you will then deliver a completed system that works rather than one destined to fail.

The other approach is to go ahead and proceed with the design you know is destined to fail. You deliver the system on schedule and everybody is happy until the system goes down. In some cases, you may even be able to blame the system failure on the weather or some other mysterious "glitch" in the power supply. The system is down and the users are sitting around waiting for you to fix the system. You may catch a lot of heat for a poorly designed system or you may even look like the good guy by getting the system up and running again.

No matter which approach you take, you should be prepared to throw the design away in certain cases. This involves not only throwing the actual code away, but also throwing the mindset away. If a previous approach has failed, then approach the problem from a new angle. Most likely, you will have learned from the problems encountered with the last design.

Anticipating Future Growth

Designing systems that will survive years of abuse and are easily maintained can be quite challenging. If a program is being written that will sort and list data to the printer and never be used again, that program can be written with virtually no standards enforced. The only requisite is that it work right away.

On the other hand, a system that has to survive for years and tolerate many changes during that time had better have very tight standards. Recall that Chapter 3 discussed techniques used to make development and maintenance of code easier. The use of modular programming, top-down design, naming conventions, and adequate documentation allows a future programmer to understand an application even if you are not around anymore.

Quite often a programmer and a system become "married." They live together quite happily for several years and then one day the programmer leaves the relationship. The system that is left is very often a complete mess. What has happened is that the programmer *was* the standard. The programmer knew where everything was and what everything meant, but nobody else could read the code.

Tight standards dictate that every variable and every field be defined with standard naming conventions. The same goes for naming functions and procedures. The code should be as readable as possible. You should add appropriate clarification if a section of code does something that is not immediately obvious. Design the databases and functions with considerable forethought. If you can design the functions in such a way that they can be used in several parts of the application, you can then store them in a library, document them, and make them available for general use.

Design databases with the ramifications of at least two to three years of growth in mind. How large will the databases get? Will the backup mechanisms be sufficient? How many users will be accessing the database at any one time? Following are two examples from two real systems to give you some ideas on the subject.

Database Expansion Issues

A collections system for a large lending institution had a note field where comments on the progress on the collection of outstanding debt were recorded for each customer. The note field was of type memo. A memo field creates a 512-byte record when you type in the first character. The average note was 60 characters long, so most of the space in the memo was unused. The support .DBT file grew to enormous proportions as the number of records in the system climbed. Eventually there was not enough room to reindex the file or allow further growth.

The easiest solution would be to get a larger disk drive. However, this was not possible, so alternative measures had to be taken. The solution was to create an 80-character buffer field as well as the memo field. If the note contained less than 80 characters, it was stored in the buffer field. If the note contained more than 80 characters, it was stored in the memo field. The user was unaware that any change had been made to the system. The program made the adjustments and determined where to store the data. Incorporating the new scheme reduced the size of the .DBT file by 30 megabytes. This allowed room on the disk for other operations and future expansion. In this case, the original design of the database had not included the possibility that the database would reach this size.

Flexibility Issues

In a different system, the method for adding a new customer type was to add a new logical field to the customer database. Over a period of time, many logical fields were added to the database, leading to extensive maintenance problems. Databases had to be revised frequently, and a great number of custom reports were created to access the various customer types.

The solution to this problem was to replace the numerous logical fields with a single-character "flag" field. The user could assign any customer type he or she wanted to each of the positions within the field. The reporting mechanism was rewritten so that any user could create any type of report for any type of customer, and any customer could have any number of types associated with him or her. This drastically reduced the workload of the programmer servicing the system since the users themselves could create their own reports.

Bottleneck Functions

A good way to build rugged, maintainable, and changeable systems is to push actions through generic functions. These functions are sometimes referred to as *bottleneck functions* since a great deal of the activity is routed through them. Instead of individual function calls to all the various Clipper facilities, the calls are made to the bottleneck functions. When changes need to be made to the way the system works, the programmer can concentrate on the bottleneck functions. This eliminates the need to make wholesale changes throughout the application.

You might develop a bottleneck function to handle windows in your application. Here are samples of calls to a bottleneck function called window() to demonstrate the concept:

```
window("CREATE",10,10,20,20)
window("DESTROY")
```

These examples call on a window() function to open and close a window on the screen. The type of window frame, the color, and other configuration information is hidden within the window() functon. This means you could drastically change the way the window() function works by modifying the internal workings of the window() function without affecting the calls to the function. If you wanted to add new capabilities to the application, you could do it in one function rather than hundreds of places throughout the application.

The window() function could maintain an array of windows that had been opened and the colors used. The functions SAVESCREEN() and RESTSCREEN() could save and restore the various screens using array elements. A color array could capture the colors used by every overlapping window and thus restore them correctly. It would be easy to modify the window() function to add shadows or other features by making the modification within the window function.

Here is another example in which the routing of all file-related actions is routed to a bottleneck function:

```
file("OPEN","Customer")
file("INDEX","Customer","Lname+Fname")
file("CLOSE","Customer")
```

The same principle applies to the file() function in this example. Since all the work is done in the file() function, you could make changes to that function that would affect the way the entire system works. Suppose you wanted to allow files to be opened in exclusive mode on a multiuser system. You could modify the function to accept a variation of the function call like this:

```
file("OPEN EXCLUSIVE","Customer")
```

The internal workings of the file() function would change slightly but would not affect any existing calls to the function. If you make the file() function handle all the actions, you can handle a problem easily by adding the appropriate code to the function. Here is what the file() function would look like:

```
FUNCTION file(command,item)
DO CASE
   CASE command == "OPEN EXCLUSIVE"
      IF FILE(item+".dbf")
         l_pos := ASCAN(openfiles,item)
         IF l_pos <> 0
            comment(;
            item+" is already open in request for "+command
            RETURN .T.
         ENDIF
         USE &item NEW EXCLUSIVE
         l_emptypos := ASCAN(item,"")
         IF l_emptypos == 0
            AADD(openfiles,item)
         ELSE
            openfiles[l_emptypos] := item
         ENDIF
      ELSE
         comment(item+" does not exist in request for "+command)
```

```
        ENDIF
     CASE command == "CLOSE"
         * more code
  ENDCASE
  RETURN .T.
```

In this example, the CASE statement branches control of the program depending on the command passed as a parameter. The function could be easily modified to handle the OPEN EXCLUSIVE command. If you desired, you could keep an array to keep track of the currently opened files to ensure you are not attempting to open the same file again. An error message is displayed if the file already exists in the array. Otherwise, the file is opened and added to the list. A CLOSE command would remove the file to be closed from the list.

The comment() function presented in the sample application in Chapters 4, 5, and 6 is also considered a bottleneck function since it handles all the messages to the user. You could drastically modify the comment() function without changing any of the calls to it. Any changes made to the comment() function would also affect any functions calling the comment function.

The expandability comes into play when you move to a network. As an example, the file() function can then include the appropriate file locking, as shown with the EXCLUSIVE example. The file() function could also be expanded to store the names of users using each file. The data would have to be stored in a central database since arrays are available only to the user on the current machine. The names of the users of a database can be stored in the form of a log that would contain the time and date the file was opened and the activity it was going to be used for. You could easily switch off the logging of users by adjusting the file() function if it was no longer necessary.

The advantages of this approach are immense. Suppose the client was concerned about security issues. A password mechanism could be set up so only certain users could gain access to various files or data entry screens in the system. The user log could even provide the client with information concerning which users are accessing the various databases and what changes were being made. The client would know that John Doe opened the employee file on a certain date and increased his hourly rate or that Jane Doe made modifications to the commission file that increased the commissions due for a given month.

As another example of the bottleneck approach, you could control all database actions through a database() function, which would be called in this manner:

```
database("SKIP","Customer")
```

If you then switched database engines, you would have to change only the database() function. A *database engine* is the method of performing the file handling of a database system. Clipper uses dBASE III format databases and performs actions pertaining to this file structure. Another database engine might involve SQL or some other file structure. If all the file handling were done through bottleneck functions, switching to a different database engine would be easier. If all the screen handling were done through the screen() function, switching from a text-based system to a graphical interface such as Windows 3 would be easier.

This bottlenecking approach makes system maintenance a lot easier. File and window handling are only a couple of the bottlenecking actions you can take to simplify coding and improve maintainability. Remember that bottlenecking pays a speed penalty and should not be used too aggressively unless you feel sure that enhancements such as SQL or Windows will be part of your application's future.

Key Points

Problem Solving

It is best to think of yourself as an analyst who is attempting to bring together the overall system, not just the programming aspect of the system.

Your main goal as a problem solver is not necessarily to always have the answer in your head. It is to be able to get the correct answer when required.

continues . . .

Keeping Current

There is a continuous stream of new developments and technology. It is your job to keep on top of all the new information—a very difficult task. You must continue to study if you intend to be a professional in this field.

Communication

There are two parts to communication that must be done effectively in order for a project to succeed. The first part is listening and understanding what the other person is attempting to say. The other part is telling the other person what you want to say and providing him or her with an understanding of what you are saying.

Estimating Work

It is always a good idea to assign time estimates to programming requests. This ensures that you work on the requests that are considered valuable.

Application Design

Design is probably one of the most neglected areas of custom programming. You must convince the customer that the cost of designing a system is money well spent.

continues . . .

Future Growth

A system that has to survive for years and tolerate many changes during that time had better have very tight standards. These standards include the use of modular programming, top-down design, naming conventions, and adequate documentation.

Bottleneck Functions

A good way to build rugged, maintainable, and changeable systems is to push actions through generic functions. These functions are sometimes referred to as bottleneck functions since a great deal of the activity is routed through them.

CHAPTER

Advanced Features

*T*his chapter reveals the heavy-hitting parts of Clipper. Because this book is intended to be an introductory book, only a brief overview of each topic is covered. You should be aware of the capabilities discussed and be able to tap into them whenever appropriate.

This chapter covers code blocks, user-defined commands, compiler macros, and the ability to interface with C and assembly languages. In addition, there is a brief discussion of object-oriented programming and the various object classes available in Clipper.

Code Blocks

A *code block* can be considered as a data type and is similar to other data types, such as date, character, logical, and numeric. Clipper treats code blocks the same as other data types except when executing them. They can be stored to variables and copied from one variable to another just like data types. They can also be named and passed as parameters.

Recall from Chapters 1 and 7 that you can store Clipper expressions to character strings and evaluate them by using the & macro operator. The code block is very similar to a character string that is compiled and executed using the & macro operator. The difference is that macros are compiled on the fly—each time the statement is encountered. A code block is compiled at compile time. The code block is faster than the macro since it does not have to be compiled while the application is running.

Code blocks are evaluated using the EVAL(), AEVAL(), or DBEVAL() function in much the same way that the & macro operator is used to evaluate macro strings. The following example demonstrates the difference between using the macro operator and using a code block:

```
var := "DATE() - 27"
? &var        // will display today's date minus 27 days
```

The expression is stored in the variable called *var* and compiled and executed at run time by using the & macro operator. The same result could be achieved by using a code block, as shown here:

```
var := {|| DATE() - 27}
? EVAL(var)    // will display today's date minus 27 days
```

Every code block must be enclosed by an opening curly brace { and a closing curly brace }. You use the | | symbols to indicate a code block and also to enclose parameters used within the code block. The first line of this example assigns the code block (DATE() – 27) to the variable called *var*. The EVAL() function executes the code block called *var*. The first parameter of the EVAL() function is the name of the code block.

Here is an example of a code block that also has parameters that are declared within the | | symbols:

```
var := {|x| DATE() - x}
? EVAL(var,27)    // will display today's date minus 27 days
```

The parameter called *x* is placed within the | | symbols. The value to be assigned to *x* is passed as the the second parameter of the EVAL() function.

Additional parameters can be passed in the same way as in the preceding example. The parameter list of the code block is separated by commas if there is more than one parameter, as in this example:

```
var := {|x,y,z| DATE() - x + y + z}
? EVAL(var,27,10,20)
```

You use a comma to separate the parameters within the | | symbols. As before, the code block name is passed as the first parameter of the EVAL() function. The next three items passed match up with the parameters declared in the code block statement. When the code block is evaluated, the resultant expression will look like this:

```
DATE() - 27 + 10 + 20
```

and the answer of the expression is returned as the value of the EVAL() function.

You can include more than one expression within the code block and separate them by commas, as shown here:

```
var := {|x| QOUT(x),DATE() - x}
```

```
? EVAL(var,27)
```

The code block defines two expressions that will be executed. The first expression uses the QOUT() function to display the value of the parameter. The second expression performs date arithmetic to subtract the value of the parameter from the current system date. The result of the last expression in the code block is returned as the value of the EVAL() function.

The AEVAL() function processes the contents of each element of an array by using a code block. Here is an example that demonstrates the AEVAL() function:

```
var := {"Jim", "Beth", "Ryan", "Daniel"}
AEVAL(var,{|x| QOUT(x) })
```

The first statement creates an array with four elements by assigning the literal values enclosed in the curly braces. The code block is executed four times by using the AEVAL() function—one time for each element in the array. Each element of the array is passed to the code block and printed by using the QOUT() function. The screen display of the example would look like this:

```
Jim
Beth
Ryan
Daniel
```

Multidimensional arrays are processed slightly differently. The value passed to the code block is the subarray of the current array element. Curly braces must be used to access the subarray elements, as shown in this example:

```
var := DIRECTORY("*.*")
AEVAL(var,{|x| QOUT(x[1]),QQOUT(" "),QQOUT(x[2])} )
```

Recall from Chapter 7 that the DIRECTORY() function returns a multidimensional array containing file information. A file mask ("*.*") is passed to the DIRECTORY() function. In this example, the directory information is returned to the variable called *var. var* is passed as the first parameter of the AEVAL() function. The code block is executed one time for each row in the array. The information passed to the *x* parameter within the code block is a subarray containing information for a single file. The file is displayed by using the QOUT() function so that it starts on a new line. The QQOUT() function then displays a space and the size of the file. Suppose you have a directory with the following files:

MYPROG.PRG
PROG1.PRG
PROG2.PRG
MYPROG.LNK

The filename and file size information will be displayed as shown here:

```
MYPROG.PRG          39
PROG1.PRG           21
PROG2.PRG           21
MYPROG.LNK          53
```

The DBEVAL() function processes the contents of records in a database. The parameters of the DBEVAL() function look like this in definition:

DBEVAL(*code block*,
       FOR *condition*,
       WHILE *condition*,
       NEXT N *records*,
       RECORD,
       REST)

The first parameter passed is the code block that performs the action on the record. It is the only required parameter.

The FOR parameter is a scoping condition similar to that used with the LIST command described in Chapter 7. This clause allows you to specify the desired records the code block should act on by specifying a condition, such as State==*l_state*. This parameter must be a code block.

The WHILE parameter is also a scoping condition. The code block will process records while a condition specified in this clause is still TRUE. At the point that the WHILE condition is no longer true, the execution of DBEVAL() terminates. This parameter must be a code block.

The NEXT parameter allows you to specify the number of records that should be processed. This parameter must be numeric.

The RECORD parameter allows you to specify one particular record that should be processed. This parameter must be numeric.

The REST parameter is a logical parameter that indicates whether DBEVAL() should process all records or process the remaining records starting at the current record. If the REST parameter is FALSE, all records will be processed. If the REST parameter is TRUE, all records starting at the current record will be processed. The WHILE and FOR parameters are still in effect no matter what is passed as the REST parameter.

Here is an example of the DBEVAL() function that processes each record in the database:

```
DBEVAL( {||QOUT(Lname)} )
```

This example processes each record in the database since only the first parameter was passed—the code block indicating the action to take. The QOUT() function displays the field called Lname.

You might want to use the FOR or WHILE parameter to select the criteria of the records you want to process, as shown here:

```
DBEVAL( {||QOUT(Lname)},{||State==l_state},;
              {||SUBSTR(Lname,1,1)=="A"})
```

In this example, the QOUT() function displays the *Lname* variable, provided the FOR and WHILE code blocks evaluate to a TRUE value. This DBEVAL() function displays a list of last names where the State field matches the variable *l_state*. The listing will continue until the first character of the field Lname is no longer an uppercase "A."

The ability to place functions within a code block provides you with virtually unlimited capabilities. The code block provides the flexibility of a macro while eliminating the need for run-time compiling.

Code blocks allow blocks of code to be passed as parameters to a function or procedure. You can write procedures and functions that take code blocks as parameters. This allows the logic within a procedure or function to change depending on the code block passed.

When deciding to use code blocks, keep in mind that **debugging code blocks** is a little more difficult since there may be multiple expressions in a single statement.

Language Extension

Clipper provides you with the ability to make up your own commands. One of the important features of Clipper 5 is the addition of the preprocessor. The *preprocessor* makes a first pass of your program before the compiler does its work. It performs actions such as making constant substitutions and merging include files. The preprocessor also handles user-defined commands. Suppose you want to create the following four commands:

```
ROSES ARE RED
VIOLETS ARE BLUE
HERE IS A POEM
MADE JUST FOR YOU
```

You would use the #command directive to define the commands in the following manner:

```
#command ROSES ARE RED => roses()
#command VIOLETS ARE BLUE => violets()
#command HERE IS A POEM => poem()
#command MADE JUST FOR YOU => made()
```

You must create the associated functions called roses(), violets(), poem(), and made() in order to use these commands. The first statement in this example causes the preprocessor to translate the statement ROSES ARE RED into the function roses(). The => symbol is used to separate the left side, which contains the command, from the right side, which contains the conversion.

Clipper uses the #command directive to define (or redefine) Clipper commands. As an example, Clipper uses the #command directive to convert any SET COLOR TO statements to the SETCOLOR() function. The file called std.ch in the \CLIPPER5\INCLUDE directory contains the #command directives for Clipper commands. Here is one of the #command directives included in the std.ch file:

```
#command SET COLOR TO ( <c> )   => SetColor( <c> )
```

This #command directive converts any SET COLOR TO statements to the SETCOLOR() function. The <c> indicates a parameter passed to the SET COLOR TO statement. The <c> on the left side of the statement is called a *regular match marker.* You specify a regular match marker by enclosing the Clipper variable in angle brackets (<>). When the match marker is used on the right side of the statement, it is called a *regular result marker.* The preprocessor replaces it with the value of the regular match marker.

For the many commands that have more than one parameter, you use a *list match marker* on the left side of the #command directive. You use a *list result marker* on the right side of the #command directive. Here is an example of the use of the list marker:

```
#command ?   [ <list,...> ]       => QOut( <list> )
```

When you use the ? command to print or display text, the command is converted to the QOUT() function by the preprocessor. As an example, the statement

```
? Fname," ",Lname
```

would be converted internally by the preprocessor to

```
QOUT(Fname," ",Lname)
```

In these examples, the Clipper commands are converted to functions by the preprocessor.

You use the *restricted match marker* to match a series of inputs. If a match succeeds, the appropriate value is set on the right side. Here is an example of the use of the restricted match marker:

```
#command ROSES ARE <var:RED,WHITE,PINK> => roses(<"var">)
```

In this case, the ROSES ARE command can have RED, WHITE, or PINK as its last word. A compiler error will occur if a different parameter is passed. The roses() function will receive a *stringified* version (one converted to a string) of RED, WHITE, or PINK, as in "RED", "WHITE", and "PINK". The roses() function can then use a CASE statement to decide which value was chosen and take the appropriate action. As an example, the roses() function could call an external program that would switch to graphics mode and paint a photograph of a rose of the appropriate color. The command ROSES ARE RED will then paint a red rose on the screen.

The following example demonstrates the use of the *logify result marker* to determine if various keywords were passed in the command line:

```
#command ROSES ARE [<var1:RED>] [<var2:WHITE>] [<var3:PINK>] => ;
               roses( <.var1.>,<.var2.>,<.var3.> )

ROSES ARE RED PINK

function roses(parm1,parm2,parm3)
   ?
   IF parm1
      ? "ROSES ARE RED"
   ENDIF
   IF parm2
      ? "ROSES ARE WHITE"
   ENDIF
   IF parm3
      ? "ROSES ARE PINK"
   ENDIF
return NIL
```

The program sets up the #command directive ROSES ARE so that logical variables are created as TRUE or FALSE, depending on the items passed as part of the ROSES ARE command. If RED is passed, the *var1* variable is set to TRUE; otherwise, it is set to FALSE. If WHITE is passed, the *var2* variable is set to TRUE; otherwise, it is set to FALSE. If PINK is passed, the *var3* variable is set to TRUE; otherwise, it is set to FALSE.

The variables are passed to the roses() function, where the ? command is used to display the results depending on logical values. The example produces the following screen output:

```
ROSES ARE RED
ROSES ARE PINK
```

If the command is changed to ROSES ARE RED WHITE PINK, the following is displayed on the screen:

```
ROSES ARE RED
ROSES ARE WHITE
ROSES ARE PINK
```

All three lines are displayed since the three parameters passed to the roses() function are TRUE.

This section is intended to give you an overview of the #command preprocessor capabilities. By modifying the #command directives, you can actually change the way the Clipper commands work. Refer to the Clipper reference manual for a more detailed description of the #command directives. There are many other options available, and they may become very complicated, as shown in this example of the Clipper USE command:

```
#command USE => dbCloseArea()

#command USE <(db)> ;
            [VIA <rdd>] ;
            [ALIAS <a>] ;
            [<new: NEW>] ;
            [<ex: EXCLUSIVE>] ;
            [<sh: SHARED>] ;
            [<ro: READONLY>] ;
            [INDEX <(index1)> [, <(indexn)>]] ;
            ;
    => dbUseArea(<.new.>, <rdd>, <(db)>, <(a)>, ;
        if(<.sh.> .or. <.ex.>, !<.ex.>, NIL), <.ro.> ) ;
        [dbSetIndex(<(index1)>)] [;dbSetIndex( <(indexn)> )]
```

The preprocessor makes all the conversions necessary for creating the variables that will be passed to the dbUseArea() and dbSetIndex() functions.

The use of the #command directives allows you to make global changes to the commands in the Clipper language. Suppose your client wants you to add a feature that reminds the users of your application of sales appointments. You write the modifications to allow appointments to be maintained, but you also need to modify the existing application so the appointments can be constantly checked. If it is time for an appointment, you want your application to stop whatever it is doing and pop up a reminder message. Since some types of processing take a long time, you cannot afford to wait until the processing is completed before checking the appointments—the user might miss appointments. You need to check the appointment file at least every minute or two, no matter what your program is doing.

You first need a function that checks the employee's appointments, using the system time. The function would look something like this:

```
function chksched()
STATIC counter := 0
counter++
IF counter > 10000
   counter := 0

   * check schedule and display message if time for appointment

ENDIF
RETURN .T.
```

Recall that the STATIC initialization occurs the first time the statement is encountered. The first time the chksched() function is called, the variable called *counter* is initialized to zero. The *counter* variable is incremented each time the function is called. If the counter value exceeds 10000, the appointment file is checked to see if there are any appointments. The counter is used so that you are not constantly checking the appointment file; that would take too much time.

You could easily modify the menu of your program to call this function while waiting for the user to select a menu item. The problem is that there are hundreds and maybe thousands of DO WHILE loops throughout your programs. It would be a major undertaking to add the chksched() function to all the DO WHILE loops in your system.

You could use the #command directive to make all the changes by making a simple adjustment to the WHILE command, as shown here:

```
#command DO WHILE <exp>   => while <exp> .and. chksched()
```

Note that the chksched() function was added to the end of the #command directive. The chksched() condition is added to all the DO WHILE loops in your application by making one change. If you have a DO WHILE statement that looks like this:

```
DO WHILE .NOT. EOF()
```

the addition of the #command directive causes the preprocessor to change the statement to look like this:

```
DO WHILE .NOT. EOF() .AND. CHKSCHED()
```

You do not have to make any adjustments to any of the DO WHILE loops in your program; the preprocessor does the work for you. Keep in mind that you pay a speed price when you add the function check to the DO WHILE loop, but this may be necessary at times to accomplish what the client wants.

Compiler Macros

The previous section discussed how the preprocessor provides the ability to modify Clipper commands. The preprocessor also allows for the creation of compiler macros. A *compiler macro* can be defined as a function that is inserted directly into the source code by the preprocessor. However, compiler macros are not functions in the normal sense of the word since they do not have a name in the symbol table. Here is an example of a function that could be replaced with a compiler macro:

```
?  area(2,4)

FUNCTION area(l_length,l_width)
RETURN l_length * l_width
```

Using a function called area() would cause the name of the area() function to be placed in the symbol table. The area() function could be changed to a compiler macro, as shown here:

```
#define AREA(Length,Width)     (Length * Width)
```

```
? AREA(2,4)
```

Both methods will produce the same result. However, in the second example, the preprocessor has picked up the #define directive, transposed every reference to AREA, and substituted (Length * Width), which in this case is

```
? 2 * 4
```

This method saves memory as there is no need to compile and store a function. The program will also run slightly more quickly.

There are drawbacks to this method. The preprocessor is case sensitive, so uppercase AREA() would need to be specified. Lowercase area() would be ignored, and you would be likely to get a link error. It is harder to debug the code since no formal function exists that the debugger can use as a place marker.

You must take special care in processing numerics by using parentheses. For example,

```
#define AREA(Length,Width)  (Length * Width)
```

```
? AREA(2+4,5)
```

will be preprocessed into

```
? 2+4*5
```

Multiplication would be performed first and the result would be 22. To solve this particular problem, you could add parentheses to the compiler macro, as shown here:

```
#define AREA(Length,Width)  ((Length) * (Width))
```

The extra parentheses would cause

```
? AREA(2+4,5)
```

to be translated into

```
? (2+4) * (5)
```

which would return the intended result.

As an alternative, you could use the #translate or #xtranslate directive. These directives are not case sensitive. The #translate command directive recognizes the first four characters, which means that two directives such as DATE() and DATEGONE() would be seen as the same function—DATE(). The #xtranslate command recognizes the whole word. These commands follow the same rules as the #command directive. Here is an example:

```
#translate tochar(<number>) => LTRIM(STR(<number>))
```

This converts any code in your program from the tochar() function call to the LTRIM(STR()) format prior to compiling.

C and Assembly Calls

Since this is a book focused on teaching the beginning programmer how to use Clipper, you may not know anything about C or assembly language. However, if your client or your boss asks if Clipper can talk to C and assembly, you can answer with a resounding "Of course!" If you are then asked to do some C or assembly language programming, you can rush down to your local computer store and pick up a C or assembly compiler and supporting books and take a crash course.

Clipper was compiled with Microsoft C 5.1, and this is the most compatible C compiler to use with Clipper. Microsoft has since introduced C 7.0, and a C++ version of its normal compiler is due to be released soon. Borland has introduced several excellent C compilers, including Turbo C, Turbo C++, and Borland C++. The professional versions include an assembler. If you use an assembler, make sure it is compatible with Microsoft MASM 5.0 or above.

The problem with communicating with C and assembly from Clipper is in the way parameters are passed to and from the C or assembly code.

To solve this problem, you need to take a few simple actions. Let's illustrate them with some samples of code. Here is a sample C program:

```
#include "extend.h"

CLIPPER quad()
{
double number;
double answer;
if(PCOUNT == 1 && ISNUM(1))
  {
   number = _parnd(1);
   answer = number*number*number*number
   _retnd(answer);
  }
else
 _retnd(errcode);
}
```

The quad() function is used to multiply a number by itself four times. If 5 is passed to quad(), the result will be 5*5*5*5, or 625. The header file extend.h must be included in the C program. It includes definitions for the words PCOUNT, CLIPPER, and ISNUM. The special functions _parnd() and _retnd() are part of a larger team of functions responsible for getting data to and from Clipper. A normal C program has a main() function as its starting point. Since Clipper is considered the main function, a main() function should not be created in the C program. The command line for compiling a Clipper-compatible C program under Microsoft C 5.1 is

```
CL /c /AL /FPa /Gs /Oalt /Zl <filename>.c
```

To link the file with your Clipper code, use RTLINK:

```
RTLINK FILE myprog, myCprog LIB CLIPPER, EXTEND, LLIBCA
```

Note that LLIBCA is a library supplied by the C compiler, in this case the Microsoft C compiler.

The preceding program, quad(), is declared as type CLIPPER, which has been defined in extend.h as "void pascal." This is a calling convention indicating how the function should pass and receive parameters and return values.

In the C program example, quad() initializes two values called *number* and *answer* as doubles. *Doubles* are like integers but are usually four bytes long, or double the length of an integer. Larger numbers can be stored to doubles. PCOUNT is used to see if a parameter was passed to the function. ISNUM checks to see if the parameter passed is numeric. If everything is okay, the first parameter is assigned to the variable called *number* by using the _parnd() function, which is a Clipper-supplied function for passing numeric doubles. The 1 between the parentheses indicates the first parameter. The number is then multiplied by itself three times, and the result is stored in the variable called *answer*. The value in *answer* is then returned to Clipper by using the Clipper _RETND() function, which returns numeric doubles.

The following table lists the Clipper functions that support data transfer to C programs:

Function	Purpose
_parc()	Character
_parclen()	Length of character
_pards()	Date to character string
_parinfa()	Type or length of array parameter
_parinfo()	Parameter count or data type
_parl()	Logical to integer
_parnd()	Numeric to double
_parni()	Numeric to integer
_parnl()	Numeric to long

The following table lists the functions used in C that support data transfer from C programs:

Function	Purpose
_ret()	NIL value
_retc()	Character
_retclen()	Character length
_retds()	String to date

Function	Purpose
_retl()	Numeric to logic
_retnd()	Double to numeric
_retni()	Integer to numeric
_retnl()	Long to numeric

The next table lists the functions used in C programs to change the values of Clipper variables:

Function	Purpose
_storc()	Character
_storclen()	Character length
_stords()	Character string to date
_storl()	Logical
_stornd()	Double to numeric
_storni()	Integer to numeric
_stornl()	Long to numeric

The next table lists the functions that are used to manipulate Clipper's memory area:

Function	Purpose
_xalloc()	Allocates memory
_xfree()	Frees memory
_xgrab()	Allocates memory and generates error if failure

There are many variable types supported by C to accommodate the differences between Clipper and C. The C language does not have a date type or a logical type, while Clipper does not have an integer type, a long type, or a double type.

The purpose of this section is to show you that it is possible to call C and assembly from Clipper. The real problem is learning the C or assembly language. Once you are able to write the programs, it is relatively easy to link those programs to your Clipper application.

The primary reason for writing functions in C or assembly rather than Clipper is speed. Both C and assembly will process a particular set of code more quickly than the same set of code written in Clipper. Another reason to use C or assembly is the hardware at a low level, such as polling the communication port; Clipper would not be able to handle communications quickly enough to handle the data coming across a modem.

Object-oriented Programming

Object-oriented programming, or OOP, has received a fair amount of visibility lately. You should explore OOP at least at a basic level since Nantucket will introduce more and more OOP technology into Clipper. The definition of OOP is based on certain capabilities within the language.

Definition of Object-oriented Programming

There have been many methods developed for constructing software. These include some of the methods discussed in Chapter 3, such as modular programming and top-down design. The *object-oriented* approach to developing software offers even greater advantages than previous development approaches. Object-oriented programming revolves around objects. An *object* contains both programs and data necessary to perform a task. These objects resemble the real world more than previous approaches. The programs in an object are called *methods.* Each object contains information about its own status (data) as well as the programs (methods) that define the behavior of the object.

As an example, a window object would contain data providing information about its size and color. The methods would provide the means to draw the window, destroy the window, resize the window, and other actions relating to the window.

Clipper provides a small number of predefined objects (discussed in the section "Objects in Clipper" later in this chapter) but does not provide a direct method to create new objects. However, the ability to store code blocks to variables in Clipper allows you to come very close to creating objects. In addition, several third-party software vendors provide the ability to create objects in Clipper.

Classes

A unique combination of data and methods is called a *class.* A class might be considered a template that defines the methods and data types to be included in an object. In the nonelectronic world, there would be a superclass called dogs and a subclass called poodle. In Clipper, you might have a window class that would define the data and methods. An object is a single *instance* of a class. The object's methods and data types are defined in the class and its values are defined in the instance. The data elements within the object are called *instance variables.*

Inheritance

You can create a subclass from a class. The data and methods from the original class are included in the subclass, and new attributes can be assigned. The subclass can define methods and data that override any of the inherited characteristics. A subclass can be created from more than one class. The result is a new subclass that contains a combination of the multiple class attributes.

Operator Overloading

Overloading is defined as the ability to use the same operator or function for more than one purpose. As an example, the plus sign (+) is used to add numbers and to combine character expressions. The expressions 1+1 and "abc"+"def" use the same operator in different ways. This is an overloaded operator in action. There are, in fact, two completely different flavors of the + operator. One does arithmetic, and the other does string concatenation. Methods can also be overloaded in objects. A method can operate in different ways depending on the class that has called it.

The ability to use a single method for a wide variety of purposes is called *polymorphism.* Various objects can call the function and pass different parameters to achieve different methods. New objects can be created that draw on the methods that already exist in the system. As an example, the plus(*numeric,numeric*) function would be different from the plus(*character,character*) function because different parameters were passed to the function.

Constructors, Destructors, and Messages

Constructors create objects from classes. An object that is created from a single class is called an instance of the class. An object is able to send and receive messages. A *message* is a request for the object to carry out a method and return the result of that action. Messages are used to provide interaction between an object and the entities outside of the object. *Destructors* are used to destroy an object when it is no longer needed.

Objects in Clipper

As already mentioned, Clipper does not allow you to define true objects. In Clipper, you can think of a class as a multidimensional array with default data and code blocks in it. An object would be a copy of the class array. The data in the array would be called the instance variables, and the code blocks would be called the methods. Messages would be used to act on the data in the array or to cause the code blocks to be executed.

Messages are passed to cause an action to be taken by the object. Here is a sample of sending a message to the BROWSEOBJ object:

```
browseobj:pageup()
```

In this example, BROWSEOBJ is the name of the object. The colon indicates you are sending a message to the object. Pageup() is the message you are sending to the BROWSEOBJ object. This tells the object to move to the next page of data in the Browse window. Notice that the message has parentheses indicating a method. If you want to imagine what the equivalent function call would be, you can flip the example, as shown here:

```
pageup(browseobj)
```

This looks a little more familiar. The syntax of the object message is a little different from a function call. This is done so that objects are set apart from the normal Clipper function calls.

You change the data (instance variables) within the object in the following way:

```
browseobj:freeze := 1
```

This freezes the first column while allowing scrolling to the right of the remainder of the columns. If you think of the word "freeze" as a constant equal to a number, say 5, the preceding assignment would look like this:

```
browseobj[5] := 1
```

Changing the value in this element would cause actions to occur in the browse window. This is the equivalent of the recalculation capability of a spreadsheet. You modify a multidimensional array and then recalculate the data in the array, which affects the way the Browse window is presented to the user. The array would also contain a table of words mapped to methods passed to the object. Suppose the following command is issued.

```
browseobj:freeze := 1
```

This is internally translated into

```
RECALC(browseobj,"freeze",1)
```

which causes the appropriate actions to take place.

Clipper objects are hardcoded. This means you can make copies of them but you cannot change them. You can modify their behavior by changing instance variables or sending messages. At this point, Clipper does not allow you to create your objects or create subclasses of existing objects.

TBROWSE Object

The TBROWSE object allows a database to be browsed. The Browse window looks like a grid on the screen, with the records being rows and the fields being columns. The grid may actually be bigger than the screen size. The data will pan left and right and scroll up and down to enable the user to access all the data in the grid.

Think of TBROWSE as a two-dimensional GET/READ. You load up the grid with data, let the user view and/or change the data, and then exit. You can compile, link, and run the sample program called TBDEMO.PRG in the \CLIPPER5\SOURCE subdirectory. This will give you a hands-on approach to TBROWSE. Simply make changes to the instance variables or send one of the various TBROWSE messages and watch the effect.

Data retrieval and file positioning are all performed by the use of user-supplied code blocks. The behavior within the Browse window is completely programmable. These features provide you with unlimited flexibility and control over the browsing of data.

TBCOLUMN Object

The TBCOLUMN object is a simple object that contains the information needed to define a single data column of a TBROWSE object. TBCOLUMN objects have no methods since TBROWSE handles all the activity.

GET Object

The GET object allows sophisticated implementation of the GET/READ command. There is a predefined array called *getlist* and a function called READMODAL(). When you issue a series of GETs and a READ, you are actually loading the *getlist* array and issuing the command

```
READMODAL(getlist)
```

The READMODAL() function handles the processing of the GETs, which includes the behavior of the control keys, pre- and postprocessing of the GETs, and so forth.

The READMODAL() function is written in Clipper and is located within a file called GETSYS.PRG in the \CLIPPER5\SOURCE subdirectory.

The following example demonstrates the creation of a GET object and the activation of the object by the READMODAL() function:

```
l_var := SPACE(12)
myget := GETNEW()
myget:row := 10
myget:col := 10
myget:name := "l_var"
myget:block := { | input | ;
                 IF(PCOUNT() > 0, l_var := input, l_var)}
myget:picture := "@!"
myget:colorspec := "BG+/B, W+/BG"
myget:postblock := { | input | .NOT. EMPTY(input) }
READMODAL({myget})
```

The variable called *l_var* is created and initialized to 12 spaces. A new GET object is created for the *l_var* variable using the GETNEW() function. The various instance variables are modified to assign the row, column, name, and picture of the object. In addition, the block instance variable is also modified. A code block used to associate the GET object with the *l_var* variable is stored in the block instance variable.

Notice that READMODAL() receives an array. In this case, the GET object is passed as a single literal element. If more than one GET object had been created, then all could be passed to the READMODAL() function as literals, as shown here:

```
READMODAL({myget1,myget2,myget3})
```

Another way is to create the array and pass the array itself to the READMODAL() function, as shown here:

```
myarray := {myget1,myget2,myget3}
READMODAL(myarray)
```

The first line in this example assigns the literals within the brackets to create a three-element array called *myarray*. The array is then passed to the READMODAL() function, which then activates the full-screen data entry session.

Study the GETSYS.PRG program in order to get a good idea of how the GET system works. Keep in mind that you can take control of the GET system at a very low level. This provides you with a great deal of flexibility in your applications.

ERROR Object

The last of the Clipper objects is the ERROR object. Its instance variables are read only, with the exception of the instance variable called *cargo*. The ERROR object contains information about run-time errors. When a run-time error occurs, an error block is created and passed to the error handler block.

Here is an example of the redefinition of the ERROR object:

```
#include "error.ch"
lasterrblock := ERRORBLOCK(;
            { | currenterr | myhandle(currenterr) })
* your own code goes in here
RETURN


FUNCTION myhandle(incoming)
DO CASE
    CASE incoming:gencode == EG_PRINT
        IF incoming:canretry .AND. incoming:tries < 20
            RETURN .T.    // retry
        ELSE
            ? "Your printer's busted"
            QUIT
        ENDIF
    CASE incoming:gencode == EG_OPEN
        ? "Unable to open "+incoming:filename
        QUIT
ENDCASE
RETURN .T.
```

This example demonstrates how you can use the ERROR object to create your own custom error-handling routines. In this example, the standard Clipper error-handling object is stored to *lasterrblock* so that it may be restored at a later time. The new error-handling object is set up so that when an error occurs, the function called myhandle() will be executed.

The CASE statement in the myhandle() function checks for only two error conditions—a printer error and a file open error. The error codes for these (*EG_PRINT* and *EG_OPEN*) are constants defined in the header file called error.ch.

You can build generic error handlers or specific error handlers, depending on the circumstances in your application. You can save or restore the most recent error object or assign a new error object using ERRORBLOCK(). When an error occurs, the error object last posted by ERRORBLOCK() is the one that will be filled. You instruct ERROR-BLOCK() to post the error object to your function by declaring it in the code block.

Key Points

Code Blocks

You can consider a code block to be a data type similar to other data types, such as date, character, logical, and numeric types. Clipper treats code blocks the same as other data types except when executing them.

Code blocks allow blocks of code to be passed as parameters to a function or procedure. This allows the logic within a procedure or function to change, depending on the code block passed.

Preprocessor

One of the important features of Clipper 5 is the addition of the preprocessor. The preprocessor makes a first pass of your program before the compiler does its work. It performs actions such as making constant substitutions and merging include files. The pre-processor also handles user-defined commands.

continues . . .

User-defined Commands

The use of the #command directives allow you to make global changes to the commands in the Clipper language.

Compiler Macros

A compiler macro can be defined as a function that is inserted directly into the source code by the preprocessor. However, compiler macros are not functions in the normal sense of the word since they do not have a name in the symbol table.

C and Assembly Calls from Clipper

It is possible to call C and assembly functions from within Clipper. The real problem is learning the C or assembly language. Once you are able to write C or assembly programs, it is relatively easy to link those programs to your Clipper application.

Object-oriented Programming

The object-oriented approach to developing software offers even greater advantages than previous development approaches. Object-oriented programming revolves around objects.

continues . . .

An object contains both programs and data necessary to perform a task. These objects resemble the real world more than previous approaches. The programs in an object are called methods. Each object contains information about its own status (data) as well as the programs (methods) that define the behavior of the object.

Classes

A unique combination of data and methods is called a class. You can consider a class as a template that defines the methods and data types to be included in an object.

Instance and Instance Variables

An object is a single instance of a class. The objects, methods, and data types are defined in the class and its values are defined in the instance. The data elements within the object are called instance variables.

Overloading and Polymorphism

Overloading is defined as the ability to use the same operator or function for more than one purpose.

The ability to use a single method for a wide variety of purposes is called polymorphism. Various objects may call the function and pass different parameters to achieve different methods.

continues . . .

Constructors and Destructors

Constructors are used to create objects from classes. Destructors are used to destroy an object when it is no longer needed.

Messages

An object is able to send and receive messages. A message is a request for the object to carry out a method and return the result of that action. Messages are used to provide interaction between an object and the entities outside of the object.

Index

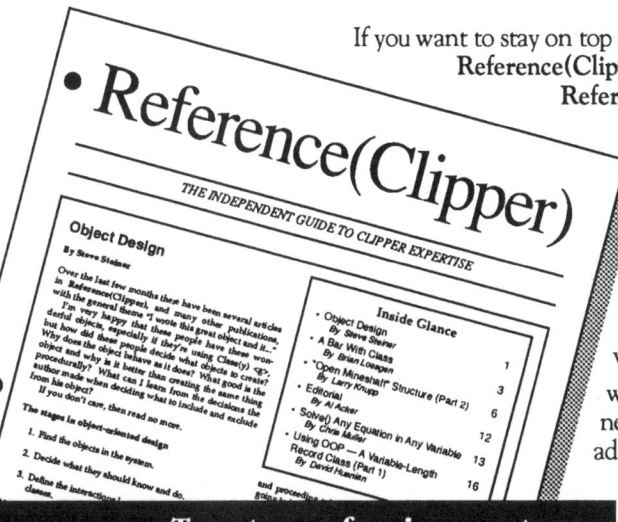

BUSINESS REPLY MAIL
FIRST-CLASS MAIL   PERMIT NO. 283   KENT, WA

POSTAGE WILL BE PAID BY ADDRESSEE

Pinnacle Publishing, Inc.
PO BOX 1088
KENT WA 98035-9910

You're important to us...

We'd like to know what you're interested in, what kinds of books you're looking for, and what you thought about this book in particular.

Please fill out the attached card and mail it in. We'll do our best to keep you informed about Osborne's newest books and special offers.

▶ *YES, Send Me a FREE Color Catalog of all Osborne computer books*
To Receive Catalog, Fill in Last 4 Digits of ISBN Number from Back of Book (see below bar code) 0-07-881 _ _ _ – _

Name: _____ Title: _____

Company: _____

Address: _____

City: _____ State: _____ Zip: _____

I'M PARTICULARLY INTERESTED IN THE FOLLOWING (*Check all that apply*)

I use this software
- ☐ WordPerfect
- ☐ Microsoft Word
- ☐ WordStar
- ☐ Lotus 1-2-3
- ☐ Quattro
- ☐ Others _____

I use this operating system
- ☐ DOS
- ☐ Windows
- ☐ UNIX
- ☐ Macintosh
- ☐ Others _____

I rate this book:
- ☐ Excellent   ☐ Good   ☐ Poor

I program in
- ☐ C or C++
- ☐ Pascal
- ☐ BASIC
- ☐ Others _____

I chose this book because
- ☐ Recognized author's name
- ☐ Osborne/McGraw-Hill's reputation
- ☐ Read book review
- ☐ Read Osborne catalog
- ☐ Saw advertisement in store
- ☐ Found/recommended in library
- ☐ Required textbook
- ☐ Price
- ☐ Other _____

Comments _____

Topics I would like to see covered in future books by Osborne/McGraw-Hill include:

_____

IMPORTANT REMINDER
To get your FREE catalog, write in the last 4 digits of the ISBN number printed on the back cover (see below bar code) 0-07-881 _ _ _ – _

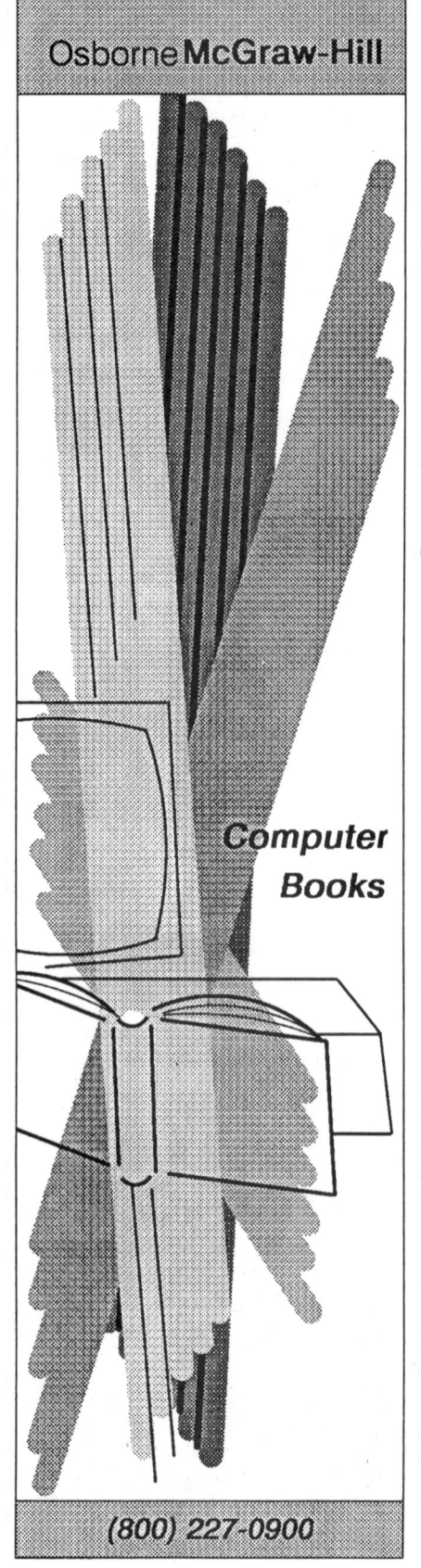

Osborne McGraw-Hill

Computer
Books

(800) 227-0900